Cochlear Implants

Cochlear Implants

A Handbook

by
Bonnie Poitras Tucker

McFarland & Company, Inc., Publishers
Jefferson, North Carolina, and London

The figure on page 8 is from *Human Information Processing: An Introduction to Psychology* by Peter H. Lindsay and Donald A. Norman, ©1972 by Harcourt Brace and Company, and is reproduced by permission of the publisher.

The present work is a reprint of the library bound edition of Cochlear Implants: A Handbook, *first published in 1998 by McFarland.*

LIBRARY OF CONGRESS CATALOGUING-IN-PUBLICATION DATA

Tucker, Bonnie P., 1939–
    Cochlear implants : a handbook / by Bonnie Poitras Tucker.
    p.   cm.
    Includes bibliographical references and index.

    ISBN 978-0-7864-4514-1
    softcover : 50# alkaline paper

    1. Tucker, Bonnie P., 1939–   2. Cochlear implants.
3. Hearing impaired—Rehabilitation.   4. Deaf—Rehabilitation.
5. Deaf children—Rehabilitation.   6. Hearing impaired
children—Rehabilitation.   7. Deaf children—Education—
United States.   8. Hearing impaired children—Education—
United States.   9. Deaf lawyers—United States—Biography.
I. Title.
RF305 .T83   2009
617.8'9—dc21   98067679

British Library cataloguing data are available

Cover image ©2009 Shutterstock.

Manufactured in the United States of America

McFarland & Company, Inc., Publishers
  Box 611, Jefferson, North Carolina 28640
  www.mcfarlandpub.com

To all users of cochlear implants—and to the wonderful new beginning that cochlear implants represent for all of us.

Also to Dr. Bill Luxford, Dawna Mills, Maxine Turnbull, and my family, particularly my mother, Thelma Poitras.

Acknowledgments

My progress with my cochlear implant would not have been possible without the help of Dr. Bill Luxford, Dawna Mills, Maxine Turnbull, and my family, particularly my mother, Thelma Poitras. Thank you for sticking with me and for giving me your encouragement and support.

Thanks go also to all of the contributors to this book, who have generously given of their time and expertise to make the public aware of the new world of hearing that people who are severely or profoundly deaf may now enter. We who are deaf owe all of you our heartfelt gratitude.

And I thank my assistant, Robin Praytor, whose help in producing this manuscript was invaluable.

Contents

Preface

Cochlear implants represent a new beginning for people with severe to profound hearing losses. Unfortunately, misinformation and disinformation about cochlear implants abound. Because cochlear implants have the potential to ameliorate or eliminate the ramifications of deafness, they are opposed by Deaf culturists—a group that claims that deafness is something to be proud of and that efforts to "cure" deafness or ameliorate its effects are immoral and unethical. Deaf culturists view cochlear implants as a form of genocide—a means of killing Deaf culture. Thus, members of this group and their spokespeople have expended considerable energy disparaging cochlear implants. As a result, the general public—including many deaf individuals, professionals who work in the field of deafness, and parents of deaf children—are unclear about what cochlear implants are, how they work, for whom they do (or do not) work, and most particularly, *whether* they work. This book is intended to answer those questions, in terms that are understandable to laypeople as well as professionals.

The first chapter, written by Michael F. Dorman, Ph.D., explains the basic concept, history, and evolution of cochlear implants and provides a summary of the significant research on cochlear implants and of the recipients of cochlear implants to date. Dr. Dorman is a well-known and admired pioneer in the field of cochlear implant research. His comprehensive yet simple explanation of how cochlear implants work is uniquely presented.

The second chapter presents the story of one adult recipient of a cochlear implant: an adult who has been profoundly deaf (and unable to wear hearing aids) from at least the age of two, and who did not hear for fifty years, until she received an implant at the age of fifty-two. The author, who was a clinically "bad" candidate for the implant and one who is not considered a "successful" user of the implant, offers her story to graphically illustrate the advantages of the implant even to those who are unable to realize maximum benefit from implantation. Statements from the author's audiologist, Dawna Mills, who works with the author and her implant, and from the author's auditory-verbal therapist for the first year and a half following implantation, Maxine

Turnbull, are also included so that the reader may compare their opinions and thoughts about the author's ability or lack of ability to use the implant with the author's own opinions and feelings.

The next section of the book presents summaries of over three hundred questionnaire responses received from adult cochlear implant recipients and parents of children with cochlear implants. The responses provide a fascinating and enlightening picture of how cochlear implant recipients, and parents of children with implants, view the success, or lack thereof, of their implants or their children's implants.

The questionnaire responses are followed by summaries, case studies, and general information provided by some of the foremost clinicians who work with children and adults who have received cochlear implants:

Carol Flexer, Ph.D., CCC-A, FAAA, Cert. AVT, Professor of Audiology in the School of Speech-Language Pathology and Audiology at the University of Akron;

Denise Wray, Ph.D., Cert. AVT, Professor of Speech-Language Pathology in the School of Speech-Language Pathology and Audiology at the University of Akron;

Elizabeth Fitzpatrick, M.S., AUD(C), Cert. AVT, Coordinator of the Cochlear Implant Program at Children's Hospital of Eastern Ontario, Ottawa, Canada;

Linda Daniel, M.A., M.S., Cert. AVT, who works with numerous children with cochlear implants in her private practice, "HEAR in Dallas";

Sally Tannenbaum, M.A., M.Ed., C.E.D., Cert. AVT, who also works with numerous children with cochlear implants in her private practice in Chicago, Illinois;

Judith I. Simser, O. Ont., B.Ed., Cert. AVT, a renowned therapist on leave from Children's Hospital of Eastern Ontario, Ottawa, Canada, training Chinese teachers and developing three auditory-verbal centers in Taiwan;

Catherine McEnroe, B.A., M.A.T., a therapist in private practice in New York and Vermont; and

Nancy Young, M.D., Head of the Section of Otology and Neurotology, Medical Director of the Cochlear Implant Program, Medical Director of the Department of Audiology at the Children's Memorial Medical Center in Chicago, and Assistant Professor at Northwestern University Medical School.

The segments written by these esteemed experts provide a wealth of insightful information about how and when cochlear implants ameliorate the ramifications of deafness and assist implanted children (and adults) to live within the mainstream of hearing society. One of the most significant factors repeatedly articulated by these experts is that children who have severe to profound hearing losses and who receive cochlear implants before the age of three are often able to function as hard-of-hearing, sometimes as only slightly hard-of-hearing, in this hearing world. Cochlear implants provide these children with sound in the full spectrum of the speech range. With proper auditory-verbal training and commitment to learning to listen, many or most of these children are able to understand speech in many or most situations and are able to develop spoken language at appropriate age-level ranges.

As reported in May 1998 to the Advisory Council of the National Institute on Deafness and Other Communication Disorders (one of the National Institutes of Health): "It has now been demonstrated that the long term benefits of cochlear implants in children are not limited to speech recognition but extend into dramatically improved language learning and language skills" (report of Dr. Ralph F. Naunton, Director, Division of Human Communications, May 7, 1998).

The book also contains a section on educational issues, written by experts who explain that a special auditory-oral educational setting for children with implants during the early years of schooling can do much to enhance the ability of some children to maximize the use of their implants. (Some children with implants, however, do not require a special educational placement.) The authors of the excerpts in this section are also renowned for their expertise: Jean Sachar Moog, M.S., Director, Moog Oral School, and Director, Oral Deafness Programs for the Oberkotter Foundation; Sister Joyce Buckler, Ed.D., long-time principal of St. Joseph Institute for the Deaf; Sister Roseanne Siebert, M.A., Supervisor of the Speech Program at St. Joseph Institute for the Deaf; and Patrick Stone, Ed.D., Director of Tucker-Maxon Oral School.

Next, the book contains a discussion of the Deaf culture controversy and explains the fallacy behind the reasoning espoused by Deaf culturists for opposing cochlear implants.

This is not a scientific research book. Rather, it is for parents, professionals, and the average, ordinary man or woman who may or may not have some connection with deafness or with individuals who are deaf or hard-of-hearing, all of whom may want to understand something about the incredible new beginning that is available for millions of severely and profoundly deaf children and adults.

Read it to learn. Read it to understand. And read it to rejoice. Good things *are* happening for people who are deaf.

Chapter 1

An Overview of
Cochlear Implants

Michael F. Dorman, Ph.D.

Michael Dorman received a Ph.D. in Developmental Psychology from the University of Connecticut. He is currently a professor in the Department of Speech and Hearing Science at Arizona State University and an adjunct professor in the Department of Surgery, Division of Head and Neck Surgery/Otolaryngology at the University of Utah Health Sciences Center. He directs research programs for individuals with cochlear implants at both Arizona State University and the University of Utah Health Sciences Center.

Many individuals with severe to profound hearing losses derive little or no benefit from conventional hearing aids. For these individuals, the sounds of speech either can't be made loud enough to be heard or are too loud and or indistinct to be understood. These conditions arise because critical structures in the inner ear, or cochlea, have been damaged in such a way that they no longer respond normally to sound. However, these damaged structures can be bypassed, and the nerve fibers that remain intact in the face of hearing loss, or even complete deafness, can be stimulated directly. The device that accomplishes this direct stimulation of nerve fibers and that, in the best of cases, restores hearing and speech understanding to individuals who have lost all or most of their hearing, is called a *cochlear implant*.

Cochlear implants are not new. The first reports of cochlear implants were published in the late 1950s and early 1960s. However, great strides have been made in the past handful of years in the level of speech understanding that the devices can produce. Now, more than half of the adults who receive an implant can understand sentences with 80–100 percent accuracy. Children who are born deaf and who receive an implant at an early age can acquire speech and language skills appropriate for their age. The aim of this chapter is to introduce, in a relatively painless manner, the anatomy, physiology, and technology behind this revolution in the treatment of severe to profound hearing loss.

An introduction to cochlear implants cannot be completely painless because neither the anatomy and physiology nor the technology behind an implant is trivial. However, the material is not difficult to follow, especially if you attend carefully to the illustrations that accompany the text (this is the same advice I give my undergraduates—if you can follow the illustrations in the textbook, you will probably pass the exam!). So look at the illustrations, and read on.

Components of an Implant

The components of a cochlear implant are shown in Figure 1. A microphone (1), worn at ear level, picks up signals and sends the signals over a small cable (2) to a pager-sized signal processor (3). The battery-powered signal processor performs a series of operations on the signals to make them appropriate for electrical stimulation of the auditory system. The processed signals travel by cable (4) to a radio-frequency transmitter (5), which, in turn, sends the signals across the skin to a receiver (6), which has been surgically implanted under the skin slightly above and in back of the ear. The signals are then sent down a set of very fine wires to electrodes (7), which have been inserted into the inner ear, or cochlea.

To understand the design of a cochlear implant, and the history of cochlear implants, it is useful to understand both the nature of the signal (speech) that the implant must reproduce and the nature of the biological system (the peripheral auditory system) that the implant must replace. We begin, first, with the speech signal.

Speech Signals

The speech signal contains frequencies from approximately 125 Hz (the pitch of a male voice) to 7,000 or 8,000 Hz (the "s" sound in the word "Sam"). (Hz is an abbreviation for Hertz. Heinrich Hertz was a German physicist who, in the late 1800s, was the first to broadcast and receive radio waves. Hz means the same as "cycles per second.") Speech can be understood with near perfect accuracy when frequencies of 300 Hz to 3,000 Hz are transmitted (this is the frequency bandwidth of a telephone line). So a cochlear implant should be able to reproduce frequencies at least from 300 to 3,000 Hz. Most devices, in fact, reproduce signals over the range 100 to 5,000–7,000 Hz.

Each of the sounds of speech has a different acoustic signature, that is, each is characterized by a unique set of frequencies. For example, the "s" in "Sam" has frequencies in the range 4,000–7,000 Hz (for a male voice). At the other extreme, the "m" in "Mary" has frequencies around 300–400 Hz. The vowel sounds in a language are characterized by multiple frequencies. For example, the vowel in "beet" is characterized by frequencies at 300 Hz and

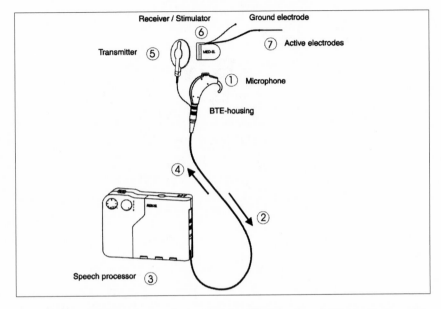

Figure 1. Components of a cochlear implant. The numbers indicate the sequence of steps from pickup of a signal by the microphone to stimulation of electrodes in the inner ear.

2,100 Hz. The vowel in "bit" is characterized by frequencies of 400 and 1,800 Hz. The signatures of the two vowels differ by only a few hundred Hz. Overall, then, an implant must transmit a range of frequencies and must have sufficient resolution for frequencies within that range so that the sounds of the language can be individually identified. It is the latter job, the resolution of small differences between sounds, that is the most difficult to accomplish.

Anatomy and Physiology

Two facts about normal hearing make a cochlear implant possible. The first is that the frequency of a sound is coded by where, or the place at which, stimulation occurs in the inner ear. The second is that the neural fibers that respond to where stimulation occurs can be jolted into responding by an electrical current as well as by the normal, somewhat involved, means. Thus, if electrodes can be placed at several places in the inner ear of a completely deaf individual, and if there are neural fibers left to stimulate, the component frequencies of sounds can be coded and, in the best case, speech understanding can be restored.

Normally it is the job of the peripheral auditory system to transmit to the brain the acoustic signatures of speech sounds. The structures that make up

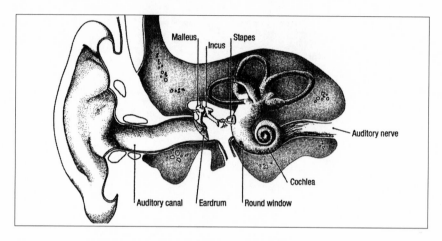

Figure 2. Structures composing the peripheral auditory system. (Figure reproduced with permission of Harcourt Brace and Company.)

the peripheral auditory system are shown in Figure 2. Sounds first travel down the external auditory canal and cause the tympanic membrane, or eardrum, to vibrate. This vibration is transmitted by the three middle ear bones—the malleus, the incus, and the stapes—to the oval window of the cochlea, or inner ear. The inward and outward movement of the stapes in response to the vibration at the eardrum causes fluid in the bony, hard-walled cochlea to be displaced.

As shown in Figures 3a and 3c, the coiled cochlea is composed of three fluid-filled compartments separated by two membranes. The basilar membrane is of crucial importance. When the fluid in the cochlea is displaced by the movement of the stapes (remember, the stapes moves because it follows the movement of the eardrum), the basilar membrane moves up and down and the place along the coil where the movement is greatest varies with the frequency of the sound. High-frequency sounds cause a maximum movement near the oval window, or the base, of the cochlea, and low-frequency sounds cause a maximum movement near the far end of the cochlea, or the apex (Georg von Békésy received the Nobel prize in 1961 for, among other discoveries, his demonstration of this effect). The relationship between the place of maximum movement and the frequency of the incoming sound is shown in Figure 3b. The 4,000 to 6,000 Hz energy in "s" causes a maximum displacement toward the base of the cochlea. The 300 Hz energy in "m" causes a maximum displacement much farther toward the "top" of the cochlear spiral. Thus, the basilar membrane acts as a frequency analyzer and begins the chain of events that leads to the perception of the sounds of our language.

Between the basilar membrane and the tectorial membrane are two groups of cells—the inner and outer hair cells. As shown in Figure 3c and, in cartoon

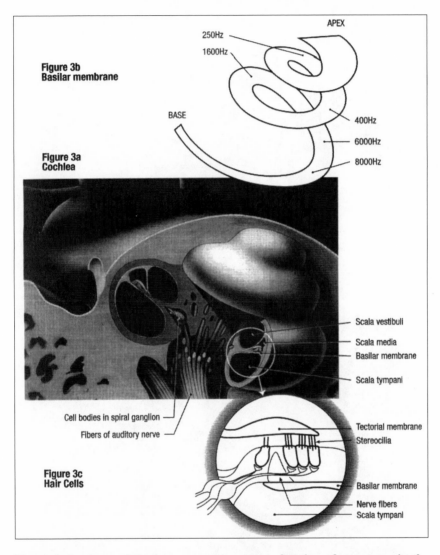

**Figure 3b
Basilar membrane**

APEX

250Hz

1600Hz

BASE

400Hz

6000Hz

8000Hz

**Figure 3a
Cochlea**

Scala vestibuli

Scala media

Basilar membrane

Scala tympani

Cell bodies in spiral ganglion

Fibers of auditory nerve

Tectorial membrane

Stereocilia

**Figure 3c
Hair Cells**

Basilar membrane

Nerve fibers

Scala tympani

Figure 3. Anatomy of the inner ear: (a) cutaway drawing of structures in the cochlea (illustration courtesy of Cochlear Corporation and Ed Zilberts); (b) frequency locations along basilar membrane; (c) enlargement of a portion of the cochlea.

fashion, in Figure 4, protruding from the top of these cells are thin rods of protein named stereocilia—the "hairs" of hair cells. When the basilar membrane moves up and down, the stereocilia move as if hinged where they exit from the body of the hair cell. The movement of the stereocilia starts a series of electrochemical events that generate a brief electrical discharge—an action

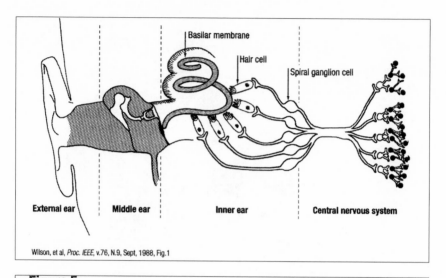

Basilar membrane

Hair cell

Spiral ganglion cell

External ear   Middle ear   Inner ear   Central nervous system

Wilson, et al, *Proc. IEEE*, v.76, N.9, Sept, 1988, Fig.1

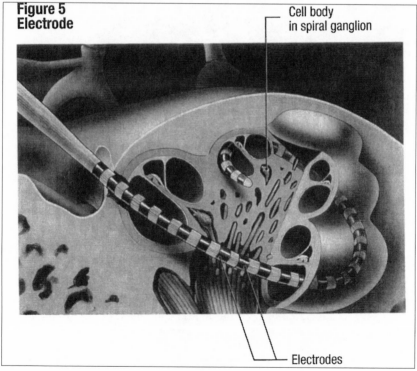

**Figure 5
Electrode**

Cell body
in spiral ganglion

Electrodes

Figure 4. Schematic illustration of structures involved in hearing.
Figure 5. An electrode with twenty-two rings inserted into the scala tympani (illustration courtesy of Cochlear Corporation and Ed Zilberts). The current from the electrodes stimulates the nerve fibers and cell bodies in the spiral ganglion.

potential, or spike discharge—along the fibers that terminate at the bottom of the hair cells. These fibers form the auditory nerve and, after making many connections in the brain stem, reach the auditory area in the cortex of the brain. When the electrical discharge, which began at the level of the cochlea, reaches the brain stem and cortical centers, we "hear."

As noted above, one of the aspects of physiology that makes the restoration of hearing possible for individuals who are deaf is that an electrical discharge can be started in the fibers of the auditory nerve either by the normal mechanism, that is, the movement of the stereocilia and the resulting electrical and chemical events, or by passing an electrical current across the fibers. The brain doesn't know how the electrical discharge was started—it knows only that a discharge took place. And because frequency is coded by *which* fibers "fire" at a given time (the ones at the base of the spiral, which code high frequencies, or the ones at the "top" of the spiral, which code low frequencies), if electrodes, inserted through the round window, can be placed at different locations along the cochlear spiral, as is shown in Figure 5, the perception of different frequencies can be restored to individuals who are deaf.

Best-Case and Worst-Case Physiology

The hair cells, the cell bodies in the spiral ganglion, or central core of the cochlea, and the fibers that make up the auditory nerve are shown in cartoon fashion in Figure 6. On the left side of the figure is a "normal" cochlea, without the bony shell, in which there is a full complement of hair cells and fibers. On the right side of the figure is a cochlea from an individual with a long-standing, profound hearing loss. Almost all of the hair cells have died, and as a consequence, the fibers that terminated at the bottom of the hair cells have degenerated. Restoring hearing to the cochlea on the left would be relatively straightforward, since all of the neural elements are available to be stimulated. Restoring hearing to the cochlea on the right would be very difficult, since there are few fibers or cell bodies to stimulate. Unfortunately, there are no tests to determine the state of neuronal survival before a patient is implanted with a device to restore hearing. Thus, no matter how good the device, there will always be some people who receive little or no speech understanding from an implant.

The First Cochlear Implants

Cochlear implants got off to a very modest start in the United States in the early 1960s. The first report of an implant in 1957, by Djourno and Eyries, was written in French and appears to have been unnoticed on this side of the

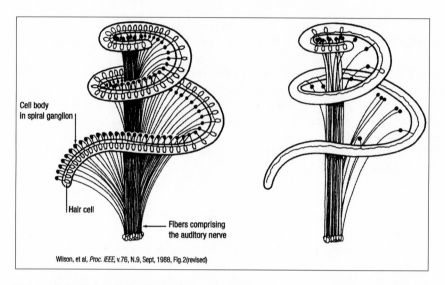

Cell body
in spiral ganglion

Hair cell

Fibers comprising
the auditory nerve

Wilson, et al, *Proc. IEEE,* v.76, N.9, Sept, 1988, Fig.2(revised)

Figure 6. On left: schematic drawing of basilar membrane, hair cells, cell bodies in the spiral ganglion, and fibers of the auditory nerve in the inner ear of an individual without hearing damage. On right: structures remaining in the cochlea of an individual with long-term deafness; there are few cell bodies or nerve fibers to stimulate.

Atlantic. A patient brought a newspaper account of the article to Bill House, a Los Angeles surgeon. In 1961 House implanted one patient with a single-electrode device and implanted another patient first with a single-electrode device and then with a five-electrode device.

Both patients reported a sensation of "hearing" when the speech signal, picked up by a microphone, was directed to the electrode. Neither patient was able to understand speech. The devices were removed within weeks of implantation due to a concern over infection or a reaction to the silicone covering of the electrode bundle. Encouraged by the outcome—that both patients reported "hearing"—House and an engineering colleague, Jack Urban, spent the next several years improving the design of both the external and the implanted electronics.

In 1964 Blair Simmons, at Stanford, in an attempt to directly stimulate cell bodies in the spiral ganglion (see Figure 3a), inserted a six-electrode array into the central core of the cochlea. The patient could hear changes in pitch up to a frequency of 300 pulses per second and could recognize speech signals as speech. The patient did not receive any speech understanding. Perhaps as interesting as the modest results was the reaction by other researchers to the results: few appeared to care. Worse, when the results were submitted for presentation at a meeting in 1965 for surgeons, the paper was turned down as being too controversial.

First Generation Implants

By 1969 House and Urban had sorted out some of the bioengineering issues connected with implantation. In that year, House began another series of tests with patients. After experimenting with five electrode systems and finding no better performance than with a single-electrode system, House settled on a single-electrode system. Single-electrode systems were also implanted by Robin Michelson at the University of California at San Francisco (UCSF). As in the early experiments, the patients did not report that they could understand speech. One patient wrote: "Speech reminds me of a long-distance, short-wave transmission with too weak a signal, or off-frequency radio setting that prevents intelligible speech. Music reminds me of listening to the Mormon choir years ago on an old radio with poor reception."[1]

Although the single-channel implant did not allow speech understanding by sound alone, the implant was a godsend to most patients. A patient wrote:

> I was deaf for 12 years, but now I hear. This is a modern miracle to me with strong religious overtones. Using the new device has opened the world to me. My current progress can be described as changing from profoundly deaf to just hard of hearing. (Tonight for the first time in all these years I can hear the bell that tells me I am at the right hand margin as I type). ... I get tremendous help and enjoyment hearing the bells at school, traffic noises on the highway, a mockingbird calling, the cat meowing, a twig breaking under foot, bacon frying, the doorbell ringing, and on and on. ... Now when I am camping and hear the chipmunk stealing the peanuts out of the sack beside me, I know that I am no longer deaf.[2]

If patients' reactions to implants were enthusiastic, professional reaction was cautious. Part of the caution stemmed from the absence of articles in professional journals on the performance of implant patients. Implant patients received a fair amount of publicity in the media, which prejudiced the case for implants in the view of scientists who wanted to see "real data," not television interviews. Indeed, as late as 1978, applications for funding for research on cochlear implants from the National Institutes of Health were turned down on "moral" grounds.

The need for an independent review of the performance of cochlear implant patients led to a landmark study of House's and Michelson's patients' directed by Bob Bilger of the University of Illinois and published in 1977, the report confirmed that, for some patients, implants (1) improved scores on tests of speech understanding when the patient could both watch and hear the speaker, (2) increased the awareness and recognition of environmental sounds, and (3) aided in the control of the speaking voice.[3] The publication of this report made implants respectable.

Second Generation Implants

The first single-electrode implants provided very little or no speech understanding by sound alone. Although the preliminary experiments by House hadn't shown any benefit of multiple electrodes, it was clear that if speech was to be understood, multiple electrodes would have to be used to stimulate different sections of the cochlea and thus stimulate the different frequency regions necessary for the coding of the frequency components in speech. In the 1970s, research groups in several countries began work on multiple-electrode (or multichannel) implants. In the United States, researchers at the University of California at San Francisco, at Stanford University, and at the University of Utah developed implants with multiple channels. Multiple-channel devices were also developed at the University of Melbourne, Australia, and in Paris. By the early 1980s, several of the projects had shown sufficient promise that commercial companies were formed.

The principal multichannel implants in the United States in the 1980s were devices with radically different designs. One was the design of the group originally at the University of Melbourne. This implant, marketed by Cochlear Corp. as the Nucleus 22, had twenty-two electrodes placed very close together (.75 mm apart) to give good frequency resolution; it used a microphone, a signal processor, an external radio frequency transmitter, and an implanted receiver to deliver signals to the electrodes. The other design was that of the group originally at the University of Utah. This design, marketed first by Symbion Inc. as the Ineraid, delivered stimulation, picked up by a microphone and processed into four frequency bands, to electrodes spaced relatively far apart (4 mm) in the cochlea. The microphone and the sound processor were connected to the implanted electrodes by a graphite connector, approximately the size of the nail on your little finger, which protruded through the skin above the ear. The through-the-skin, or percutaneous, connector was used so that only the electrode wires were implanted. This was thought to be a good idea because there were no implanted electronics that could fail, thus requiring additional surgery.

By 1985 it became clear that another independent study of the effectiveness of cochlear implants was needed, since there were, once again, many claims about the effectiveness of the new commercial devices offered in the United States. For example, the very first patient implanted with the commercial Ineraid device in 1983 turned out, in retrospect, to be one of the best-performing patients with any device, including devices marketed today. He promptly was whisked off on an around-the-world trip to promote the device. Given the specter of publicity before science, the National Institutes of Health awarded a grant to Bruce Gantz and Richard Tyler at the University of Iowa Hospital to conduct an independent test of single-channel and multichannel devices. The design of the study eliminated the possibility of assigning a given implant only to patients who might do well with the device. The early results were straightforward—patients who were implanted with the multichannel devices performed far better than patients implanted with single-channel devices. Indeed, performance with the single-channel devices was so poor that implantation of the single-channel systems at Iowa was terminated.

In spite of the differences in design, the two multichannel devices (the Ineraid and the Nucleus 22) produced very similar scores on tests of speech understanding. The average score for words in sentences was around 30 percent correct. Importantly, however, the *range* of scores was 0 to 92 percent correct. Some patients, then, could understand sentences with near perfect accuracy by means of either device. The scores for the Nucleus device were not a surprise because the device used twenty-two electrodes to stimulate a wide range of fibers in the cochlea. However, the similar scores for the Ineraid patients were puzzling because of the relatively few (four) channels of stimulation. How could four channels produce speech-understanding test scores that were equal to the scores produced by twenty-two channels? We will return to this story later.

Third-Generation Implants

In 1982 the Neural Prosthesis Program (NPP) of the National Institutes of Health awarded a contract to develop new speech processors to a group of researchers at Research Triangle Institute (RTI), North Carolina, headed by Blake Wilson. The new processors were originally designed for the multichannel implant patients at the University of California, San Francisco. At the same time the NPP awarded contracts to Graham Clark at the University of Melbourne and to Robert White at Stanford University to continue work on the multichannel implants developed at those universities. These contracts led to the signal processors now used in the cochlear implants marketed in the United States.

The design of a "generic" signal processor is shown in Figure 7. An incoming speech signal is picked up by a microphone and is directed to filters that cover the range of frequencies in the speech signal. The energy in each filter is estimated and is then squeezed, or compressed, into a range appropriate for electrical stimulation. This is necessary because the tolerable range of electrical stimulation is much smaller than the range of intensities of sounds in the speech signal. Then a pulse is generated in each channel with an amplitude that represents the energy in the channel. This operation codes the intensity of the signal in each channel. Pulses from low-frequency filters go to electrodes at the "top," or apex, of the cochlea, and pulses from high-frequency filters go to electrodes at the "bottom," or base, of the cochlea. The pulses are sent in sequential fashion, one after the other, to the electrodes. This

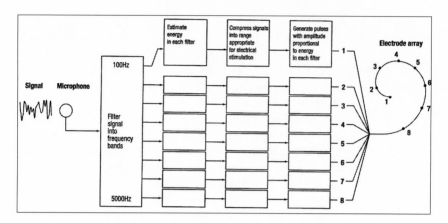

Figure 7. The design of a "generic" cochlear-implant signal processor.

interleaving of the pulses is important because pulses sent at the same time can interfere with each other and distort the representation of the frequencies in the speech signal.

The devices originally produced by Clark's group at the University of Melbourne, and now marketed by Cochlear Corporation, have undergone many changes since their beginnings in the 1970s. The hallmark of the present devices is the use of twenty filters connected to twenty electrodes. The energy in each filter is estimated, and the six to ten channels with the most energy are determined every few milliseconds. This operation is designed to pick out the multiple frequencies that characterize each of the sounds of English.

Wilson's group at RTI first developed a number of processing strategies for patients with the University of California at San Francisco (UCSF) multichannel device. Among the strategies was a "peak picking" strategy very similar to the one described above for the present University of Melbourne/Cochlear Corporation device.

Some of the UCSF patients had through-the-skin (percutaneous) connectors; others used a transmitter-receiver to send signals from the signal processor to the electrodes. The transmitter-receiver system proved unwieldy for research because it limited the types and ranges of stimuli that could be specified for the electrodes. In contrast, the direct electrical connection from the processor to the electrodes provided by the percutaneous connectors imposed no such limitations.

In 1986–87 the RTI group turned to patients who used the Ineraid's through-the-skin connector and six intracochlear electrodes in order to develop new signal-processing strategies. The result of many years of work was the continuous interleaved sampling (CIS) strategy—a strategy that is now implemented in one way or another on most commercial implants. (Even though all implant systems now offered commercially use a transmitter-receiver link, that link is adequate in most cases for support of a CIS strategy. The Ineraid system, with its percutaneous connector, is no longer manufactured or marketed.)

The hallmark of the CIS strategy is that pulses are sent out at a very fast rate in a staggered order to the electrodes. The high rate of stimulation defines the variation in time of the components of the speech signal better than a low stimulation rate.

As happens only sometimes in science, spectacular results were obtained with the first Ineraid patient tested with the CIS system. The patient obtained nearly perfect scores on tests of sentence understanding. These scores, given previous data, were not particularly surprising. What was surprising was a score of 80 percent correct on a very difficult test of words presented in isolation. Further refinement in the CIS processor boosted the patient's single-word score to 98 percent correct, a score well within the range of scores for normal-hearing listeners. Of course, not all patients did this well—scores on the test of words in isolation ranged from 5 to 94 percent correct—but Wilson and his colleagues were clearly on the right track.

It is worth noting that the RTI made a decision early in its work to donate all results from its NIH-sponsored research on cochlear implants to the public domain. This has facilitated use of the technology by manufacturers of implant systems and thereby helped bring the benefits of the technology to recipients of cochlear implants. CIS or CIS-like processors are now offered in implant systems manufactured by Advanced Bionics Corporation of Sylmar, California (the Clarion devices); Med El Corporation of Innsbruck, Austria (the COMBI 40 and COMBI 40+ devices); Cochlear Pty. Ltd. of Sydney, Australia (as a processing option in its new CI24M device); and Bionic Systems of Antwerp, Belgium (the LAURA device). Ironically, the manufacturer of the Ineraid device decided not to utilize this technology and instead discontinued the Ineraid product line, thus denying the benefits of the technology to the very patients with whom the technology was developed!

The Current State of the Art

How well do patients understand speech with the current generation of cochlear implants? Scores for words in sentences for patients who use the eight-channel Clarion CIS processor are shown in Figure 8. The most common score is 90–100 percent correct. Similar scores are found for patients who use Cochlear Corporation's Nucleus 22–Spectra processor, which is the most widely used processor in the world (with over 15,000 units worldwide). However, for any device used, some patients, perhaps 10 percent, score in the 0–10 percent correct range. As we noted in the section on anatomy and physiology, inevitably some patients will have very few fibers to stimulate and, as a consequence, will not be able to code the multiple frequencies in the speech signal.

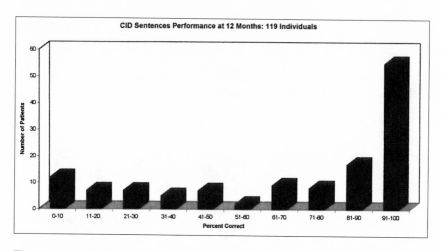

Figure 8. Identification of words in sentences by 119 adults fit with a cochlear implant. Slightly more than half of the individuals achieved scores between 80 and 100 percent correct.

Even the best-performing patients do not get all the information in the speech signal. Patients who achieve scores in the sentence test of between 90–100 percent correct average only 58 percent correct when tested with individual words without sentence context (the best-performing patients achieve scores between 70 and 90 percent correct). Thus, it appears that the best-performing patients recognize many, perhaps most, individual sounds and rely on sentence context to fill in the identity of the sounds they cannot resolve.

What does an implant sound like to the best-performing patients? One patient writes: "Speech sounds perfectly natural to me now. ...it is easy to distinguish voices, even over the telephone. Also important, I can hear all the little intonations and inflections in speech with which we color the mood and meaning of what we say. I would say that speech is very clear, although I find that when I begin to listen to someone with a heavy accent, it takes me a bit before I get a good grip on what they are saying."[4] Another patient wrote:

> In my everyday situation ... I deal with customers in person and on the phone. ... I really don't run into any problems at work except for some children who might ask me a question, or a customer who is looking in the opposite direction and is talking to me. So I have to ask the person to turn around and face me. With the telephone I can understand at least 90 percent of the time. Sometimes I have to have them spell their names for me when they are reserving movies and ... kids at certain age levels are hard for me to understand. The only other situation [in which I have trouble] is when we are with a lot people and everyone is talking.[5]

A patient with *average* scores on tests of word intelligibility wrote: "I receive a sharp clear signal when the person articulates properly. I don't do well with mumblers and foreign accents. [I don't hear] as well as I would like in everyday situations ... [but] most are very satisfactory. [I don't hear as well as I would like] in group meetings [but] do pretty well with an FM system when [I can] move the microphone around."[6]

One patient with *very poor* speech understanding wrote:

> It [the implant] is incredibly useful for environmental sounds ... the door-bell, the microwave signal, the two different phone lines at home (one is a TDD) ... and so on. I was thrilled to hear crickets again—even though everyone else with normal hearing seems to complain about them. It is just wonderful to hear birds again and when I was in Belgium on vacation last year I heard a rooster crow. It was the first rooster I had heard since I was a child. I also enjoyed listening to the train whistles and ... the wonderful church bells. I would stop in the middle of a street to listen in wonder to those bells! I recognized speech as such when I heard it for the first time, but it sounded to me like when I was little and was sent to bed ... when we had company. I'd strain my ears to hear what the adults were talking about through closed doors. I couldn't understand what they were saying but could recognize the voices. ... I can tell men's voices from women's. I can tell singing from speech.[7]

Results for Adults Who Were Deafened at Birth

The results described above were for patients who had been deafened relatively late in life and who had memories of what speech sounds like. What happens if an adult (as distinguished from a child) who has *never* heard before is given an implant? There are several reasons to suspect that understanding speech by means of the implant would be very difficult for these individuals. First, the individual would have no memory of what the consonants and vowels of language sound like. Second, it is likely that the individual's auditory system would have been damaged as a result of the deprivation of sound. It has been well documented that the size of cell bodies in the core of the cochlea and in the central nervous system shrink, or atrophy, as a consequence of not being stimulated by sound. Furthermore, stimulation during infancy drives, or shapes, the formation of neural connections in the central nervous system. Neural interconnections will not develop normally in the absence of stimulation. This does not suggest that the auditory system will not respond to sound following a long period of deprivation but rather suggests that the neural responses to sound will be abnormal. Thus, we should expect that adults who were deafened at birth and who receive an implant as an adult will "hear" but will have great difficulty, perhaps unsurmountable difficulty, in understanding speech.

The data support the prediction. Tests conducted in several countries indicate, overwhelmingly, that patients who were deafened at birth and who were implanted as adults obtain little speech understanding by means of an implant.[8] Of all the patients reported in the literature, only a few individuals achieve speech understanding scores at a level above chance. Yet many individuals who obtain no speech understanding wear their implants daily and derive a high level of satisfaction with the devices. This is because (1) the implant allows them to "hear"; (2) the implant allows them to recognize some environmental sounds, such as a dog barking or a telephone ringing; (3) the implant provides improved self-monitoring for speech production, which leads to better voice quality; and (4) the implant assists with speechreading.

There is a growing population (primarily teenagers and young adults but some older adults), also deaf from birth, who are receiving cochlear implants. Generally, they are profoundly hearing-impaired, are considered good hearing aid users (in contrast to the individuals described in the previous paragraph, who did not wear hearing aids), communicate through auditory and oral means, and have been mainstreamed through their school years. These "borderline" cochlear implant candidates can articulate eloquently the differences between hearing with their hearing aids and hearing with their implants. This group is too new yet to have contributed to the pool of research data. Clinicians are finding that many—or even most—of these individuals understand speech with their implants.

Why Aren't Devices with More Electrodes Better?

It was noted above that one of the puzzles about cochlear implants is that devices with a relatively small number of electrodes allow the same levels of speech understanding as devices with many more electrodes. The results of experiments at RTI and the House Ear Institute suggest that most patients cannot take advantage of more than a relatively small (perhaps six to seven) number of electrodes, or channels, in the course of speech understanding. The factors underlying this limitation are not well understood. Perhaps the current electrode designs restrict, for some unknown reason, the number of channels that can be accessed. If this is so, then perhaps different electrode designs would allow more channels to be accessed in the service of speech perception.

How Many Channels Are Needed?

In the previous section we indicated that implants with relatively few channels allowed the same level of speech understanding as devices with relatively many channels. We also indicated that the patients who achieve 90–100 percent scores on tests of word understanding in sentences average only 58 percent correct on tests of words in isolation. So, how many channels are needed to get a perfect, or near perfect, score on words in isolation, or alternatively, how many channels are necessary to correctly identify each of the sounds in an isolated word?

To answer this question, my colleague Philip Loizou and I have processed words through a simulation of a cochlear implant's signal processor with four, six, and eight channels and have presented the words to normal-hearing listeners for identification. The results indicate that eight channels of stimulation allow 95 percent of the sounds in the words to be identified. Thus, if an implant patient were able to extract from eight channels all the information that a normal-hearing individual could extract, eight channels, or eight electrodes, would be sufficient to allow a very high level of speech understanding.

Children and Implants

An adult who loses his or her hearing and who then is fitted with a cochlear implant has a lifetime of linguistic knowledge to aid in the interpretation of the new, slightly degraded, or greatly degraded sounds delivered by the implant. Thus, the largely tacit, or unconscious, knowledge about what sequences of sounds are permissible in English and which words usually follow each other in a normal sentence has a large influence on the intelligibility of speech transmitted by an implant. A child who has acquired language, and subsequently loses hearing, may respond to an implant as well as an adult if the child has developed adult-like linguistic knowledge. However, the child deafened at birth does not have a set of linguistic rules to guide the interpretation of the impoverished sounds provided by the implant. Indeed, the child must discover the rules of spoken language by means of the degraded signal.

Learning a language by means of a degraded speech signal is not a circumstance unique to children with cochlear implants. Children with mild to profound hearing losses have always faced this challenge. We should imagine that the performance of hearing-impaired children on tasks of speech perception, speech production, and language acquisition could be used to generate a reasonable set of expectations for the performance of implanted children. However, the speech and language skills of "normal" hearing-impaired children vary widely. On the one hand, there are ample data to suggest that even a mild hearing loss, if undetected, can result in a delay in the acquisition of language skills. On the other hand, a relatively small number of individuals, such as the author of this book, have acquired speech and language skills— in this instance, the skills appropriate for a professor of law—and have acquired those skills with the aid of very little hearing for a very short period of time. Nonetheless, the usual outcomes of losing hearing early and profoundly are delays in the acquisition of language skills and disorders in both speech production and, of course, speech perception.

The first children to receive implants were given single-channel devices by Bill House in 1980. The children obtained very little speech understanding by means of the device (remember that a single-channel device cannot represent the multiple frequencies that characterize each of the sounds of speech). The average level of speech-perception skill was being able to discriminate the difference between a one-syllable word and a two-syllable word. Understanding words in sentences by sound alone was near zero except for one or two children. The results for these single-channel patients are important for several reasons. One is that the results established that children could obtain some information even from a very impoverished signal. The second reason is that the relatively meager results have allowed those who do not approve of implants in children, on principle, to say that implants do not "work" in children or to say that "no child has acquired language by means of a cochlear implant."

Of course, as implants improved from single-channel devices to second- and third-generation, multichannel devices, so also did the performance of implanted children. In the United States, large studies of the speech and language skills of implanted children who were deafened before they learned language (prelingually deafened children) have been conducted, and are still under way, at the University of Iowa, the University of Indiana School of Medicine, the Central Institute for the Deaf, and the New York University School of Medicine.

Before the results of these, and other, studies are summarized, several factors that have affected the results need to be considered. First is the nature of the device used. For obvious reasons, very long-term data are available only from children who were implanted with either single-channel implants or early versions of multichannel implants. Second is the nature of the disorder that produced the deafness. Some pathologies damage parts of both the peripheral and the central nervous system. Thus, some implanted children must struggle with both a degraded signal and learning disabilities. Other pathologies result in a cochlea that is not fully developed and in which only a small number of electrodes can be inserted. The task of understanding speech will be especially difficult (but not necessarily impossible) for these children. Third is the age of the child at implantation. Given that early stimulation shapes the organization of neural connections from the auditory periphery to the cerebral cortex, it stands to reason that the earlier the children are implanted, the better their performance will be later in childhood. The population of children for whom there are the most data were implanted relatively late in childhood. Only recently have children age 2 years or younger received implants. Fourth is the type and amount of rehabilitation and or parental attention the child receives. Studies have found that children in classrooms where hearing and listening are the sole means of communication score better on tests of speech intelligibility than do children in classrooms where listening and speaking are only one of the possible means of communication.[9] The more time spent in aural rehabilitation, the better is the performance. Finally, not all parents have had the time and the skills to aid their children in adapting to sound. Given the factors cited above, we should expect to find, and do find, a wide range of test scores in children. The current data on the speech and language skills of children with implants serve best as a hint as to the level of skills that will be acquired by children who will use advanced sound-processors, who will be implanted early in childhood (age 2 or before), and who will receive intensive rehabilitation.

Speech Understanding by Prelingually Deafened Children

The results on a test of understanding common phrases for thirty prelingually deafened children fitted with third-generation cochlear implants are shown in Figure 9.[10] The children were implanted at ages 3.5 to 7.5 years and had used their implant for only a year. Ten of the thirty children achieved

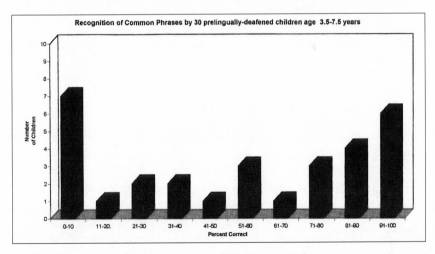

Figure 9. Identification of words in common phrases by thirty prelingually deafened children who were fit with an implant between the ages of 3.5 and 7.5 years and who had used the implant for a year. Thirty-three percent of the children achieved scores between 80 and 100 percent correct. Twenty-seven percent of the children achieved scores between 0 and 20 percent correct.

scores between 80 and 100 percent correct. However, seven of the thirty achieved scores between 0 and 10 percent correct. The low scores are not surprising given the number of factors working against acquiring speech-perception skills immediately following a long period of auditory deprivation. Moreover, data from other studies indicate that children who score 0 percent correct at one year after implantation can achieve scores of 100 percent correct two, three, four, or five years following implantation.[11] Indeed, a study of one hundred children in England reports that 85 percent of the children were able to understand common phrases three years after implantation.[12] Clearly, after a relatively short period of adaptation, many children are able to achieve high scores on tests of sentence understanding. Several chapters in this book provide further discussions of this topic.

The Intelligibility of Speech Produced by Prelingually Deafened Children

The average intelligibility of speech produced by profoundly hearing-impaired children is about 20 percent. The intelligibility of speech produced by a sample of implanted children at the Central Institute for the Deaf—children, who use second-generation multichannel implants, who were implanted at age 4, who had used their implants for at least two years, and who attended oral schools—is 48 percent, with a range from 14 to 93 percent.[13] Like the scores for speech understanding, the scores for speech intelligibility vary greatly. And again, it is encouraging that some of the children achieved scores of 90 percent intelligibility or better. The study of one hundred children from England reports that five years after implantation, 83 percent of the children produce speech that is sufficiently intelligible and that the children use speech as their primary mode of communication.

Language Acquisition

Children who are profoundly deaf generally develop language at less than half the rate of normal-hearing children, that is, at a rate of approximately five months' growth in one year. At age 5 years, for example, a profoundly deaf child may have the expressive language skills of a normal-hearing child of 2.4 years. As a consequence, children implanted at, for example, 5 years of age will be delayed in language structure, vocabulary, and language content. A critical issue, then, is whether an implant can restore a normal rate of language development. Recent results from the study at the Indiana University School of Medicine indicate that the answer to this question is "yes."[14] Children implanted at age 4 years (on average) were tested for expressive language skills at six-month intervals for a period of two and one-half years following implantation. In each six-month interval, the implanted children's scores increased as much as the scores from a group of normal-hearing children. In contrast to the six-month gain in language score found for normal-hearing and implanted children in each six-month interval, the gain in language scores for a group of not-implanted, profoundly deaf children was approximately 2.5 months. The different rates of acquisition of language skills in the implanted and not-implanted children demonstrate the effectiveness of the implant in fostering the acquisition of spoken language. These data argue eloquently for early implantation of children—the earlier children are implanted, the less language delay they will have to overcome. The case studies provided later in this book reinforce this concept.

If an implant can restore a normal rate of language acquisition, is it the case that children implanted, for example, at age 5 years are doomed throughout childhood to be 2.6 years behind in language skills? The answer to this question is "no." As documented in the case studies in this book, the language skills of implanted children can—and do—catch up with the language skills of normal-hearing children.

On Reading and Hearing

Many studies have shown that there is an important relationship between reading skills and the ability to segment, or divide, the speech signal into syllables and sounds. Poor readers have more difficulty than good readers in identifying the number of syllables in words and the number of different sounds in words. It follows from this that children who cannot hear, or produce, the syllables and sounds in a language will begin the processes of reading at a marked disadvantage. Early poor reading skills act, in turn, to limit the addition of new words to a child's vocabulary (new words appear to be added to a vocabulary principally from reading new words and discovering their meaning from context). The third-grade reading level, on average, of profoundly deaf high school graduates documents the difficulty in learning to read when an individual does not have access to the sound system of his or her language. This is not to say that perceiving and producing speech auditorily is an absolute requirement for reading. However, it is undeniable that learning to read is enormously easier if an individual can hear or produce the speech sounds that most writing systems seek to mimic. And adding words to an individual's vocabulary is very much easier if the meanings of new words encountered in print can be inferred from an already large vocabulary.

Cochlear implants assist deaf children in improving their reading scores by providing the children with the ability to access our sound system. Thus, as the case studies presented later in this text illustrate, implanted deaf children increasingly demonstrate reading scores at age-appropriate levels.

The Look of Devices in the Near Future

One aspect of the near future is already clear—companies will offer smaller devices, ones that fit behind the ear like a hearing aid. It remains to be seen whether the smaller devices—with, perhaps, restricted computational power—will allow the same level of performance as the larger devices that are currently manufactured. The signal processing of the devices produced by different companies will, most likely, function in very similar ways. All will offer variable rates of stimulation, and all will use the continuous interleaved sampling (CIS) strategy or a version of this strategy. Each device will have a "feature" that distinguishes it from other devices. The newest device from Cochlear Corporation, the CI24m-ACE, features two new electrodes that allow the device to be run in one of a number of modes of stimulation (e.g., monopolar or bipolar electrode stimulation), and features a faster pulse rate than previous models. The Clarion device offers an electrode design that differs from other designs, and the device can be programmed with a variety of pulse-stimulation schemes or with the analogue signal as output to the electrode array. The Med El Combi 40+, which is currently being tested in the United States, offers an electrode array that can be inserted deeper into the cochlea than other electrodes and offers both a CIS stimulation scheme and a stimulation scheme similar to that of the Cochlear Corporation device. There is some evidence that each of the features of each of the devices might be of benefit to patients. At present, it is difficult to argue that any of these features will make a large difference in performance. However, all of the devices will provide the opportunity for individuals who have lost their hearing to hear once again and the opportunity for children, and some adults, who have never heard to hear for the first time.

Further Reading and Viewing

Perhaps the best way to become acquainted with cochlear implants is to view videotapes of adults and children who use implants. An impressive tape is *The Story of David*, documenting Warren Estabrooks's work with a child fitted with a cochlear implant. This tape can be obtained from Cochlear Corporation, 61 Inverness Drive East, Suite 200, Englewood, CO 80112. Another impressive, and short, tape is *Samples of Speech Production and Language in Children with Cochlear Implants* which documents the ability of several children who use cochlear implants. This tape can be obtained from Dr. Emily

Tobey, Callier Center for Communication Disorders, University of Texas at Dallas, 1966 Inwood Rd., Dallas, TX 75236. A video of adults who use cochlear implants is *Symphony of Life*. This tape can be obtained from Cochlear Corporation, 61 Inverness Drive East, Suite 200, Englewood, CO 80112.

Good sources of technical information about cochlear implants can be found in the following texts: R. Tyler (ed.), *Cochlear Implants: Audiological Foundations* (Singular Publishing Group, 1993); G. Clark, Y. Tong, and J. Patrick (eds.), *Cochlear Prostheses* (Churchill Livingstone, 1990); D. Allum (ed.), *Cochlear Implant Rehabilitation in Children and Adults* (Singular Publishing Group, 1996); G. Clark, R. Cowan and R. Dowell (eds.), *Cochlear Implantation for Infants and Children* (Singular Publishing Group, 1997); M. E. Nevins and P. Chute (eds.), *Children with Cochlear Implants in Educational Settings* (Singular Publishing Group, 1996); and A. Geers and J. Moog (eds.), "Effectiveness of Cochlear Implants and Tactile Aids for Deaf Children: The Sensory Aids Study at Central Institute for the Deaf," *Volta Review* 96, no. 5 (1994).

Each company that manufactures cochlear implants has publications describing its products. The address for Advanced Bionics Corporation is 12740 San Fernando Road, Sylmar, CA 91342. The address for Cochlear Corporation is 61 Inverness Drive East, Suite 200, Englewood, CO 80112. The address for Med El Corporation is P.O. Box 14183, Research Triangle Park, NC 27709. In addition, information and referrals may be obtained from the Alexander Graham Bell Association for the Deaf, 3417 Volta Place NW, Washington, DC, 20007 (202-337-5220), and from Auditory-Verbal International, 2121 Eisenhower Ave., Suite 402, Alexandria, VA 22314 (703-739-1049).

NOTES

1. W. House, "Case Histories," *Annals of Otology, Rhinology, and Laryngology* 86 (supp. 38) (1977).
2. *Ibid.*
3. R. Bilger, F. Black, N. Hopkinson, E. Myers, J. Payne, and N. Stenson, "Evaluation of Subjects Presently Fitted with Implanted Auditory Prosthesis," *Annals of Otology, Rhinology, and Laryngology* 86 (supp. 38) (1977): 1–176.
4. Personal communication to M. Dorman.
5. *Ibid.*
6. *Ibid.*
7. *Ibid.*
8. T. Zwolan, P. Kileny, J. Kemink, C. Spak, and L. Lougheed, "A Closer Look at Cochlear Implant Use by Prelingual Adults" (paper presented at the Third International Cochlear Implant Symposium, Innsbruck, Austria, 1993).
9. M. Osberger, A. Robbins, S. Todd, and A. Riley, "Speech Intelligibility of Children with Cochlear Implants," *Volta Review* 96, no. 5 (1994): 169–80.
10. Data provided by Dorcas Kesler of Advanced Bionics Corporation.

11. S. Waltzman, N. Cohen, R. Gomolin, J. Green, W. Shapiro, R. Hoffman, and J. T. Roland, *American Journal of Otology* 18 (1997): 342–49.

12. Gerald M. O'Donoghue, Queens Medical Center HHS Trust, Nottingham, England, personal communication.

13. Osberger, et al., "Speech Intelligibility."

14. A. Robbins, M. Svirsky, and K. Kirk, "Implanted Children Can Speak, but Can They Communicate?" (paper presented at the Sixth Symposium on Cochlear Implants in Children, University of Miami School of Medicine, Miami, 1996).

Chapter 2

Me and My Implant: The Story of an "Unsuccessful" Cochlear Implant Recipient

BONNIE POITRAS TUCKER, J.D.

Professor Tucker received her law degree from the University of Colorado in 1980. She served as law clerk to the honorable William E. Doyle, U.S. Court of Appeals, 10th Circuit, was a litigation partner in the firm of Brown & Bain, P.A., and is now Professor of Law at Arizona State University College of Law. The author of numerous articles and books (including the autobiographical The Feel of Silence*), Professor Tucker has been profoundly deaf (and unable to wear hearing aids) since the age of two. She received a cochlear implant at the age of fifty-two.*

Let's Do It (Making the Decision)

Silence for fifty years and then the prospect of sound—the possibility was mind-boggling! What would I hear? Would I really "hear" anything? Would the sounds make any sense? Would my brain be able to tolerate this terrible invasion of heretofore unknown noise? Would my mind, and body, rebel? Would I be driven mad by the distraction of constant whirring and whining sounds, a never-ending irritable disruption of my quiet peace? My God, whatever possessed me to do this?

These thoughts, and others, went through my mind as I lay on the hospital cot awaiting cochlear implant surgery—surgery that I, against my surgeon's recommendation, had insisted on having.

And then came that most terrifying thought, a thought that I fought my damnedest to keep from popping into the forefront of my brain but that stubbornly refused to stay hidden, like a clever child with years of experience playing hide-and-seek running circles around a trusting, less cunning, adult: Would this intrusive barrage of noise destroy my ability to concentrate and prevent me from doing what I do so well—speechreading?

But it was too late to turn back now. The fight had been fought, and I had *won*. Or had I?

I was fifty-two years old. My parents had discovered that I was profoundly deaf when I was two, and I was never able to wear hearing aids. Despite my profound deafness, however, as a result of good training and a lucky innate ability to *inhale* speech and language, I had very good speech—those familiar with the speech of deaf people might think I was hard-of-hearing, but those not familiar with deafness or deaf speech thought I had an accent of some sort. And I was one fantastic speechreader. Really. I could speechread almost anyone in a one-to-one, face-to-face conversation. It was due to these skills that I was able to function successfully in the legal profession, first as a trial attorney and later as a law professor teaching large law school classes in the Socratic (question-and-answer) method.

Excellent speech and speechreading abilities notwithstanding, I was still deaf. And I hated being deaf. I hated not being able to use the telephone. I hated having to rely on an interpreter in court, in large law school classes, at meetings, on the telephone, etc. I hated not being able to use the telephone. I hated not being able to watch television, go to movies or plays, hear music, communicate in a dark place or after the sun went down. I hated not being able to use the telephone. I hated not being able to understand my youngest grandchildren (toddlers are almost impossible to speechread). And, in case you haven't gotten the message yet, I hated not being able to use the telephone.

Since I so hated being deaf, it should not come as any surprise that when the multichannel cochlear implant began getting some publicity, and people who had once heard but had became deaf began showing good results with cochlear implants, I decided that I would be implanted. But don't let me deceive you. This was not a simple, sudden decision.

Several years before, I had seriously considered having the single-channel cochlear implant, after being contacted by several doctors and researchers who wanted me to serve as a "guinea pig." But my research showed that I could expect very little benefit, if any, from the single-channel implant. The possible benefits did not seem worth the time and energy that I would have to expend, particularly since I was a struggling law student and single mother of three children. Ultimately, I declined.

By 1990, however, vast progress had been made in the field of multichannel cochlear implants. People with short-term deafness, people who were deaf but had previously heard, people with long-term deafness who had worn (and received considerable benefit from) hearing aids for some time, and children who were implanted in their early years were showing what I (and most professionals) considered to be remarkable results with cochlear implants. I was ready.

Having made my decision, I was shocked to learn that the powers that be were not ready for me! I thought it was a simple matter of *me* making up *my* mind to be implanted. After all, doctors had wanted to implant me years before, and it was I who had said no. Naively, I thought that now that I had said yes, we would all just get on with the job—not so. Now that doctors and audiologists knew more about cochlear implants, they decided that I was not a good candidate for the implant. My long-term deafness was against me. Medical wisdom had changed.

The latest theory was that since my brain had not had auditory input for so long (assuming it ever did—we have no way of knowing how much I heard before the age of two), it would not know what to do with the auditory input it would receive from the implant. To put it bluntly (and the "experts" did), I was a "bad" candidate. I would not "do well" with the implant. Having explained that to me, the medical experts assumed that I would acquiesce in their decision that I should not have an implant.

I did not acquiesce. The more I learned about multichannel implants, the more determined I became to be implanted. Maybe the doctors and audiologists were right. The reality was that no one—not me, not the doctors, not the audiologists—could know for sure whether an implant would help me hear. We could talk about probabilities and possibilities and plausibilities forever; as far as I was concerned, that was all irrelevant. I knew that it would take two things to make the implant successful: hard work and perseverance on my part, and some physical capability of the ear and brain. The first I could guarantee; I was willing to take my chances on the second.

So I set about persuading Dr. William Luxford of the House Ear Institute in Los Angeles to perform the surgery.

Dr. Luxford, of course, opined that I should not have the implant, for the same reasons I had heard a hundredfold times before: I already spoke and speechread so well that the implant would give me little practical benefit; since I had been deaf all my life, the chances of my receiving any substantial benefit were slim to none; I would probably hear just background noises that might drive me crazy; the implant would do nothing to change my life in any significant manner; etc., etc. After a few weeks, however, I finally persuaded the good doctor that the decision should be *mine*, not his. Even though I respected his opinion and recommendation, and recognized the substantial possibility (probability?) that he was right, I still wanted to try. Dr. Luxford agreed to perform the surgery, on my sworn promise that no matter how much I hated the implant, I would wear it for at least a year and a half and perhaps two years, the minimum amount of time he felt it would take for me to see any real benefit from the implant—if, that is, I was ever going to see such benefit.

Our agreement was signed, sealed, and delivered with a vengeance. There I was on a hospital cot awaiting surgery to be implanted with a Cochlear Corporation Nucleus 22 device while visions of the proverbial monster sauntered unwelcomely through my mind.

The Surgery

On December 10, 1991, the day before my cochlear implant surgery was scheduled, I flew to Los Angeles. I spent the night with a friend, who dropped me off at the hospital on her way to work the next morning. I was given a battery of routine preoperative tests (EKG, blood tests, x-rays), filled out the usual mountains of paperwork, and early that afternoon was officially checked into the hospital for an overnight stay. Shortly after being shown to my hospital bed, I had chats with Dr. Luxford and the anesthesiologist, was given a sedative, and after the usual "wait on the cot in the hallway," during which I tried not to think about what might be in store for the future, was wheeled into surgery.

The next thing I knew it was about three and a half hours later and I was in the recovery room, feeling crummy. My head hurt. I was sick to my stomach. I had bandages over half of one side of my head. I could feel the bump, slightly behind my ear, that would stay with me for the rest of my life—the place where the internal implant stuck out, the place where a magnet would be attached to connect the internal device to the external processor. I closed my eyes and willed myself to remember that by the same time tomorrow I'd feel a lot better.

The next morning my daughter, Ronale, arrived from her home in San Diego at about 10:30. After Ronale swore to act as my bodyguard-nurse and after some more bureaucratic paperwork was completed, I was allowed to check out of that first-class hotel. Ronale and I went to Brentwood, walked around a few shops (I even bought a new blouse), had lunch at an Italian restaurant, and drove to the airport for my flight home. My parents met me at the airport in Phoenix, took one look at me, and drove me to my house, where I fell into bed.

It doesn't sound *too* bad, does it? And in truth, I don't remember it as being too bad. (On the other hand, I obviously didn't remember childbirth as being too bad, else how could I have had three children?)

I stayed around the house for a couple of days, until I got all the anesthetics out of my system and could make a halfhearted stab at washing the ends of my hair without wetting my scalp (try that someday). On about the fourth day after surgery, I went back to work. I felt dizzy off and on for a while and had some minimal discomfort, but nothing I couldn't live and work with. The biggest aggravation was trying to comb my already too thin hair over the bald spot. (I haven't decided whether it's more important in my next life to come back with thick hair or hearing. I sure hope I don't have to choose.)

The *really* hard part was waiting to be "hooked up." That was a *very long* month. I couldn't sleep for wondering what would happen when we made the magic connection. Would it work?

Hooking Up the Processor

A month later, on January 9, 1992, I again flew to Los Angeles. This time I rented a car and drove to the House Ear Institute. I was alone; I had not asked any friend, foe, or family member to come along. Dr. Luxford and his audiologist, Dawna Mills, had warned me not to expect much at the initial hookup. I hadn't wanted to risk anyone else's disappointment if I couldn't hear with this thing; it would be all I could do to handle my own disappointment.

Hooking up the implant was to take three days. It was not just a simple matter of connecting the external processor to the internal device. Each of the twenty-two electrodes had to be individually programmed by Dawna, via computer, to provide noise that my brain could process as intelligible (hopefully) and tolerable (hopefully, again) sound. In view of my fifty years of silence, the ability of my ear-brain to process information was expected to fluctuate greatly for some time. Thus, at a minimum, I would need to spend a few hours a day for three consecutive days working in a cooperative effort with Dawna and her magic computer (actually, I think it's half Dawna's magic and half the computer's magic), struggling to devise for my processor a program that I could go home and play with for three weeks or so before my next compulsory visit to L.A.

Once I arrived at Dawna's office, the initial lessons began. It seemed to take forever just to get the magnet placed on the bump on my head so that it would not fall off. Then I had to figure out how to get the microphone around my ear and still keep my glasses on my head. Sigh. Already I felt like a creature from *Star Wars*, and I had yet to figure out what to do with the long, forty-inch cord that ran from the magnet and microphone (which were connected by a short cord, not to be confused with the long cord) to the processor. I stuffed the longest cord inside my blouse and hoped for the best. Then I pulled it out again to connect it to the processor.

Ahhh, the processor. It was about one and a half times the size of a cigarette box and the weight of at least three cartons of cigarettes. Where was I going to *put* it? I wondered. But now was not the time to think about such mundane matters. It was time for the real fun to begin.

After we got all the paraphernalia organized on various parts of my person, Dawna plugged my processor into the computer. We would program each electrode separately, Dawna explained, and after we had programmed all of the electrodes, we would create a "map" for my processor. The map was sort of like a roadmap. It would tell us where the sounds were going, in terms of direction and intensity (plus a few other things that remain too complicated for me to understand, much less explain).

Dawna turned on the first electrode, number 20 (we started with the low-frequency electrodes), and told me to let her know the first time I heard a noise—that would be my "threshold" level for that electrode. She played with the dial, increasing the sound on that electrode. A few seconds later I heard it—sound. Real sound. It was unmistakable. Not a vibration, not my imagination, but S O U N D. I was overwhelmed—part happiness and part fear. Tears welled behind my eyes but did not fall. I refused to let them.

We played with that electrode for a while. Dawna kept making the sound louder until, as instructed, I told her that the noise was as loud as I could tolerate it for a period of a minute or so. We had now established my "comfort" level for that electrode. The span between my threshold and comfort levels was my "range" for that electrode. Our job with electrode 20 was over for the moment.

Dawna turned electrode 20 off and turned electrode 19 on. And the process began all over again with electrode 19. We repeated the process for a few more electrodes. Already I was exhausted. Just the pinpricks of sound were overwhelming. I had a headache accompanied by nausea that I tried to ignore. I would have *loved* to take a nap (and I think I've taken only three naps in my entire life).

There was no time for a nap. We had to balance the electrodes we had already programmed. This involved playing a sound on each electrode in turn, one after the other in fairly rapid succession, to be sure that all the programmed electrodes were set at approximately the same loudness level. If one electrode was louder, Dawna lowered it; if one was softer, she made it louder. Finally, all the electrodes seemed to be balanced—they seemed to be at approximately the same loudness level.

And now it was time to turn on all the electrodes we had programmed. Dawna warned me not to expect much. We had programmed only a few of the electrodes. And I was getting very little sound from each of them. My ranges were extremely small—only 3, 4, or 5, which meant that the sound could travel only a minuscule distance on each electrode. Experienced and very successful cochlear implant users often have ranges between 50 and 100 or more on each electrode, Dawna explained (although some do well with smaller ranges). I thought of an accordion. It seemed logical that sound traveling through the full range of the accordion would be fuller and richer than sound traveling through just one inch of the accordion. Until I could build up my ranges from the first inch of the accordion to the second, third, and ultimately—if I was lucky—to the fiftieth or however many inches the accordion would stretch to, the sound that I would hear would be very limited in quality. So I tried to prepare myself to expect just "a little" sound.

On came the sound. And out came my tears. This time all my efforts could not hold them back.

"It's too loud, I know," said Dawna. "Is it painful?"

"No," I managed to reply.

In truth, the tears were not falling because of discomfort. They were falling because I was overwhelmed to be hearing sound. I did not have the words to describe what I felt, and I didn't even try. How could I explain what it felt like to experience sound to someone who has known sound all her life? Anything I said then, and anything I say now, would be anticlimactic.

Sound. I heard it.

Sound. It was amazing.

Yes. Sound.

I won't bore you with the rest of the process. Dawna and I spent several hours a day for the next two days doing more of the same, and I flew home to Phoenix with a "map" of sorts.

Surviving the First Year

Well, I had the implant. And I had the best map that could be created at the moment, which wasn't saying much.

I didn't like it.

That's an understatement.

I hated it.

All I heard were dots. Little beep, beep, beeps. Dot dot dot dot dot dot dot dot dot ... They made no sense at all. And they were downright unpleasant. I wanted those incessant dots to *stop*.

And I had a couple of other complaints as well. First, I started to get dizzy. A couple of times I even fell after losing my balance. I saw Dr. Luxford, who declared that I had developed something called cochlear hydrops, which results in an accumulation of fluid around the cochlea when hearing fluctuates. Dr. Luxford put me on steroids, which got rid of the problem for the time being, and placed me on a diuretic to keep water from forming around the cochlea and causing future episodes. (I continue to take the diuretics. I've had three or four other episodes of hydrops in the five years since my implant—all of which were resolved with steroids in a matter of a week or two.)

Second, I developed tinnitus (ringing in the ears) when I took the implant off. The loud ringing in my head was very distracting. I thought it was some deity's way of telling me that I was meant to keep the implant on at all times— something I intended to do anyway and had promised Dr. Luxford I would do. But I did have to take the implant off when I went to bed at night. And on more than one occasion, the tinnitus kept me from sleeping. I began to think that I'd better see some progress with this implant soon or I'd be *really* annoyed.

I was destined for more annoyance. Because I didn't see any progress.

That's not to say that I wasn't hearing things, however. I heard things, all right.

I heard the toilet flushing—and not just when I flushed it, but also when others flushed it. It sounded like I imagined Niagara Falls would sound. It was *loud* and *horrible*. I started to talk about conserving water by flushing the toilet only once a day. That didn't lead to as unpleasant a situation as you might think because I also started limiting the number of times a day I used the toilet, which meant that the toilet didn't *need* to be flushed as often—but that's not why I limited my use of it. I limited my use of the toilet for two reasons.

First, I wouldn't use the toilet when anyone else was around. I learned that you can *hear* someone using the toilet. My God, whatever happened to privacy?

Second, it was just too much trouble to use the toilet with this implant. I had finally figured out a way to wear the processor without looking like a Martian. I ran the long cord from behind my ear through my clothing as far as a pocket inset into the right side of whatever I was wearing on the lower half of my body. I poked a hole on the inside of the pocket with a scissor, and pushed the cord through the hole before inserting it into the processor. Then I stuck the processor, still attached to the cord, into the pocket. Voila, almost invisible. The problem was that most of the clothes I had with inset pockets were pants. So I took to wearing only pants. The cord, however, was still forty inches long, and it did not stretch. To pull my pants down to go to the bathroom, I had to bend completely in half to avoid being choked to death by the cord (which, if you will recall, went from the processor in my pocket past my neck and around my ear to the microphone and magnet). Then I would slowly ease my bent body onto the toilet. It was a pain in the neck and also a pain in the back—a general pain.

(I don't know why I am using the past tense, since the situation remains the same today. I have, however, taken to wearing skirts and dresses again. I take everything to a tailor, who insets a pocket in every piece of clothing I purchase. I have even gotten creative and had a pocket of sorts put into the short sleeve of a sequined cocktail dress, since the dress was too fitted and the sequins too delicate to allow a pocket to be placed on the side of the dress.)

I heard more than toilets, though. I also heard motorcycles. Every time a motorcycle drove in the vicinity of wherever I happened to be, I almost went crazy. It hurt; it *really* hurt. I heard thunder too, if it was close. And I heard the washer, the dryer, the dishwasher, and a hundred and one other appliances and gadgets that all sounded (and continue to sound) most unpleasant. Were all appliances and gadgets invented by deaf people?

I heard dogs bark—big dogs. I could no longer take walks in certain places because I was terrified of the huge dogs I heard barking behind fences— dogs that I had heretofore not known existed, since the fences kept them hidden. Now I was convinced that those dogs would break down the fences to attack me.

This is why I had the implant?—I wondered during the first six months after hookup.

Not exactly: there were still the dots to contend with—my individual Morse code, which I took to calling, in my mind only, the "dittydots." What were the dittydots trying to tell me? I was in the midst of my own personal mystery story, and I turned out to be a lousy Nancy Drew. Try as I might, drawing on every discernible clue, I seemed to create only more confusion and chaos. I couldn't even distinguish between music, someone speaking, or static on the car radio.

But I wasn't alone with my struggles. Every week on one day after work, usually at about 5:30 in the evening, I met for about two hours with my friend Maxine Turnbull, an auditory-verbal therapist. Maxine's job was to provide me with auditory "therapy"—training that would teach me how to make sense of the dots. This was a unique experience. That Maxine and I are still friends to this day is no small feat.

Maxine and I did not seem to be working with the same vocabulary. Maxine would pick an innocuous topic—days of the week, for example.

"Today we are going to distinguish between the days of the week," Maxine would announce.

Fine with me. No problem.

So we would begin. Maxine would place a bunch of papers on the table, each one spelling out the name of one day of the week. While I stared at the papers, Maxine would voice the name of one day while covering her mouth with a sheet of cardboard so that I could not see any part of her face except her eyes.

"Monday," Maxine would say while my eyes darted among the bits of paper, looking for clues.

"Dot-dot," I heard. Was that Monday, Tuesday, Thursday, Friday, or Sunday? About the only day of the week I could eliminate was Saturday, because Saturday had *three* dots instead of two, although sometimes, on my good days, I could eliminate Wednesday, which Maxine seemed to say in a way that I heard two and a quarter dots. So I'd repeat to Maxine what I heard—"dot, dot," I'd say.

"Those are not dots," Maxine would reply.

"To me they are—that's exactly what they sound like," I'd insist. "How can you possibly expect me to make sense of two dots," I'd whine.

So we'd put the dots in context.

We'd write a bunch of sentences on two pieces of paper: "Sunday is the first day of the week." "Tuesday is the second day of the work week." Or some such drivel. Real exciting stuff for two people with forty-plus years of schooling between us to spend time working on. I would take one piece of paper in hand, scrutinize it fiercely, and Maxine would take the other and read one of the sentences to me from behind the cardboard curtain. I would impatiently count the dots as Maxine recited the sentence, and I would try to figure out which one she was reading. The most fun I'd had since nursery school!

Fun or no, I concentrated—*hard*. And I finally got so that I could guess half or so of the sentences correctly. A milestone. So we progressed, to bigger and better things—to the months of the year, to numbers, to colors, and then to all four together: On a Thursday in April I wore a yellow dress in size ten. The dots were getting more difficult to keep track of. All this, of course, was done with sentences in hand for me to read. Without my cheat-sheet, I couldn't do a thing. But I was following the dots faster. And sometimes I began to hear dashes—the dots seemed to last longer. I accused Maxine of distorting the words she spoke. It got harder to count. Two dots, three dashes, four dots—it's easier to count the cards in each of the four suits while playing bridge. But after three or four months of this, I became a master dot and dash counter. So then we moved to nursery rhymes.

Why nursery rhymes, you ask? Because I *knew* all the nursery rhymes, having recited them all to each of my three children ad infinitum, and was able to say them all in perfect rhythm. Jack and Jill went up a hill—the cadence is quite a bit different from Diddle Diddle Dumpling, my son John. So now I was counting—and trying to remember—dots, dashes, and the pauses between them. It sounds ridiculous, I know, but I actually began to want to show off my newfound skills. After a while I had the months, days of the week, colors, numbers, and nursery rhymes down pretty well, and Maxine could test me on those even without my cheat-sheets in front of me. I really got good on the nursery rhymes because I was beginning to get some "pitch" information from the implant and could get a bit of the inflection. By following the unique inflection of a particular nursery rhyme, I could almost disregard the dots and dashes. Relief at last!

Unfortunately, however, I couldn't find any place in the real world where people talked in nursery rhymes or spoke to me s-l-o-w-l-y in short, concise sentences about such lively topics of conversation as numbers and colors. So our approach became more pragmatic. After six months or so, Maxine and I moved on to the weather. We took to studying the weather column in the newspaper. Our dialogue went something like this:

"It's sixty degrees in San Diego today," Maxine would say to me behind the newspaper that covered the lower half of her face.

"Really," I would reply. "How nice that it is fifty degrees in Santa Anna today."

The two sentences had the same number of dots, dashes, and spaces, but with a lot missing in between.

And from the weather we progressed to "practical sentences" that someone might actually say to me, sentences such as "What is your name?" "Where do you live?" "What do you do for a living?" After weeks of repetition, I got so that I could recognize most of those sentences. But how much was understanding and how much was memory was anyone's guess.

The saving grace is that after Maxine and I played at these games for a couple of hours or so, we would go out and drink two glasses of wine with dinner. On "therapy" days I would collapse into bed at 9:00 P.M., totally exhausted from stress, strain, and two glasses of wine. I think therapy is a misnomer for this type of training.

And then came the day we decided to show off for my parents. Maxine came to my house, where my parents met us. Hands folded in their laps, my mom and dad sat on the living room couch and waited for the big event. We all felt a bit awkward, not the least Maxine, who must have felt out of place in that scenario of parents watching their fifty-plus-year-old daughter do circus tricks. By that time we had progressed to items of clothing. I distinctly remember Maxine saying to me, behind the piece of cardboard, "Your mother is wearing a blue blouse." And then, "Today, on Friday, your father is wearing brown pants." And like a good little parrot, I repeated both sentences back word for word (although Maxine did have to repeat them a couple of times).

What I mostly remember is the tears in my mother's eyes. "I've never seen you understand anything without watching the speaker's lips," my mom said tearfully.

It really was a parlor trick, though. Because, remember, my entire repertoire included only numbers, colors, months, days of the week, the weather, a few mundane sentences, plus one or two equally cosmopolitan topics of conversation. And I also had the clues in front of me. Today *was* Friday, and I could see that my father *was* wearing brown pants. But we took our progress as we found it, in tiny increments.

Or rather, Maxine took our progress as we found it. I, to the contrary, bitched. I should be ladylike, I know, and say I complained. But the truth is I *didn't* complain; I bitched. I don't know precisely how to define the difference between complaining and bitching, but I know bitching when I see it, and that's what I did. I would say that I spent a good third or half of my two hours a week with Maxine bitching.

I want to hear words, not count dots, dashes, and pauses, I bitched.

I'm tired of these silly games, I bitched.

This is too hard, too stupid, too time-consuming, too futile, too nonsensical, too annoying, too childish, too frustrating, too nonuseful, too (fill in the blank), I bitched.

We're wasting our time, I bitched.

And Maxine sat and let me bitch.

But not once did I say I wanted to stop. Nor *did* I want to stop. I just wanted to vent my frustration. I wanted to *hear speech*. And I clearly wasn't doing that.

A year had passed, and I wasn't understanding speech.

A whole year.

But I kept trying.

Most of the time I practiced alone, as best as I could. I practiced trying to make sense of the noises all around me; trying to get comfortable enough to ask people around me what the noises were that I heard. Picture this: There we are, four law professors, talking at the law school about some issue of faculty concern. I am trying to decipher when a new speaker starts talking so I can flip my head in the right direction and look at the speaker before he finishes what he is saying. But wait—there's a loud noise that keeps me from hearing *anyone's* speech.

"What *is* that loud noise?" I wonder aloud, exasperated.

"What loud noise?" asks one of my fellow law professors.

"*That* loud noise," I retort. Obviously if I could *explain* what the loud noise was, I wouldn't have to *ask* what it was, I think to myself.

Unfortunately, no one but me seems to hear any loud noise. Whatever the noise is, it's something my colleagues are so used to hearing that they don't even consciously recognize it. Perhaps it's the air conditioning, someone suggests. Or perhaps it's the sound of people talking outside the room, the sound of a computer printing out paper, or the pencil sharpener someone is using. No one knows.

How do I explain a sound I can't identify? I'm reminded of that old Abbot and Costello routine. Who's on first? No, Whose on second, Whats on first:

What's that sound?

What sound?

That sound!

What sound is that?

That sound I heard.

Sigh. I guess you had to have been there. This loses something in the translation.

I tried using books on tapes for a while, following along with the written version of the tape while listening to the spoken version, but found that *much* too frustrating. Despite all representations to the contrary, the speaker simply did *not* say every word that was written, and more often than not I became lost, never to find my place again. And it drove me *crazy* to read so slowly—my usual pattern is to read the average size book in just a few hours.

I tried the television too—watching the closed captions and listening at the same time; that worked pretty well with *Jeopardy*, so I took to taping *Jeopardy* every day and watching it faithfully. And I concentrated *hard* on *listening* to everything everyone said.

I also tried a bit of music. I had spent hundreds and hundreds of hours learning all the Christmas songs as a young girl, word by word and sentence by sentence by repetition and banging on the piano. I had even learned to read a little music, and had trained my voice to move up or down in pitch based on the number of notes between each word. So, since I could sing the Christmas songs in reasonably good tune, Maxine and her co-worker, Pat, made a tape of Christmas tunes for me to practice "listening" with.

We couldn't just buy a tape. The combination of music and words was too much—just overwhelming. The tape I used had to be very simple, just the melody with someone singing—no band, no loud background noise to drown out that melody. I think Maxine and Pat spent hours making that tape. And I spent many hours trying my utmost to use it with a borrowed walkman.

Unfortunately, it didn't work.

What can I say? Obviously, the singers just didn't sing the songs as well as I did (smile). I couldn't follow the melodies, much less the words. The singers didn't follow the pattern I expected them to follow. They sang too fast; they sang too slow; they paused where no pauses were called for (per my interpretation!). I sang along merrily at my own pace. Unfortunately, I usually finished singing either a minute or two before or after the singer finished.

To preserve my sanity, if not my sense of humor, I decided to put music on hold for a while. First things first. Back to the dittydots.

And back also I went to Los Angeles and Dawna, my implant team audiologist. For my visits with Dawna composed the third part of the scheme to acquire meaning from my cochlear implant.

I've racked up a lot of frequent-flyer miles in the years since my implant, flying back and forth between Phoenix and the House Ear Institute in Los Angeles. That first year alone I visited Dawna at least fifteen times. Initially I went every two or three weeks for a new map, visits that gradually petered out to once a month. Those visits were imperative. My "hearing" fluctuated so much during that first year it was incredible. My brain seemed to be doing flip-flops trying to adjust to the new sounds. So a map that would sound good when I left Dawna's office and for a few days thereafter would sound unbelievably bad just a week or two later. It was all I could do to hang in there until the next trip to L.A. could be arranged.

Dawna tells me that she has made more maps for me than for any other of her more than approximately two hundred multichannel cochlear implant patients. Each time I visit Dawna, we make at least ten to twenty new maps. And oftentimes after I finally leave Los Angeles with a map that seems workable, once I'm back in Phoenix, in my real world, I find that the map is not workable at all. Then Dawna and I Federal Express processors back and forth. Dawna makes a change to my map based on my complaints (i.e., it's too loud, it's too soft, it's too high-pitched, it's too low pitched). She then programs the newly revised map into a loaner processor, and Federal Expresses the loaner to me overnight. I send my processor back by return Fed Ex and try out the new map on the loaner for a day. If the new map is acceptable, Dawna inputs the new map into my processor and Fed Exes it back to me; when I receive my processor, I Fed Ex the loaner back to her. If the new map is not acceptable, Dawna programs yet another map into my processor, and we go back to square one, beginning the game anew. We played this game a *lot* that first year. We still play this game, but not as often these days.

The slightest nuance in a map makes a humongous difference to the overall sound pattern that I hear. It is mind-boggling. During that first year, Dawna tried every strategy known to post-implant era man to devise a map that was palatable to my brain. As I became more knowledgeable about the mapping strategy, I would add my creative thoughts to Dawna's, and together we would try to generate magic. We played around with (and continue to play around with) all kinds of things that make no sense to normal people—the loudness growth curve, the gain, the frequency allocation tables, the comfort levels, the threshold levels, and a bunch of other things that sound equally like gibberish. A change of just one point or one degree on any one of these factors, in just one electrode, can make a big difference in my ability to tolerate or understand sound (something Dawna and others insist is a real rarity). This continues to be a tough process. The part of my brain that regulates hearing remains uncooperative and is sometimes downright combative. We discovered almost immediately that the combativeness manifested itself in a couple of unique differences.

First, no matter how we struggled, we could not activate the high-frequency electrodes. Dawna and I have finally become resigned to the fact that my brain will not accept electrodes one through five. I just can't tolerate the piercing sounds.

Second, we've had very little success increasing the ranges (between the threshold and comfort levels) on the electrodes that were activated. At the end of the first year, my ranges were minuscule. Even today, after nearly seven years with the implant, my ranges are between 10 and 35. In this regard, I seem to be truly one of a kind.

Despite those problems, over that first year Dawna and I made minutely incremental but meaningful progress—although I usually failed to see the progress at the time. I would frequently leave the House Ear Institute discouraged, if not despondent. Patience is not my strong point.

I was not enthralled with the pace of my progress.

While Maxine and Dawna raved about the benefits they saw from my implant, I was less than enthusiastic.

A year had passed. I'd hoped to explode firecrackers. I'd expected at least to brandish some sparklers. All I'd gotten to do was light the matches.

Did I like the implant?

No, not really.

Was I ready to give it up?

Not by a long shot.

Years Two through Six

The next four years were not radically different from the first with respect to the implant. There *were* some radical differences in my life, however. First,

I was invited to spend a semester as a visiting professor of law at Cornell Law School in upstate New York. I took a semester's leave from ASU College of Law and embarked to cold country. Finding a place to live and a car to drive while living more than two thousand miles across the country was no problem. Arranging to rent my Phoenix house to snowbirds from Canada and to keep my car at a friend's house was no problem. Getting my work sent between ASU and Cornell was no problem. Even leaving my children and grandchildren was no problem. I did have one problem, however—finding people to work with me and my implant while I was away from home.

Luckily, I was able to arrange to work with Pat Chute, the audiologist at the Manhattan Eye and Ear Institute. Pat was equally as experienced and as competent as Dawna in mapping implant processors. Taking small planes from Ithaca to New York City in the midst of a series of snowstorms was more adventuresome than flying from Phoenix to L.A. and sometimes considerably more frustrating. The weather rarely cooperated (that was the winter of the blizzard of '93), and the planes were never on time. Nevertheless, I flew to New York about four times that semester to get new maps from Pat.

I also arranged to receive auditory therapy of sorts from an audiology student at Ithaca College. The student I worked with, Roni, was patient, nice, and willing to do what needed to be done. Unfortunately, however, neither of us knew what needed to be done. Roni had only cursory knowledge of cochlear implants and auditory-verbal therapy. She was eager to learn, but I had little to teach her. Between the two of us, we managed to work out a system that seemed to serve its purpose. Once a week for that entire semester, I visited Roni, and we would talk for an hour. We'd carry on conversations, with Roni talking from behind a pad of legal-sized paper so that I could not see the lower half of her face. In that way, I would practice listening.

Roni thought our "therapy" of dubious value. There were days when I could not understand a word she said, even when she repeated every sentence four times. There were other days, however, when we could converse for five consecutive minutes intelligibly. No matter how hard we tried, however, we could never figure out why what worked some of the time did not work all of the time. I compared it to my tennis backhand. But this did seem to be a bit worse—even a lot worse—than my erratic backhand. We bumbled on nevertheless, sometimes talking about the most inane subjects to keep the conversation going. The progress, if any, was infinitesimal.

After six months in New York, I returned to Phoenix and ASU, during which time Maxine and I resumed our auditory-verbal therapy for another semester. At the end of that semester, I packed up and left for Australia, where I had been invited to teach at Monash Law School in Melbourne while I took a semester's sabbatical from ASU College of Law.

It was in Australia that I began to really appreciate the benefits of the implant. I'd been to Australia before. I remembered the Australian accents and how difficult they were to speechread. I remembered too that many Australians did not move their lips much. And I knew that Australia was full of people from other countries—all with their own various accents, equally difficult to speechread. I hired Maxine to come to Australia when school started to serve as my oral interpreter in my law school classes and on the telephone.

I should digress and tell you about my oral interpreters. As I've said before, I'm a speechreader. I rely on watching people's lips and faces to understand what they are saying. Obviously, I can't do that when I'm talking to someone on the telephone, when I'm talking with a large group of people—of whom many are too far away to speechread, when the speaker is not facing me or when I'm behind the speaker, when a speaker has a mustache and beard that completely cover his lips, when a speaker has a heavy accent, when a speaker doesn't move his or her lips when speaking, or when I am participating in group discussions during which it is impossible to figure out who is speaking before they finish what they are saying. When I began practicing law, I had to devise a means of understanding speech in all of these situations. The solution was to train my secretary to orally interpret.

This system is quite simple. As a practicing attorney, when I argued in court or attended large meetings or depositions and in other instances when speechreading was impossible, my secretary accompanied me. She would sit next to me and silently mouth the words of any nonspeechreadable speaker, and I would read her lips and face rather than the lips and face of the speaker. As a law professor, I follow the same practice. In large law school classes or presentations, for example, where the students and participants will be interacting with me in a Socratic dialogue, my secretary-assistant sits in the front row and silently mouths the words of the speakers in the classroom or audience. If I can speechread the speaker, I do so directly. If the speaker is too far away or is for some other reason not speechreadable, I speechread that speaker's words as my assistant mouths them.

There is very little delay in this system. My assistant keeps right up with the speaker; she is at most only one or two words behind. I look alternately at the speaker and my assistant, so I maintain some eye contact with the speaker. It is a very effective system; in most cases, few people are aware of any difference in the communication methodology.

I use a similar system on the telephone. I have two receivers on my office telephone. I speak into one, and my assistant listens on the other and silently mouths what the speaker on the other end of the line is saying at the same time that the words are spoken. The mouthpiece on my assistant's receiver has been disconnected so that any inadvertent coughs or whispers are not heard by the person on the other end of the line. Most people I speak with are not aware that I use an interpreter on the telephone.

These were the tasks I hired Maxine to perform in Australia (in addition to some administrative tasks). Unfortunately, however, due to the accents and speech patterns of students from Australia and numerous other countries, Maxine was unable to understand the speech of my students well enough, or quickly enough, to interpret their speech for me in class. Initially, I panicked. How would I conduct my classes in the discussion mode that was necessary in a law school setting without adequate interpreting services?

Gritting my teeth, I strained to understand the students via a combination of speechreading and the sounds that I heard from my implant. After a couple of false starts, I found I could actually do it—I could understand the students on my own! Students with Australian accents, German accents, Indian accents, African accents, I was almost always able to understand them. The implant proved to be a godsend. With the little hearing the implant provided me, in combination with speechreading, I was able to understand people in Australia even better than many Americans, such as Maxine, were able to. (Of course, I still had to use Maxine to interpret on the telephone—the implant did not work without speechreading. But in time Maxine improved considerably on the telephone, and telephone interpreting was quite a bit easier than classroom interpreting, so we were able to manage quite nicely.)

Score one big one for the implant—finally.

While regaling in the implant's first big success, however, I continued to confront one of the implant's biggest failures—apparently unique to my case. From the beginning, I have found it nearly impossible to talk in group settings or on the telephone with the implant activated. Cochlear implants are supposed to *improve* the speech of deaf people. For me, the implant does the opposite— it actually hinders my speech. Oh, I can talk fine to one or two people with the implant activated. But when I talk in a group setting, when four or more people are together, no one can understand me when the implant is turned on. And things are even worse when I speak at a meeting or when I teach or give a presentation. In all settings where more than three people are present, I must turn the implant off when I speak.

I am constantly fiddling with the little volume-control dial on my processor. I have my hand on that processor at all times. I turn the dial up to a volume of three when others are speaking, and I listen to the speech of others in conjunction with speechreading. When I speak to more than three people or on the telephone, however, I turn the volume completely off. I've worn out at least three processor dials (not to mention my already limited patience) due to this constant fiddling.

We've tried to figure it out—to no avail. *Why can't I speak properly with the processor turned on?* No one seems to know. We speculate a lot. Perhaps it is because my voice sounds so loud to me with the implant on that I lower the volume of my speech so much that people cannot hear me. Both Dawna and Pat Chute tell me, once again, that I'm one of a kind. Sigh.

Score one on the minus side for my implant.

But there *have* been numerous plus scores for the implant, in addition to my Australian experience. The benefits have been slow in coming and are not always noticeable at once. They creep up on me, and suddenly I realize that I am able to do or enjoy something that I never used to do or enjoy. Here are a few of those somethings.

The Birds

I learned to appreciate hearing birds in Australia. Australia is famous for its birds, you know. They are everywhere. And some of them are quite beautiful to look at, very colorful. I enjoyed hearing the birds outside the window of my apartment and while I took various hikes throughout that glorious country.

But now that I can hear the birds, how do I turn them off? There's a very large crow family living in the trees in the backyard of the neighbor right behind me. The strident, rackety noises those birds make all day long drive me to distraction. Don't they ever sleep?

The Mystery Noises

Hardly a week goes by that I don't find myself pondering the meaning of some mystery noise. One of the latest puzzles was the most exasperating.

I was lying peacefully on my bed, reading class papers. And then I heard it.

Beep, beep, beep.

I looked around. It wasn't birds I was hearing through the open door to my patio. I can recognize bird sounds by now. But just to be sure, I shut the bedroom door.

Beep, beep, beep.

Whatever it was, it was still there.

I checked the alarm clock; it was not on. I checked the toilet and water faucets; they weren't dripping. I checked the air conditioner; it was off. I checked the washer, the dryer, the refrigerator, the fan over the stove, the smoke alarm, the computer, and every small appliance I possess. None were making a noise.

The beeping continued.

I was desperate. I went to the phone to call a friend and ask if she wanted to come over for a glass of wine and, coincidentally, to check out my mystery noise.

Lo and behold, the phone was off the hook. And that off-the-hook phone was beeping like mad.

No one ever told me that when phones are off the hook they talk to you and tell you to hang them up!

And did you know that blue jeans squish when you walk in them—the tighter the jeans, the more they squish? It took me a long time to figure out what that noise was. I'm no longer comfortable wearing blue jeans; all that squishing is quite disconcerting.

Functions

Now when I go to meetings or functions at an auditorium in which an infrared system is used, I can almost do away with interpreters. With an infrared cord plugged into my processor, all I need is to be able to see a single corner of the speaker's mouth. Using the combination of the clear, direct sound I receive from the infrared system and minimal speechreading, I'm able to understand most speakers — even when the microphone the speaker is using covers most of his or her lips.

I've even been to a few plays and enjoyed them using this type of system. I still have to sit front and center to allow speechreading, of course, and I don't understand all of what is said, but I get enough to enjoy some shows. I had never enjoyed *any* show before receiving the implant.

Children

I really can hear my grandchildren well with this implant. If I have to take the processor off, such as when we are swimming, I find the little ones very hard to understand. They never stay still, and unlike my children, they don't remember to look at me when they talk. A special benefit is that I can hear them cry from another room, so when I'm babysitting I don't have to check on them every ten minutes, as I did my own children. I don't know how I managed to raise three children without this implant!

Teaching

Although I cannot give up my interpreter altogether in the classroom, I no longer have to use the interpreter as often as I used to. Now I bring my assistant only to classes in which there are more than 35 students. With the combination of speechreading and the sound I get from my implant, I'm able to manage in classes of 35 or less, even with the lively class discussions we have in my classes (the students talk about a third of the time). And even in the larger classes, in which I have 70–130 students, I don't have to rely on my assistant to interpret as often as I used to. Usually, I need her only for the students in the back of the room.

Recognizing Speech

I can often tell now when people are talking, and I will look up to see what they are saying. People don't have to come up to me and tap my shoulder to get my attention anymore. And I can usually hear someone call my name, which means that people don't have to run across a room trying to catch me when they want to speak to me. In group conversations I'm able to follow a lot better. I can tell when a new speaker starts to speak, and I'll turn and look at that speaker in time to catch at least some of what he or she is saying. On hiking trails, people can actually call me from behind. I'm sure that in some of these situations my family and friends like the implant even more than I do.

Hearing Special Sounds

I can now hear someone knock on my office or hotel room door. I doubt that the average hearing person can appreciate how wonderful it feels to be able to shut my door at work and get some privacy or to be able to hear room service knock at my door in a hotel rather than having to prop my hotel door open with a shoe and wait for the room service waiter to appear. I can hear the doorbell ring, so I don't have to be sure to remain in a room with a flashing light if I'm expecting a visitor. I can hear a phone ring, so I now stop talking when I'm in someone else's office and his or her phone starts ringing. I now know when there are loud noises outside my classroom, making it impossible for the students to hear. Whereas I used to keep right on talking, now I either wait for the noises to subside or shut the door.

In short, I'm more in tune with the world around me.

Navigating the Minefield

I haven't flooded my kitchen floor, ground my silverware in the garbage disposal, or lost my keys in a while. Now I hear the water running, so I turn it off; I hear the silverware fall in the garbage disposal, so I grab it; and I even sometimes hear my keys drop on the floor, so I pick them up before they are lost forever.

I hear the signal light in my car blinking, so my grandchildren, unlike my children, do not have to keep telling me, "Your blinker is on."

I no longer drive with the radio in my car on at full blast (not knowing it is on), nor do I lean on my car horn for two minutes without realizing it.

I can even hear when the drive-up bank teller is talking to me, so I can let the teller know I am a speechreader and cannot hear what she is saying.

I no longer leave the kitchen fan running or vacuum an entire room when the vacuum is not plugged in.

The minefield is getting smaller every day.

The Telephone

There are no two ways about it—life in modern society revolves around the telephone. As much as I want to hear speech in everyday life, I want to hear on the telephone more. Because in most situations, I can understand speech by speechreading. The only way to use the telephone without hearing, however, is via a relay service or an interpreter—neither of which is conducive to natural (not to mention private) telephone conversations.

For the first year or two I couldn't use the telephone at all with the implant. Over the past three years, however, I have made some progress. Using the special telephone adapter that plugs directly into my processor, I can hear the dial tone, hear whether the phone rings or is busy, hear whether the phone is answered, and hear whether the phone is answered by a person or a machine. The real trick, however, is to determine who has answered the phone and what that person is saying.

After *much* practice, I am now able to understand a lot of what my mother, my daughter-in-law Heidi, Maxine, and Dawna say on the phone, as long as we keep the conversations fairly short, sweet, and to the point. A few sentences at a time are the most I can handle, and the topic has to be about something reasonably expected.

I can understand some of what my older son, Kevin, says, and a lot of what my eldest granddaughter, Aubreigh, says, though it helps if I ask the questions and control the conversation. I can understand my daughter, Ronale, only enough to get her on the phone and ask her to transfer to TDD, since her voice does not project. I can't understand my younger son, Scott, any better, because his voice is too deep.

I can understand a few friends if I call and we talk about plans to meet or discuss simple matters. But again, they must speak only a couple of sentences at a time, in simple terms.

I've used the voice phone to call room service at a hotel and am able to understand the speaker well enough to make my wishes known and coordinate delivery of my order. And once I used the voice phone to call 911 when 911 refused to answer the phone via TDD (not a pleasant experience).

But all of this happens only when *I* make the phone calls. I almost never *answer* the telephone on the voice phone, since usually I cannot tell who the caller is—so I have no idea who is talking.

For example, I was talking to my son Kevin on the phone one afternoon while my assistant, Robin, interpreted. Kevin said he needed to look up some information and might call me back. He didn't call back by the time Robin left for home at 4:45, but the phone rang almost immediately after Robin left. Assuming it was Kevin, I answered the phone.

"Hello," I said.

"Hello," responded the caller. "This is dot dot."

"Is this Kevin?" I asked.

"Dot, this is dot dot," responded the caller.

"Oh, hi, Kevin," I replied. "Robin has left already; I'll call you back on the TDD."

"No," said the caller, "I just wanted to ask if I could visit your class tomorrow with two people."

"You want to visit my class tomorrow?" I queried.

"Yes, is that OK?" the caller replied.

"Sure," I said. "I'll see you tomorrow at 8:00 A.M."

Later that evening I thought about that conversation. Kevin, a lawyer, was in the midst of a significant legal case. Why would he want to take the time to visit my class? So I called Kevin on the TDD and asked, "Why are you coming to visit my class tomorrow?"

"I'm not," Kevin responded. "Where did you get that idea?"

"Oh, sorry," I said. "I misunderstood what you said when you called me back at five after Robin had left. What was it you said?"

"I didn't call you back at five," said Kevin, somewhat startled.

Oh God. All night long I wondered who, if anyone, would show up at my class tomorrow. I *knew* I'd heard that correctly.

My mystery caller turned out to be a woman named Tammy who works in the admissions office of the law school and who did indeed want to bring two prospective students to visit my class.

It was the dittydots again. The name "Kevin" makes two dots. So does the name "Tammy." They sound alike to me. You can see why I don't dare answer the voice telephone. God knows what I might get myself into.

I'm still working on the telephone, but matters don't seem to be progressing very far. Telephone use does not seem in the cards with my current implant. That's discouraging.

There are other discouragements too. I can understand speech without speechreading in only a few instances. And this sometimes makes life *more* frustrating. Now I hear—and recognize—the speech sounds, so I know that I am missing something. Before the implant, I generally didn't realize that people were talking and didn't miss what I didn't know was happening. I am no longer oblivious and thus am sometimes more frustrated. I am reminded of this every time I fly. Before receiving the implant, I never knew how often the pilots, stewards, or stewardesses talked over the intercom to the passengers. Now I hear the constant messages over the intercom, and I'm in a frenzy of worry and indecision. Is something important being said? Or is the pilot simply telling the passengers to look out at the pretty clouds? Should I go and ask a stewardess what's up, or should I stay in my seat and ignore the voice overhead? Whoever said that ignorance is bliss knew what he or she was talking about.

The inability to understand what is being said is evident also in any setting where there is any background noise. In a restaurant, for example, with people talking, music playing, and silverware clanging, the background noises drown the speech sounds. My implant is useless in such a situation.

And there's yet another problem with my implant: the sounds fluctuate.

So the benefits I obtain from the implant fluctuate. The implant does not provide the same quality or quantity of sound from day to day or even from hour to hour. One day everything may sound crisp and crystal-clear. The next day everything may sound murky and garbled. Even the pitch of what I hear changes from time to time, sometimes from minute to minute. This is not all due to environmental factors such as background noise. Rather, the continuing fluctuation seems to be due in large part to factors in my head and brain, factors beyond my control. Some contributing factors are obvious, such as how tired I am or how much stress I'm under or even what type of weather we're having, although why the last should matter I do not know. But those factors alone do not explain the perplexing ins and outs of the quality and quantity of sound coming from the implant. One day I can talk on the telephone with my mother pretty well; the next day I can't understand anything my mother says on the phone. One day I can hear the students talk in my classroom clearly and distinctly; the next day I am forced to rely on my assistant's interpreting skills—another enigma. There are too many enigmas relating to my implant!

And I still don't like music much. I have to admit I've been derelict about practicing on the piano. I say it's because of lack of time, but I suspect that subconsciously I'm reluctant to brave the disappointment.

So here I am—one of a kind, strange, a "bad" implant user. I haven't achieved either of the goals I'd established pre-implantation: I can't hear speech without speechreading; and I can't use the telephone in most circumstances.

Was I wise to have the implant?

Does my "bad" use of the implant justify the surgery, expense, time, and hassle?

Yes, and yes again. I *like* my implant. I *rely* on it.

I took my eldest granddaughter, Aubreigh, on a raft trip for her twelfth birthday. I *hated* having to be without the implant for a day; it made the trip a lot less pleasurable.

I followed my three-year-old granddaughter, Ashlyn, into the pool one Saturday afternoon, forgetting about the implant processor stuck into the bra of my bathing suit. The processor shorted out after being completely submerged in water, of course, and I panicked. I was scheduled to fly to the East Coast on Monday to give a series of presentations, and I did not want to go without my implant. There was no way a loaner processor could be Federal Expressed to me on Sunday—even Federal Express employees get a day off. In desperation I called Dr. Luxford at his home and explained my predicament. Dr. Luxford arranged to call Dawna and have her come to the House Ear Institute on Saturday evening to program my map into a loaner processor. Then we arranged for me to fly to Los Angeles on Sunday morning, rent a car, and drive to the institute, where Dr. Luxford would meet me at the entrance with the loaner. This meant a lot of trouble for everyone involved and a lot of expense for me—all for a "bad" implant user.

Would I go back to total deafness?

Not voluntarily—and not without one hell of a fight.

The Future

I haven't seen any additional benefits from my implant for over a year now. This particular implant has taken me as far as it will go. It's time to move on.

So I've been doing my research and, once again, pressuring Dr. Luxford. Next summer I hope to be implanted with a new, technologically advanced, implant.

Take note, please, that Dr. Luxford has agreed to implant the second device when the time seems best and is tentatively thinking that next summer might be a good time. The good doctor, as I mentioned above, considers my implant to be "working." I've surpassed Dr. Luxford's expectations with my current implant ten times over. And although he remains conservative about the results of a second implant, Dr. Luxford is coming around nicely. It has been tentatively *noted in my medical chart* (per my insistence—always get it in writing), that next summer will be the summer of implant number two.

Am I looking forward to it? Not to the first year. Would anyone look forward to surgery and at least a year of grueling work? I am, after all, stubborn but not stupid. Ultimately, however, I look forward to seeing what progress a new implant will bring. With a little luck, maybe I'll call you on the voice telephone two years from now. Better yet, maybe you'll be able to call me—even if all you want to do is sell me a time-share condominium. I look forward to the possibility of being as aggravated with telephone sales callers as everyone else. If that doesn't happen, of course, I'll be very disappointed. But I won't be sorry I tried.

Wish me luck, please. And remember to call me in two years.

Chapter 3

Perspective of Bonnie's Implant Audiologist

DAWNA MILLS, M.A., CCC-A

Dawna Mills received a B.S. in Communication Disorders from Worcester State College in 1984 and an M.A. in Audiology from California State University Long Beach in 1986. In 1989 she became coordinator of the Adult Cochlear Implant Program at the House Ear Institute. She has worked with over two hundred adult cochlear implant recipients and has been involved in numerous research projects relating to cochlear implants.

It was evident from the beginning that Bonnie was a determined lady. I knew I was in for a challenging case. In our first discussion on the phone (through her oral interpreter), I was already preparing Bonnie for the long road that lay ahead.

Based on my experience with other implant patients who had congenital hearing losses and or had not worn hearing aids over a long period of time, I felt that if Bonnie received a cochlear implant, the very best we could hope for was a possible improvement in speechreading, identification of some environmental sounds, and better modulation of her voice. Since Bonnie was, and still is, an excellent speechreader, I doubted the implant would make a difference in her ability to communicate with others. Therefore, the big question was, what could the implant possibly provide for Bonnie?

On December 9, 1991, I saw Bonnie for a cochlear implant evaluation. Bonnie had never been able to use hearing aids, in part because of recruitment—a condition in which sounds have an abnormally rapid growth of loudness. As a result, with hearing aids, Bonnie felt pain rather than heard sound. In addition, when I tried hearing aids on Bonnie, she reported that they caused tinnitus and headaches. I became moderately concerned that a cochlear implant would produce the same adverse reaction.

We discussed the possibility that Bonnie might have a congenital reaction to an implant and that she would receive sensations rather than auditory perception. This occurs most often in people, like Bonnie, who have not had experience with hearing aids and who have early-onset profound hearing loss. We also discussed the need for long-term aural rehabilitation after receiving

53

the implant. A cochlear implant center in Bonnie's city of residence was not willing to work with Bonnie because the medical staff felt that since she was prelingually, rather than postlingually deaf, she should not be implanted. Ultimately, however, Bonnie informed me that she had arranged to work with a friend (Maxine Turnbull) who was also an aural rehabilitation specialist. One obstacle down, many more to go.

One of my biggest concerns was Bonnie's expectations for the implant. She clearly expected the implant to enable her to understand speech without the aid of speechreading. Based on my experience with other patients with similar backgrounds, I did not believe that to be an achievable goal for Bonnie. Bonnie said, "I'm going to prove you wrong." I chuckled. "I hope you do. I would be very happy to be wrong in this case."

Bonnie's surgery on December 11, 1991, followed the normal course; there were no complications. Dr. Luxford was able to insert all electrodes into the cochlea without difficulty. What followed, however, was not the typical course of events. Postoperatively, Bonnie complained of a roaring tinnitus in both the operated and the unoperated ear as well as a substantial degree of unsteadiness. Both symptoms persisted for several weeks after surgery, although they ultimately disappeared.

The next milestone was the initial fitting of the external device—the activation of the implant. I was more than a little uneasy about this day. What type of response would Bonnie have? Would she hear sound or merely feel vibrations in her chest and head? Would she be able to *tolerate* sound if she was able to perceive it? Would she hate the sound and refuse to wear the processor? If nothing else, I knew programming the implant was going to be a challenge for both of us.

I was pleasantly surprised with Bonnie's initial fitting on January 9, 1992. Bonnie was able to perceive sound on all electrodes. The congenital reaction that I feared never occurred. However, Bonnie was not able to tolerate sound from all the electrodes when they were all activated. This was not at all unexpected. I made adjustments so that speech would be at a comfortable listening level and, after a very emotionally exhausting morning, sent Bonnie on a well-deserved lunch break.

When Bonnie returned from lunch she reported that everything was painfully loud. We were back to square one. We remeasured all threshold (soft) and comfort (loud) levels and found a substantial change from the morning session. I had seen this happen before with other cochlear implant users with long-term deafness, so I was not overly concerned. After reprogramming, I gave Bonnie several listening exercises. She was able to distinguish differences in word and sentence lengths and to differentiate some of the easier vowels (e.g., *cheep* vs. *chip*). (Bonnie, however, disputes the latter.) Given Bonnie's long-term deafness, I felt that her progress for the first day was extremely good. Bonnie, on the other hand, was not at all impressed!

Bonnie returned the next day for more follow-up testing and programming. She reported that when she had turned the radio on the night before, she could not hear anything at all. After determining that there was nothing wrong with her equipment, I deduced that Bonnie's electrical hearing levels were fluctuating dramatically. Given the fact that she had very small ranges between her soft and loud levels, even small shifts in her electrical hearing thresholds could make sounds either too loud or inaudible. We reprogrammed again.

One phenomenon we see in patients with poor auditory nerve survival is auditory adaptation. When this happens, the auditory nerve is not capable of transmitting a sustained sound but instead becomes fatigued and hence inaudible. I evaluated Bonnie for this condition. I selected various electrodes along the electrode array and presented a steady tone at each electrode. As I stimulated each electrode, Bonnie informed me that the sound faded to inaudibility in approximately forty seconds. This response warranted a call to the manufacturer of Bonnie's implant. Cochlear Corporation staff suggested a few programming options; I tried all of them, to no avail. The best we could do at the time was to simply monitor the problem.

We practiced on distinguishing word and sentence length differences and on listening to nursery rhymes. Bonnie was able to correctly identify 75 percent of the nursery rhymes I read to her. We attempted some "speech tracking," which required Bonnie to repeat verbatim what I read. Speech-tracking tests can be administered in a hearing-plus-vision (speechreading) mode, a vision-only mode (speechreading alone), or a hearing-only mode. The test is scored by counting the number of words correctly repeated in a given number of minutes to obtain a word-per-minute score. I administered this test to Bonnie in both the vision-only and the vision-plus-hearing modes. The results showed that her implant *decreased* Bonnie's ability to speechread, a not unusual result when excellent speechreaders are first implanted. It would be simply a matter of time before Bonnie's speechreading was as good or better with her implant.

When Bonnie returned for a third day of programming, her ranges between soft and loud levels were even smaller, so I decided that she should keep the program we had made the day before. Bonnie reported that many sounds were still a little too loud, however. As in our first two sessions, I administered a multitude of aural rehabilitation exercises. We began by working on fairly easy exercises and progressed to more challenging ones. And then it was time to send Bonnie back home to Arizona for a few weeks before our next appointment. This was a trying time for Bonnie, as she began listening to the multitude of sounds in our very noisy world. Bonnie faced a very long road ahead.

Bonnie returned for a three-week follow-up appointment on January 31, 1992. She reported that the high-frequency sounds were making her nauseated. I felt she was making good progress with her implant. She was able to perform more difficult closed-set tasks. However, tinnitus continued to bother her when she disconnected the processor.

When Bonnie returned to Los Angeles for another follow-up visit on February 24, 1992, one and a half months after her initial hookup, she was frustrated and discouraged with her progress. She felt that the implant made her speech less discernible. Although I did not hear any difference in Bonnie's speech, she reported that more than a few people had commented that her speech sounded slurred, as though she were talking in the back of her throat. From my perspective, Bonnie was making steady progress with the implant, but she did not share my opinion. We talked many times about expectations and the fact that she could not rush the acclimatization process. Even though hard work would speed up the process, the simple element of time could not be changed, due to her lifetime deafness.

In the next several programming sessions during the course of a few months, we experimented with removing some of the high-frequency electrodes from Bonnie's map. Because of her very small ranges between threshold and comfort levels and the unpleasant sound quality of those electrodes, we ultimately removed them from the map.

Another problem appeared in June 1992. Bonnie experienced a sudden increase in loudness from her implant. After obtaining new threshold and comfort levels, we found that the range between these two levels was significantly reduced relative to the range in the last programming session. In addition, at times during that session, sounds became first piercing and subsequently too soft. An X ray showing the placement of the cochlear implant's electrode array in the inner ear revealed the array to be in the proper position. We could not explain the fluctuating levels and hypersensitivity. Bonnie continued to report unsteadiness as well. Dr. Luxford conferred with another prominent otologist who specializes in cochlear implants. They theorized that Bonnie was suffering from cochlear hydrops, a condition that can cause dizziness and fluctuating hearing. The doctors recommended that Bonnie reduce her salt intake, and they placed her on a short course of steroids and a diuretic.

Bonnie and I had many sessions over the first year, during which we attempted to improve the sound quality of her map. We tried removing unpleasant channels from the program; we tried different coding strategies. Even minor changes in the program substantially affected the quality of sound that Bonnie received. Small changes, such as a 2 percent increase or decrease in the overall loudness of the program, could (and still can) determine whether Bonnie understands or does not understand speech without speechreading. This is extremely unusual. Most cochlear implant recipients do not notice such small changes in their programs, much less notice any change in performance with the implant.

On December 15, 1992, almost one year after the initial fitting of the cochlear implant, Bonnie and I did some in-depth diagnostic testing in a sound-treated booth. The results looked very good, especially on the closed-set tasks (Bonnie had to identify sentences from a limited number of choices in front of her). What was most exciting, however, was the fact that Bonnie was beginning to demonstrate some open-set speech understanding—she was able to repeat words or sentences in the listening-alone mode, with no known context or fixed alternative choices. I felt this to be a real turning point. Bonnie could now say, "I told you I would be able to understand some words without speechreading!" I was now a believer.

We continued to have many programming sessions over the next year. Bonnie's complaints remained the same. Her two main complaints were that the sound was "croaky" and that she had to continually adjust the sensitivity control. Sounds seemed to be either too loud or too soft, and background noises were extremely bothersome. Although we have made many (and I do stress *many*) maps, we have never been able to improve on these issues. Bonnie is still unable to activate her implant when she talks on the phone or in groups because her own voice sounds too loud. Nevertheless, Bonnie and I have been able to carry on a fairly lengthy conversation on the phone without the use of Bonnie's oral interpreter. This is quite impressive for someone with Bonnie's hearing history. I never believed this would be possible for her.

We continue to monitor Bonnie's progress through semiannual evaluations. Bonnie has shown steady, albeit slow improvement over the years. During our last session I tested her "auditory-only" comprehension of sentences in settings with and without background noise. In the quiet condition (without background noise), she achieved close to the mean score for *post*lingually deafened adults using a cochlear implant. It was very interesting, however, to see how significantly background noise adversely affected her performance. In all patients we see some degradation in the ability to understand speech when background noise is present, but Bonnie did much poorer in that situation than one would expect. On average, we see a decrement of 20 percent in patients' ability to understand speech when a minimal amount of competing noise is introduced. In Bonnie's case, her ability to understand speech dropped from 56 percent in a setting *without* background noise to 9 percent when background noise is present.

At this time Bonnie is considering a second implant for the nonimplanted ear. She is still striving for better hearing. Based on a careful review of our programming sessions over the past five and one-half years, I have no doubt that we are in for more of the same problems with a second implant. I know that Bonnie is ready for the challenge. But am I?

It has been hard work on both our parts, but Bonnie's success with the implant has made our hard work worthwhile. Bonnie has far exceeded our expectations with her cochlear implant. I believe that her perseverance, hard work, and intelligence have played a large part in her success.

Chapter 4

Perspective of Bonnie's Auditory-Verbal Therapist

Maxine Turnbull, M.Ed., Cert. AVT

Maxine Turnbull has a B.A. in Elementary Education from Arizona State University and an M.Ed. in Special Education—Deaf and Hard of Hearing—from the University of Arizona. Turnbull is one of the founders of and is currently executive director and an auditory-verbal therapist for Listen Inc., an Association for Hearing-Impaired Children, a private, nonprofit organization in Tempe, Arizona, offering a wide range of services for children and adults with hearing impairments.

The telephone ring—normally a happy, unobtrusive sound—gave no indication of the emotional state of the caller. Her first words, however, left no doubt as to her extreme level of anger.

"*Do you work with cochlear implants?*" Bonnie Tucker's words came leaping through the phone, and the thought immediately occurred to me that this might be a good time to "just say No!"

After I answered "yes," Bonnie proceeded to grill me about the rehab therapy: what I would do, how I would do it, and finally, would I work with an adult—namely, her?

As we talked, the anger diminished, and Bonnie explained that she had decided to get a cochlear implant. (My first thought, which I wisely kept to myself, was, why would Bonnie Tucker, who speechreads so well, speaks so well, functions so well, and is so successful, choose to undergo implant surgery? I'm sure that I was not the only one who entertained this thought.) Bonnie explained that because of her long-term deafness, she was not considered a "good" cochlear implant candidate, and that because she was not considered an acceptable candidate for an implant by local implant centers and was going out of state for her surgery, local implant centers refused to work with her for auditory training.

As I listened to Bonnie on the telephone and later when we met in my office, it became clear that this was a fellow human being who had a consuming drive to *hear*. (It is impossible for those of us who hear to fully understand the depth of this desire and the intensity of this drive when we have known nothing else, when we take hearing for *granted*.) Bonnie was willing to go to great personal expense, undergo surgery, travel out of state monthly for remapping, commit to weekly aural rehabilitation sessions, put up with the aggravation, inconvenience, and appearance of wearing all the necessary equipment, risk the loss of some of her speechreading skill, and endeavor to tolerate, adjust to, and ultimately benefit from the *intrusion* of sound-stimulation ... in spite of not being a "good" implant candidate. Oh, and by the way, her goal was speech discrimination—*in six months*!

As a longtime auditory-verbal therapist, I had many years of experience successfully helping children with severe or profound hearing loss use hearing aids effectively to "learn to listen" and acquire language and spoken English. I had less experience with cochlear implants in general and with adults with cochlear implants in particular. What's more, all that I knew about Bonnie Tucker came crashing into focus. As a professional in the field of deafness, I had heard about Bonnie Tucker long before I met her in person. Everyone talked about her amazing speechreading ability, her highly intelligible speech, and her many achievements.

After I met and came to know Bonnie, I developed great admiration for her determination and courage, and I was inspired professionally by what she had accomplished. Being a rather calm, quiet, easygoing person, however, I was often intimidated by her assertiveness, and I was wary of her anger.

Ohmygosh—what have I agreed to??!!

Thus began an interesting, challenging, exciting, and often frustrating association. Great frustration was present for both of us—but for very different reasons.

Calm, Quiet, Easygoing met Agitated, Outspoken, and Intense on January 14, our first rehab session, which took place six days after the initial programming of Bonnie's processor. Bonnie stormed into my office without a greeting and got straight to the point: "This is too loud! At a level I can hear, my voice is too loud! I CAN'T USE THIS IN CLASS WITH STUDENTS! I CAN'T STAND THE NOISE! I CAN'T STAND THE LOUDNESS!!"

I took a deep breath, and we moved on to some of the initial activities suggested by Bonnie's audiologist: phrase length identification from the cochlear implant rehabilitation manual. Bonnie listened and followed the words on her page while I read the first four sentences. I then read one of the sentences at random; she listened, still looking at her set of sentences, and told me which one I had read. We soon added four more sentences following the same procedure, and Bonnie picked out each sentence that I read. When I commented on her success, she replied, "Any idiot can count beeps!" (So much for pointing out success!)

Bonnie's goal was very clear from the beginning: speech discrimination and use of the telephone. She had been counseled carefully and thoroughly that these might not be realistic goals for someone with lifetime deafness—

especially someone who had never worn hearing aids. Nevertheless, she never wavered in her goal, and *that became the standard by which she measured her progress.*

Although I was willing to allow that speech discrimination *might* be a possibility, I knew that six months of using the cochlear implant and hearing sound was not a realistic time frame for that to happen. My goal, then, was somehow to add months, years—maybe the rest of her life?—to her time line. I hoped that success in early and simpler tasks would help her recognize that progress was being made and that she would then be willing to expand her time frame way beyond six months.

Based on my years of experience, I know that the auditory rehabilitation process takes place consciously and systematically, step by step, moving from the known to the unknown, from easy to more difficult. Most important, it requires consistency (in wearing and using equipment, in signal, in therapy attendance, and in reinforcement in other settings); it requires meaningful repetition, time and patience. I learned quickly that "patience" is neither a part of Bonnie's vocabulary nor a part of her personality. (And we've already discussed her theory of time!) Progress throughout this process is often measured in small increments and subtle changes rather than large leaps. Going from living without sound for fifty years to "speech discrimination in six months" is one *enormous* leap!

Bonnie and I were obviously coming to our rehabilitation sessions from different viewpoints and experiences. There was *much* to cause frustration for each of us.

The First Month

My goals for each session included (1) beginning at a level where Bonnie could feel some success as quickly as possible; (2) gradually increasing the difficulty or diversity of the exercises; (3) utilizing activities and materials that might have some carryover or functional use outside the therapy session or that at least contained language Bonnie might hear in other settings; (4) pointing out progress; and (5) offering support, encouragement, and perspective on the process.

The first month of therapy was characterized by dramatic contrasts between Bonnie's words, her success with the activities, and her actions. We continued to practice some of the exercises from the Cochlear Corporation rehab manual. By the time we had progressed to the second set of ten sentences (using groups of four sentences at a time, which Bonnie looked at as I read them from out of her line of vision), Bonnie was picking out the sentence I read without an initial listening practice first. (She would ask me to repeat the sentence, sometimes two or three times, if she wasn't sure which sentence

I was reading.) By the third week, I was using a normal rate of speaking, she was asking for fewer repeats, and the process was becoming more automatic for her. She had stopped *consciously* "counting beeps!"

We used an audiotape with familiar Christmas songs, and Bonnie (with help initially) would follow the printed words. At one point she commented that she couldn't hear the "es" on "Christmas*es*." We used the written words from the Christmas songs for listening practice. Gradually she began to be able to tell the difference when I repeated lines from "Jingle Bells" in random order, which was quite significant, since each line has the same number of syllables:

> Dashing through the snow;
> Laughing all the way;
> Bells on bobtail ring;
> Making spirits bright.

Bonnie wanted me to set stations on her car radio and show her how to operate the cassette player. Then she became frustrated when she couldn't distinguish speech or music from static (in three weeks of hearing sound, mind you). "That's absurd!!" she declared. "I can't even hear an airplane overhead!" (Her father was able to hear airplanes with his hearing aids.)

In the meantime, Bonnie went shopping for pianos and keyboards and took a keyboard home to try out. She reported that she was able to hear the trombone best. By the third week, she had bought a piano! (She noted that she could hear it but that it sounded awful!)

As the month progressed, Bonnie's ability to handle sound deteriorated. She perceived an "echo" when the processor was on "N" (the normal function setting). There were "too many beeps" (i.e., more than the number of words and syllables in the sentence), and she felt she was doing better with the processor on "S" (for noise suppression). She was suffering from constant headaches and nausea, and she was unable to wear the processor for very long periods at a time.

Bonnie returned to Los Angeles and her audiologist for remapping. Threshold shifts (common in the first months) were causing her to receive too much high-frequency stimulation, so that some sounds—such as paper rattling—were making her sick. She also found that she had developed more tolerance for sound, especially in the lower frequencies, and she returned home with a map of somewhat wider ranges (although still extremely limited compared with the maps of most cochlear implant users during the early months).

The Second Month

According to Bonnie's comments, the new mapping was not better, but her tolerance of sound was better. Sound was "flat," "nasal," and "distorted."

Her voice became softer, and her speech was slower. She had not considered that the implant would have a detrimental effect on her communication abilities. Bonnie Tucker, deaf at least from the age of two, was beginning to develop an *auditory* feedback system.

And Bonnie had other complaints: "The equipment is a pain in the ass; the cord is too short; the whole thing is a huge bother! The microphone won't stay on, so I have to use my [eyeglass] earpiece to hold it, and the area is becoming irritated!" "I'm not getting enough information," she constantly complained.

In counterpoint to all of this, Bonnie made progress:

• Bonnie heard the telephone ring in her office (while working on the weekend) and was able to receive calls (via the TDD) from both her son and her daughter. (Before the implant, she had to rely on the flashing button on her telephone to alert her to the ring, and she would miss the call if she were turned to her computer or away from her desk.)

• She commented that she was surprised at the number of airplanes that flew overhead while she was playing tennis. (Three weeks before, she couldn't hear them, or she didn't recognize the sound as an airplane.)

• We started using practice sentences with the same number of syllables. Looking at her page containing the sentences, Bonnie had little difficulty picking the sentence that I read. I noted that she was beginning to make these discriminations without knowing the strategy she was using, whereas previously she would tell me what little strategies she had used to pick the particular sentence.

• We used articles from the newspaper for speech tracking. When we both looked at copies of the same article, Bonnie was able to follow what I was reading without difficulty.

• We used words with different initial consonants: bold, cold, mold; bake, cake, make. After some practice and in this structured exercise, Bonnie was able to determine which word I had said. She commented, "That's pretty good, huh?!" (A glimmer of hope, I thought!)

• We found that the more auditory information Bonnie received, the better. She perceived very little difference in vowels in single words but was able to pick the right word when it was put into a sentence (i.e., "I heard your words" versus "I heed your words").

• For the first time (*one* time), Bonnie came in relatively calm and relaxed.

By the end of the second month, Bonnie actually said out loud, spontaneously and without prompting: "I'm not ready to put it [the processor] in the drawer yet. I'll give it one year!" Endeavoring to remain calm, all I could think was ... YESSSS!

The Third Month

Bonnie was discouraged with her third trip to Los Angeles for her remapping. Although her ranges and her tolerance for sound were slowly improving, the improvements were not enough for her. "It sounds 'raspy.' 'Friday' sounds like three syllables. It sounds like something is being cut out. Like a water faucet turned on full blast, but with only a trickle of water coming out."

She came into the next session extremely discouraged. "Things are getting worse! The loudness is making me sick! Everything sounds the same!" During the same session, she also heard the cuckoo announce the hour, heard the doorbell ring, and said the *ticking* of the cuckoo clock sounded like the turn signal in her car. She reported that while on a recent ski trip, she heard a "pop" from the fireplace and jumped, and that when the telephone rang, she figured out what the sound was and answered the phone (though she didn't know who—if anyone—was on the line).

As the weeks progressed, we started using a variety of materials for listening practice in addition to some of the exercises in the cochlear implant rehab manual. The manual exercises that we did use were very carefully chosen (or were modified) because the objectives and the activities moved far too quickly for individuals who have never heard sounds and thus have no auditory memory.

It should be noted that all of the specific exercises with Bonnie were done through hearing alone, *without* speechreading; in fact, they *had* to be done without speechreading because Bonnie is such a talented speechreader. Bonnie usually obtained scores on speechreading tests in the range of 95–100 percent, so I smiled to myself when people told Bonnie that one of the big advantages of a cochlear implant was to improve speechreading abilities. In eighteen years as an auditory-verbal therapist, I have never worked with anyone else—child or adult—with whom I had to be so completely auditory! This is the *only* case in which those disparaging accusations often directed toward auditory-verbal therapists—"The therapists won't even let them speechread!" —were true!

Some of the activities Bonnie and I worked on included the following:

• Speech-tracking activities from popular books as well as newspaper articles—Bonnie could keep up with me (and often complained that I was reading too slowly); when I stopped, she would pick up and start reading at the right place. As we practiced, she was able to find where I was reading when I started in different places throughout the paragraph.

• Nursery rhymes—Bonnie already knew most of the nursery rhymes by heart. In addition to being familiar, they have rhythm, repetition, short phrases, natural pauses—all elements helpful and necessary to individuals working to acquire an auditory memory base.

• Greetings and language she might hear in the "real world"—"Hi Bonnie; Hi there; Hello, Bonnie; What's happening?; Good morning; See you _____ (later; tomorrow; next week; Monday, Tuesday)."

• Numbers—starting with index cards with a single number written on them, we worked our way through the decades, separating out and working with those that were the most difficult to discriminate (e.g., 16/15; 25/35; 35/39). Trying to vary the activity, I would read a paragraph containing several numbers and ask Bonnie to listen *only* for the number.

• Days of the week; months of the year—working from a word on a card to putting the word in a sentence and listening only for that word, we slowly began to combine days, months, and numbers to form dates.

Frequently we would go to dinner after the therapy session. Bonnie sometimes asked me about the different sounds: a cart rolling over the Mexican-tile floor; a steady flow of conversation from another table; one waitress's voice, which seemed to carry throughout the room. It was apparent that (1) Bonnie was beginning to separate out one sound from a background of continuous sound (noise) and (2) she needed someone to help identify these sounds so that she knew would know what she was hearing.

Throughout this five-month period since the initial mapping, Bonnie had continued to experience threshold shifts, and she required frequent remapping. She continued to have difficulty tolerating the loudness of sound (during one session, she was discriminating the difference between two high-frequency sounds based on which one hurt more); consistency in wearing the processor (and having it turned to the recommended level) and consistency in signal were therefore impossible. She was disappointed when she was unable to hear sounds she thought she should, such as seals barking and clapping at Sea World or the sounds of the ocean. In May Bonnie's audiologist reiterated that she didn't think Bonnie would be able to attain speech discrimination.

Bonnie and I had a major conflict with how we viewed her progress. I viewed this as a process starting from scratch: no sound awareness; no auditory foundation or memory to relate any sound to. She was having to build sound associations and an auditory memory bank with absolutely no previous experience. I thought that Bonnie was doing well, that she was making consistent progress step by step and that the progress for such a short period of time was very good—in fact, beyond the expectations and predictions of most people. Bonnie, however, measured her progress against her goal of speech discrimination, and she fell far short of that goal. Anything I tried to point out as "progress" was discounted—"Yes, but ..." Since she expected to be doing much more by this time, she began to feel anxious for progress because of her one-year self-imposed "deadline."

Eight to Twelve Months After Initial Mapping

The end of May brought the end of our weekly sessions, since Bonnie was out of town during most of the summer. Bonnie returned to therapy sessions in September following a summer that included a bout with cochlear hydrops and the dizziness and nausea that accompany it. Although new mappings had been obtained in San Diego and in Australia during her travels, she continued to have great difficulty tolerating the loudness of sound.

As Bonnie discussed her summer, the subtle and not-so-subtle indications of progress and auditory change began to emerge.

• She had just been to L.A. and had been "desperate" to get a different map before her hike to Havasupai Canyon with her grown children, so that she could hear people call her.

• She had a loaner processor, and she liked the sound better than that of her own processor, although she still was not getting "enough" information.

• It was now taking her a while to adjust to silence after she took her processor off.

• In a group, she was able to identify the speaker faster.

• She was more aware of sound. She might not know or recognize the word "Bonnie," but she was aware of the sound and could turn to the individual calling her.

We began our first session after our long delay with the same activities we'd been engaged in the previous May. Looking at a list of sixteen different sentences, Bonnie easily and quickly picked out the sentence I said. After I read one sentence, she told me that I had mistakenly read "a" instead of "the," as written. And she quickly recognized that one sentence was a question instead of a statement. (Discriminating the difference between statements and questions had been a very difficult task for her.) We practiced numbers—for the first time without cards—and she was able to tell me the number I said most of the time with very few repeats.

After Bonnie left my office, I sat reflecting on the session. I recognized that a major change was occurring for Bonnie: she was developing a "sense" of hearing that was pleasant (or at least tolerable), as opposed to something that was an imposition or intrusion in her life. Sound was becoming more meaningful. The processor and related equipment, as well as the sound, were not as aggravating. In addition, Bonnie seemed more at ease with the *process* of listening.

I also noted that Bonnie was attending to voice much faster, such as when I called her name or when I started talking without waiting for her to look at me. As she was walking down the hall to leave my office and I was walking in the opposite direction, she turned to my voice—the first time she had attended to voice at that great a distance (30–35 feet). I recalled a contrasting incident in my office just a few months before: standing right behind her, I had called her several times, even raising my voice, and she had not responded.

We began to use names of states for auditory practice. How convenient it was that the western states could be divided easily into three- and four-syllable groups (Washington, Idaho, Nevada; Colorado, California, New Mexico)! By combining a city with the state, we could practice five-syllable groups (Washington, D.C.; Ithaca, New York). I chose cities and states that are heard or seen more often or were particularly relevant to Bonnie because of her frequent travel. We started with index cards with the states written on them, but it was important to move to an auditory-only experience as quickly as possible because of the difference in processing input from visual and from auditory modalities. Bonnie discovered this herself and commented that just hearing a word is a completely different experience from both seeing *and* hearing the word.

We continued our exercises with variations. For example, before a session, I would make up a number of sentences about a particular state and would give Bonnie a paper containing a list of the words used, listed in random order in columns. I would say a sentence to Bonnie using those words, and she would repeat the sentence I had said. Or we would both read the same paragraph from a book about a national park, a famous person, or an event. Then I would make up sentences about that particular topic, and she would tell me (i.e., "figure out") what I had said. (Bonnie continuously reminded me that she was not "hearing and understanding" the sentences but rather was getting a little bit of information and guessing the rest! She also was quick to point out that this had "no practical value" for her everyday life.)

As the weeks progressed, we moved away from lists and written information to auditory-only statements and questions about my or Bonnie's current activities, upcoming holidays and events, trips one or the other of us had taken, family members and their activities. Although it was often necessary for me to repeat the same sentence several times, Bonnie began to understand entire phrases and thus figure out the rest of the sentence. For example, she understood the phrases "spoke at her graduation," "school for the deaf," "Camelback Inn"—she was particularly impressed that she understood the last, since it was a name and typically names are more difficult to understand auditorily as well as through speechreading. One evening Bonnie understood a whole sentence: "I was born in New Mexico." Her spontaneous reply—"You were born in New Mexico? I didn't know that"—told me that she had not only heard but understood the complete sentence.

I developed a list of "common questions" that might be heard in other social or professional situations: "What is your name?" "Where do you live?" "What do you do for a living?" "How long were you with Brown and Bain [law firm]?" "Do you specialize in a particular area of law?" "What courses do you teach this semester?" "How long have you been teaching at ASU?" Initially Bonnie practiced listening to these randomly stated sentences and repeated the sentence I had said. As she became more familiar with the questions, she began to answer the questions rather than repeat them, so that we were engaging in a communicative exchange closer to real life.

It became evident over time that the words and phrases that we had worked on the longest (and that Bonnie had heard more often) were the ones she began to recognize immediately. More and more often during the exercises, Bonnie would think she heard a particular word or sentence, and it would turn out to be very similar: "Harvard" sounded like "harder"; "When did you get back home?" sounded like "Where did you get that cold?" Other words sounded very clear to her—"centipede," "rock formation," "United States," "president"—all of which was very frustrating ... and tantalizing. "If some words are as clear as a bell, why not all of them?" she wondered.

In November (Bonnie's eleventh month of implant use), she reported that for the first time she had heard someone whistle. Also for the first time, she watched and listened to a guest speaker in class without her oral interpreter and was able to understand the presentation.

During one session in November, Bonnie used her direct input adapter for the telephone to dial and listen to my answering machine. Much to her surprise, she heard and understood some of the message: part of the telephone number being repeated ("66__7") and "as soon as possible." She commented hopefully, "Maybe telephone use is a possibility after all."

We began to practice listening to telephone-answering machines and recorded messages. Bonnie recognized the different telephone sounds (i.e., a ring vs. a busy signal), began to detect the beginning and end of the recorded message, and identified the signal to begin recording one's message. Each time she listened to a particular message, she understood more and more of the information. Many recorded messages, such as movie titles and show times, however, were spoken far too quickly and thus were too frustrating to use for practice.

Toward the end of December, Bonnie was in New York City. When getting into a taxi, Bonnie heard the driver ask, "How was your dinner?" Since it was dark and he had a large mustache, Bonnie knew that she had *heard* the question. About this same time, Bonnie mentioned that when watching television with captions only—without sound—she found "something missing."

On New Year's Day, January 1, 1993, Bonnie called me on the telephone! From our brief conversation, Bonnie was able to understand (without my repeating these sentences): "Today is a beautiful day," "I have a question ... about your book," "about halfway through the first part ..." A few other sentences sounded like something else: "washing clothes" sounded like "watching TV," and "this is exciting" sounded to her like "today is Friday." I recognized this initial undertaking for what it was: a courageous and significant step for

Bonnie. For me, it *was* exciting to receive a call, however brief or limited, from someone whom I had never talked to before on the telephone without either a TDD or an oral interpreter as a third party to our conversation.

As Bonnie and I discussed frequently (and sometimes heatedly), the glass can be half empty or half full—at the same time. Once as Bonnie complained because she got "50 percent of the sentences wrong," I pointed out that if she got 50 percent wrong, she also got 50 percent *right*! It was one of the few times she didn't have an immediate rebuttal.

Consistently during this first year of implant use, Bonnie discounted the sometimes small and seemingly insignificant steps that I called "progress." Being focused totally on "speech discrimination," Bonnie was unwilling or unable to look at anything less as beneficial or important. One of our discussions dealt with the meaning of "success." I endeavored to point out that success meant different things for different implant users, depending on each individual's goals and history. One person might call the implant a success because she felt more in touch with, and thus more secure within, the environment; another might consider the implant a success because it helped him hear the doorbell or the telephone ringing or other environmental sounds; still another might call the implant a success because she is able to use the telephone. Bonnie, in her own inimitable way, argued that I was wrong—success was speech discrimination, using the telephone with anyone, and conversing in the dark.

The Second Year

Bonnie went off to Cornell as a visiting law professor for the spring semester, so our regular sessions ended. She continued to feel that too much was missing from the signals she received, and she continued to have problems tolerating the loudness of the sound she *did* receive. She constantly turned the sensitivity-control dial up and down: down when she was talking because her own voice was too loud for her; up when others were speaking so that she could hear them. Despite all this, Bonnie was diligent in wearing the processor consistently and in working with a young woman in New York.

Our infrequent communication and one visit during these months again pointed out subtle changes and progress (from my standpoint). Significantly, Bonnie herself began to recognize some benefits from the implant. And when we met in New York City, I noted that she responded to sound at still greater distances, that she heard warning bells on the subway, that she heard the radio in a taxi and knew that someone was speaking, that she turned to the sound of voice more quickly and at greater distances, that she often asked about different sounds as they occurred, and that she was able to follow the song "Tea for Two" at a play (she commented that the song was "clear as a bell").

When Bonnie returned to Arizona, she determinedly set about to practice using the telephone with anyone she could "coerce" into talking to her daily!

A New Beginning—But Not the Conclusion

For me, the therapy sessions and listening experiences shared with Bonnie over the first two years of her implant use were filed with excitement, wonder, challenge, and frustration. It was a challenge to find or create activities that provided the necessary repetition, sequential development, successful accomplishment, and usefulness in the "real world" but that were not intellectually insulting—actually it was *impossible*, not just a challenge, to hit on all of these. It was a challenge to have patience with Bonnie's impatience; the major frustration for me was Bonnie's lack of recognition or acknowledgment of her progress.

For Bonnie, these sessions were filled primarily with frustration. She wanted to *hear*: to communicate with ease; to listen to music; to use the telephone; to participate more fully in the same experiences and activities that the sense of hearing affords those with whom Bonnie spends her life—people with normal hearing. And she wanted it all *now* (actually, *yesterday* would have been better!).

Bonnie's cochlear implant has given her a "taste" of possibility, although so far (at five years post-implant) she has fallen short of her goal of "speech discrimination." Though she refers to herself as an "unsuccessful" implant user, Bonnie does recognize and articulate to others many of the benefits the implant (combined with her tenacity and hard work) has provided her. Furthermore, she has become a vocal and outspoken proponent for those adults and parents who want implants for themselves or for their children. I doubt if there are many people who would use the word "unsuccessful" when referring to Bonnie and her implant use. As an individual with lifelong deafness who was never able to wear hearing aids, she has far exceeded the expectations and educated predictions of professionals involved with cochlear implants.

Out of our auditory rehabilitation association grew a friendship. Thus, I have had many opportunities to see Bonnie in all kinds of settings—professional as well as social—and to become aware of how hearing via her implant has become an integrated part of her life. I've also experienced the differences that are present now when she is without her implant.

Frequently now, I say something to Bonnie, and I *know* without question, that she has heard and understood a word, phrase, or sentence without speechreading. For a while, I was keenly aware of these incidents and was wondering if Bonnie *heard* or if she somehow speechread me when my back was turned or my mouth was full or if she could somehow speechread around corners. At a recent symphony concert at which Evelyn Glennie performed, I sat next to Bonnie as she listened, with obvious enjoyment, to some of the music at the first concert she had ever attended. I felt as though I were sitting in the midst of a minor miracle—and the tears welled up. As we walked out the door, a couple and their seventeen-year-old son, with whom I had once worked, asked Bonnie how she liked her implant. She replied, "I *LOVE* it!"

Where is that darn tape-recorder when you really need it?!

Chapter 5

Survey of Implanted Adults and Parents of Implanted Children

General

Questionnaires were sent to approximately 600 adults who were recipients of cochlear implants and 600 parents of children who were recipients of cochlear implants in the United States and Canada. This is not a scientific research study. Rather, the results of this survey are intended to add to the relevant knowledge about cochlear implants, in the form of the implant benefits and detriments as perceived by adult recipients and parents of implanted children themselves rather than the benefits and detriments noted by doctors, audiologists, and other professionals. This information is crucial to a full understanding of the overall effectiveness of cochlear implants.

Adult Responses

One hundred and thirty-nine adults with implants timely responded to the questionnaire—83 females and 56 males.[1] The mean age for the respondents at the time of implantation was 51, with a range from 11 to 79 years of age. The mean length of time reported for wearing a cochlear implant was 4.6 years, with a range from 1 month to 18 years (the individual who reported having an implant for 18 years used a single-channel implant from 1979 to 1989 and switched to a multichannel implant in 1989).

Seventy-eight percent (108) of the respondents reported being postlingually deafened, whereas 19% (26) reported being prelingually deaf or deafened.

For implants, 8 respondents use the Clarion 1.0 device, 9 the Ineraid, 12 the Clarion 1.2, 15 the Cochlear Corp. Nucleus MSP, and 90 the Cochlear Corp. Nucleus Spectra. Five did not list their implant types.

73

The overwhelming number of respondents reported being pleased with their cochlear implants: 99% reported that they like their implants; and 100% report that they are glad they received their implants. Seventy-eight percent rated their implant as very successful, 17% rated their implants as moderately successful, and 5% rated their implants as mildly successful. *No implant recipient rates his or her implant as being not successful.* This is true despite the fact that about half of the respondents indicated that they find their implants uncomfortable in noisy settings.

Some of the interesting comments (both positive and negative) made by the respondents include the following:

Positive Comments

I feel safer with the implant on.

I'm delighted with the implant. It turned my life around.

I'm happier and more confident, and people are more natural and at ease with me.

I feel more empowered.

I'm more apt to talk to strangers.

People made me feel stupid before. Now I enjoy going out and mixing with people.

I am more relaxed, and my outlook on life is more rewarding.

I don't feel left out all the time like I was of no account.

The implant has greatly improved all aspects of my life.

The implant has ... resulted in a great increase in job satisfaction and performance. There's a great increase in interaction and cooperation with co-workers.

I feel much less isolated.

The implant bolstered my self-esteem tremendously.

There is a little rhyme about a centipede that had so many legs it didn't know which was which or which to use first—at which its feelings reached such a pitch it spent time on its back in a ditch! I've been given a whole bunch of new legs.

Some aspects of the cochlear implant experience are non-verbal: e.g., music perception; environmental awareness; not having to constantly ask what's happening behind me; feeling more secure and less anxious about maintaining visual vigilance.

I took a very big leap last week and judged the state finals for IMTA piano auditions. I was more scared than the first contestant! Pretty cool, huh? My implant made me a piano judge! Amazing.

Negative Comments

I hear so much and understand so little.

My age may have something to do with my not being able to adjust to my implant.

People think that after the cochlear implant, a person is perfectly normal and they expect 100% hearing. The continuing conflict is very tiring.

After my implant my husband got jealous because I didn't have to rely on him to answer the phone for me and I wouldn't stay away from my grand-babies. (I just wanted to hear their voices.)

I feel deafer because the improved hearing in some situations makes me more aware of what I've missed.

Closed-Captioning, Telephone Relay Services, and Interpreters

Thirty-seven percent of the respondents reported that their implants reduce the need to rely on closed-captioning; 45% reported that their implants reduce their need to rely on telephone relay services; and 53% reported that their implants reduce their need for interpreters.

Telephone Use

Eighty-one percent of the respondents said that their implants help them to use the telephone.

The reported ability or lack of ability of the respondents to use the telephone with their implants is documented in Chart 1:

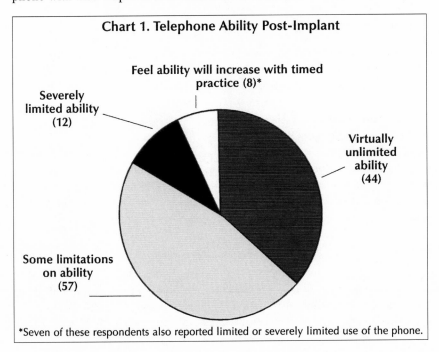

Chart 1. Telephone Ability Post-Implant

Feel ability will increase with timed practice (8)*

Severely limited ability (12)

Virtually unlimited ability (44)

Some limitations on ability (57)

*Seven of these respondents also reported limited or severely limited use of the phone.

Numerous respondents reported that their ability to use the phone post-implant developed or improved over a long period of time and with a lot of training and effort. Several respondents mentioned that the quality of the phone they (or the person to whom they are speaking) are using makes a big difference and that it is difficult or impossible to use cordless and some cell phones. Others indicated that they now use the phone at work or for business purposes.

Following is a sampling of respondent comments:

> I am thrilled with my ability to use the phone. I need it for work. It took a year to really train myself in its use.

> I can basically talk to almost anybody, strangers as well as people I know. …I even have a cellular phone, take calls at work, call a computer company for assistance, and can understand what people are saying.

> I can conduct business and social discussions, make travel plans—really do anything if I have my plug-in [telephone adaptor] device. I handled a conference call with four people and didn't miss anything. I have trouble with accents and people who speak too fast.

> I can talk to almost anyone, including cold callers (e.g., telemarketers), and can get phone numbers and addresses.

Other Areas of Improvement Resulting from Implantation

The respondents reported that their cochlear implants helped them in situations as shown in charts 2 and 3.

Prelingually Deaf or Deafened vs. Postlingually Deafened

The number of postlingually deaf respondents is approximately four times larger than the number of prelingually deaf respondents. These figures are in general accord with the overall adult population of cochlear implant recipients.[2]

Open-Speech Discrimination

Questionnaire recipients were asked: "In your opinion, how would you rate your open-speech discrimination using the implant?" They were asked to use a percentage ranging between 10 percentage points (i.e., 0–10%, 11–20%, etc.).[3]

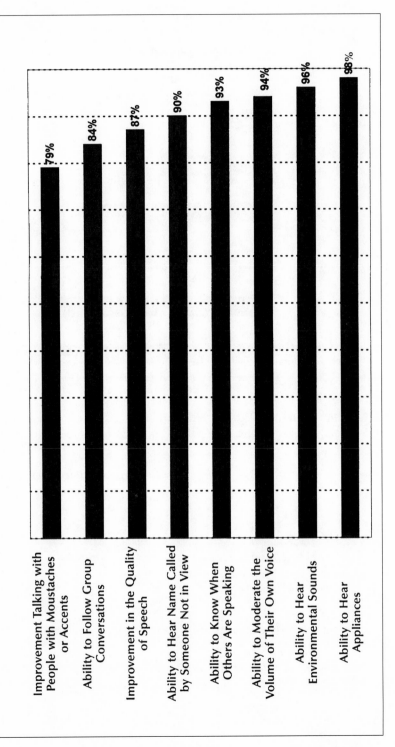

Chart 2. Percentage of Respondents Reporting Improvements

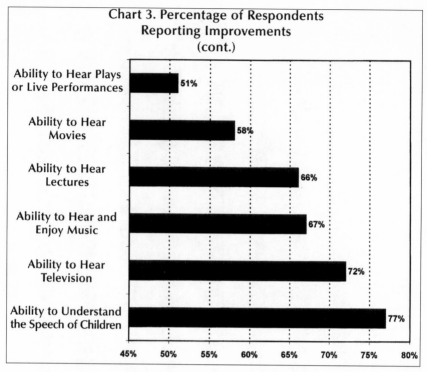

Chart 3. Percentage of Respondents Reporting Improvements (cont.)

The prelingually deaf or deafened adults, many of whom had benefited from hearing aids for some time before implantation, perceived the following:

Percent of Perceived Open-Speech Discrimination	Approximate Percent of Respondents
0–10%	23%
31–40%	5%
41–50%	22%
51–60%	5%
61–70%	9%
71–80%	14%
81–90%	22%

The postlingually deafened adults perceived the following:

Percent of Perceived Open-Speech Discrimination	Approximate Percent of Respondents
0–10%	9%
11–20%	1%
21–30%	9%

31–40%	6%
41–50%	13%
51–60%	6%
61–70%	9%
71–80%	11%
81–90%	26%
91–100%	9%

In many cases, an individual's perceived open-speech discrimination is less than that individual's tested open-speech discrimination scores, as tested by the individual's implant audiologist. By way of example, the test scores of one individual who perceives having 75% open-speech discrimination showed that individual as having 90% open-speech discrimination; the test scores of another individual who perceives having 30% open-speech discrimination showed that individual as having 80% open-speech discrimination.[4]

If the range of open-speech discrimination is narrowed to 50%-or-less versus 51%-or-more for comparison purposes, there is an 11% differential between pre- and postlingually deaf or deafened recipients. Prelingually deaf or deafened recipients are split 50%–50% as perceiving that they receive 51%-or-more versus 50%-or-less open-speech discrimination. (Those who perceive that they receive more than 50% open-speech discrimination were good hearing-aid users and benefited from auditory training pre-implantation.) In comparison, 38% of the postlingually deaf or deafened recipients reported perceiving open-speech discrimination in the 0–50% range, whereas 61% reported perceiving open-speech discrimination in the 51%-to-100% range.

The difference between the pre- and postlingually deaf or deafened respondents becomes most evident when comparing the two ends of the scale. Twenty-three percent of the prelingually deaf or deafened recipients perceive having only 0–10% open-speech discrimination, as compared with 9% of the postlingually deaf or deafened recipients who perceive having only 0–10% open-speech discrimination. Whereas 9% of the postlingually deaf or deafened recipients perceive having 91–100% open-speech discrimination, no prelingually deaf or deafened recipients perceive having open-speech discrimination in this range.

Auditory Training

Of the 20 prelingually deafened respondents who reported receiving auditory training post-implant, 76% found the training very beneficial, 15% found the training moderately beneficial, and 9% found the training minimally beneficial. Of the 66 postlingually deafened respondents who reported receiving auditory training post-implant, 68% found the training very beneficial, 20% found the training moderately beneficial, 5% found the training minimally beneficial, and 7% found the training of no benefit.

Analysis of Profoundly Deaf Respondents

General

Of the 139 respondents, 129 indicated having been profoundly deaf for some length of time:

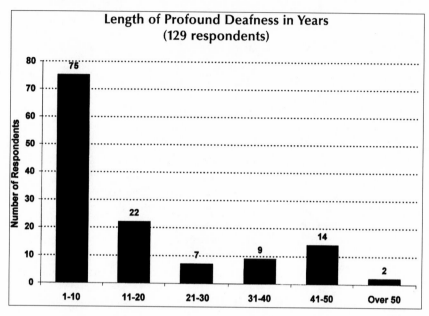

One hundred and twenty-four of these 129 respondents spend most of their waking time with hearing people. One hundred and fourteen feel that their cochlear implants have affected their interpersonal relationships: 105 reported the effects as positive; 7 reported the effects as negative. One respondent reported that her "husband became jealous of her newfound independence, because [she] no longer had to rely on him." Another respondent remarked, "During sex the cochlear implant can't be worn, and I miss what the wife says." One hundred and three of these respondents said that their cochlear implants have affected the way they feel about themselves: 94 reported positive affects; 3 reported negative affects.

Profoundly Deaf for 1–10 Years

The percentage of perceived open-speech discrimination with the implant varied most for the 75 recipients who were profoundly deaf for 1–10 years:

12% perceive having 91–100% open-speech discrimination post-implantation (the only group reporting in this range).

22% perceive having 81–90% open-speech discrimination post-implantation;

12% perceive having 71–80% open-speech discrimination post-implantation.[5]

Profoundly Deaf for 11–20 Years

The percentage of perceived open-speech discrimination with the implant also varied considerably for the 22 recipients who were profoundly deaf for 11–20 years:

32% (7 individuals) perceive having 81–90% open-speech discrimination post-implantation.

23% (5 individuals) perceive having 71–80% open-speech discrimination post-implantation.

23% (5 individuals) perceive having 41–50% open-speech discrimination post-implantation.

9% (2 individuals) perceive having 21–30% open speech discrimination post-implantation.

No one in this group perceived having less than 20% open-speech discrimination post-implantation.[6]

Profoundly Deaf for 21–30 Years

Of the 7 respondents who were profoundly deaf for 21–30 years, 1 perceives having 81–90% open-speech discrimination post-implantation, 2 perceive having 61–70%, 2 perceive having 41–50%, and 1 perceives having 31–40% open-speech discrimination post-implantation. None perceive having less than 30% open-speech discrimination post-implantation.[7]

Profoundly Deaf for 31–40 Years

Of the 9 respondents who were profoundly deaf for 31–40 years, 2 perceive having 81–90% open-speech discrimination post-implantation, 3 perceive having 41–50%, 1 perceives having between 31–40%, 1 perceives having 11–20%, and 2 perceive having 10% or less open-speech discrimination post-implantation.

Profoundly Deaf for 41 Years or Longer

The percentage of perceived open-speech discrimination with the implant varied considerably among the 16 respondents who were profoundly deaf for

41 years or longer: 5 perceive having 81–90% open-speech discrimination post-implantation; 3 perceive having 61–70% open-speech discrimination; 3 were spread evenly (7% in each 10% increment) from 21–50% with respect to their perceived open-speech discrimination; and 5 perceive having 0–10% open-speech discrimination post-implantation.

Auditory Training

The responses indicate that the longer the period of time the respondents had been profoundly deaf, the more likely they were to find auditory training post-implantation very beneficial and to continue that training for longer periods of time.

Problems/Complaints

The questionnaire respondents were asked what they feel to be the most frustrating aspects of their cochlear implants. The following were the most prevalent responses:

1. The inadequate ability of current implants to provide sufficient discrimination between sounds

2. The difficulty understanding speech with the implant because of background noise, noisy environments, and/or echoing noises

3. The difficulty of being around music or in loud environments (such as a subway station or on trains or planes), since the noise is often uncomfortable and sometimes unbearable

4. The discomfort felt when certain sounds are made (such as rattling cutlery or dishes, lawn mowers, power tools, or some appliances)

5. Long, unwieldy, and often perilous cords from the processor to the microphone; bulky processors; the inability to wear the equipment with certain clothes (such as bathing suits or sundresses); the difficulty of finding a way to keep the equipment (both microphone and processor) on the body or clothing; the lack of a comfortable place to wear the processor

6. The inability to wear the implant in the water or rain or to wear the implant comfortably while sleeping (to enable a parent to hear a crying child or to hear a person sleeping in the same bed, for example)

7. The dependency on audiologists and special computer equipment that is available only in limited places during limited times (making it difficult to schedule appointments around work schedules or to take business trips and vacations)

8. The wait for equipment when repairs are necessary, leaving the implant recipient without hearing for days or with nonfunctioning or malfunctioning parts or equipment

9. Expensive accessories, equipment, replacement parts, and insurance costs

10. The very short life span of batteries, which "die" abruptly at very inconvenient times

11. The need to protect the implant from rain and moisture, especially humidity, which is a real problem and often causes the microphone to become less effective or ineffective

12. The difficulty in "hooking up" to the telephone with cords and plugs, making it a hit-or-miss proposition as to whether an implant user will be able to answer the phone before the caller hangs up

Parent Responses

One hundred and seventy-six parents responded to the questionnaire. The 176 children discussed included 90 females and 84 males. (Two respondents did not indicate the gender of their children.) The mean age for the children at the time of implantation was 5 years, with a range from 1.7 years to 16 years of age. The mean length of time reported for wearing a cochlear implant was 2.8 years, with a range from 3 months to 12 years.

Eighty-six percent of the parents said their children were prelingually deaf or deafened; 13% said their children were postlingually deafened. The children use the Clarion 1.0 (3 recipients), Clarion 1.2 (14 recipients), Cochlear Corp. Nucleus MSP (13 recipients), and Cochlear Corp. Nucleus Spectra (141 recipients). (One parent reported her child's implant type as a 3-M House, which is a single-channel implant; four parents did not provide this information.

The overwhelming number of parents feel their children are pleased with their cochlear implants. Ninety-seven percent report that they think their children like the implants. Only two parents feel their children do not like the implants. Ninety-five percent of the parents said that *they* like their children's implants; only one parent said she does not like her child's implant.

One hundred percent of the parents said they are glad that their children received cochlear implants. Eighty-six percent of the parents rated their children's implants as very successful, 10% as moderately successful, and 2% as mildly successful. *No parent rated his/her child's implant as not successful.* Like the adult respondents, however, approximately half of the parents indicated that their children find their implants uncomfortable in noisy settings.

Some of the interesting comments from parents include the following:

Positive Comments

The cochlear implant has opened up a whole new world for our son. He is less frustrated, more in tune with his world, and has become more of a participator. He tries to talk so much more, loves music where he was never interested before. It's a medical miracle to our family.

[Our daughter] has become more confident and connected, especially when she's with a peer group. She really loves her implant and will not tolerate a dead battery for even a minute.

With the implant [our son's] speech is almost perfect.

The cochlear implant has completely changed our daughter's life. Before the implant she was shy, quiet, noninteractive. Now she initiates conversations with anyone, feels comfortable asking for help, has a very funny sense of humor, and is a delightful child.

Our daughter's ... confidence and self-esteem grew after her implantation; she is a cheerleader, takes ballet, and sings in the children's choir at church.

The cochlear implant was the best decision we ever made.... Our son ... plays on the soccer league, baseball team, loves Super Nintendo, and fights with his two sisters. He is mainstreamed in our school district.

It is the best decision I ever made for my daughter, and if I hadn't been so stubborn about educating myself about the cochlear implant, I would have had her implanted at 2 years instead of 3 years.

I told the implant team I would be happy if it gave my son enough hearing so he could hear a car-horn honk to keep him from getting run over. The implant gave him so much more. He can hear birds, dogs, his baby brother cry, the furnace start, grease popping in a fryer, and most of all, my voice saying, "I love you and I'm so proud of you."

The cochlear implant has been a miracle in our daughter's life. Her quality of life has been enriched; her speech is very clear, and she can communicate without problem with hearing people. She has been in a school for the deaf for 7 years and has now switched to the mainstream without a problem.

Negative Comments

Awareness of her deafness is just now becoming evident with statements like "I hate being deaf" or "It's not fair that I'm deaf."

Our son ... wants to join in with neighborhood kids now, but because of his "baby" language and funny voice he is often shunned or outright "ejected" from group games. This is very frustrating for him and for me to watch.

Hearing children in groups are not nice. One on one is best, but getting that from neighbor kids is hard. Schoolchildren come from all over, and when I really look at it, our daughter doesn't have a buddy like other children her age.

Following are a few interesting anecdotes:

Because our daughter was so young and active, we found ourselves requesting new cables, magnets, and microphones on a pretty regular basis. I guess we didn't realize how frequently we were getting parts delivered until our three-year-old son saw a Federal Express truck pass our car one day and immediately yelled: "Mommy look! It's a *cochlear truck!*"

[B]efore the implant I always feared the way it would look and what other people and children would think or say. Now, when older children say "he has something in his hair," I respond by telling them that my son is deaf and has a computer that allows him to hear. The kids think that is "Cool!" When adults ask, I brag! I am more than happy to tell them about this miracle.

[M]y toughest battle has been (and still is) getting or finding the right educational setting for my child after his implant. Once I decided against sign language for my son, my school district provided no support. They have no idea what my son's potential is now that he has the implant. They usually send all deaf kids to the local deaf school, where "total communication" is supposedly used but where they primarily sign. I am fighting to get him in a funded oral preschool, and I'm sure I will have to fight to get him mainstreamed when the time comes.

Areas of Improvement Resulting from Implantation

Parents reported that their children's implants help in the situations as shown on the charts on pages 86–87.

Prelingually Deaf or Deafened vs. Postlingually Deafened

Eighty-six percent of the children discussed were prelingually deaf or deafened; 13% were postlingually deafened. Thus, the number of prelingually deaf or deafened children reported in this survey is approximately 6.5 times larger than the number of postlingually deafened children.

Open-Speech Discrimination

Parents were asked: "In *your* opinion, how would you rate your child's open-speech discrimination using the implant?" They were asked to use a percentage ranging between 10 percentage points (i.e., 0–10%, 11–20%, etc.).[8] One hundred fifty-five parents responded to this question (chart at top of page 88).

Thus, 44% of the parents perceive their children as having greater than 70% open-speech discrimination; 61% perceive their children as having greater than 50% open-speech discrimination; and 84% perceive their children as having greater than 40% open-speech discrimination. Only 16% of the parents perceive their children as having less than 40% open-speech discrimination.

The perceived ability of the respondents' children to discriminate open speech is broken down by age of implantation (chart at bottom of page 88).

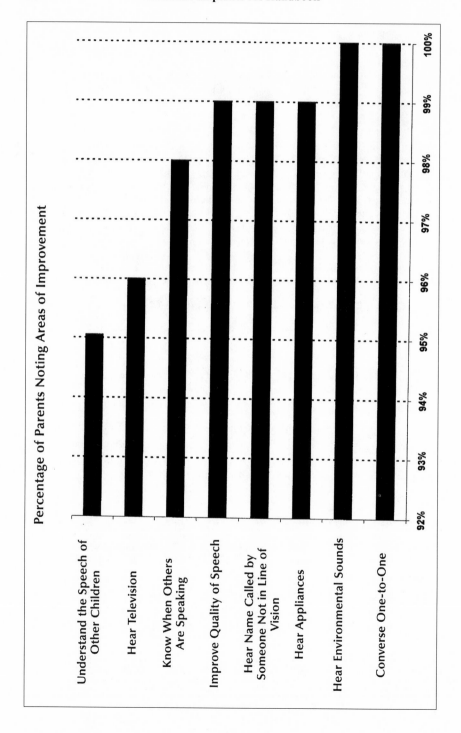

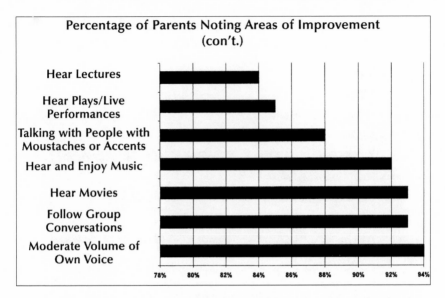

As this graph evidences, the earlier a child receives his or her implant, the more open-speech discrimination (and eventual language development) the child will acquire as a result of the implant. This conclusion is supported by the clinicians' and educators' comments presented later in this book. This conclusion is further confirmed when comparing the two ends of the perceived open-speech discrimination scale: the average age of implantation of children whose parents perceive them as having 91–100% open-speech discrimination is 2.6 years, whereas the average age at implantation for those children whose parents perceive their open-speech discrimination as between 0–10% is 7.5 years.

Auditory Training

Ninety-seven percent of the parents reported that their children received auditory training after being implanted. Ninety percent found the training to be very beneficial, and 6% found the training to be moderately beneficial. One parent opined that the training provided only minimal benefit, and one parent felt that auditory training offered no benefit.

Language Acquisition

One hundred and fifty-nine parents reported that the cochlear implant helps their children to acquire language. Three parents felt that their children had not had their implants long enough to detect the effect of implantation on language acquisition. Seven parents indicated that the cochlear implant had

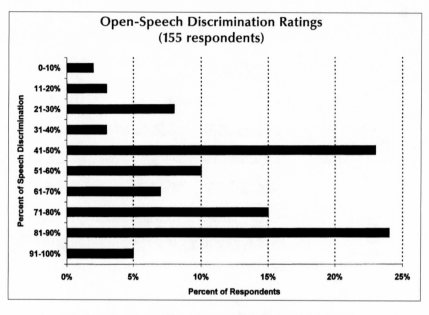

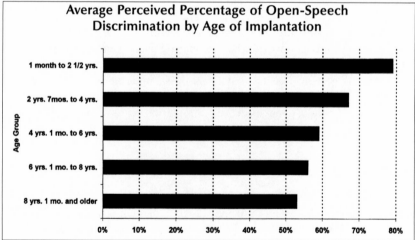

not helped their children acquire language, since those children already had good language skills at the time of implantation. Following are some of the parents' comments about language development:

> Our daughter had minimal language at 20 months of age of approximately 24 words. Now [at age 3 1/2] she converses easily with children and adults and has little trouble being understood. She tests within normal ranges for expressive and receptive language.

> [Our son's] cochlear implant has improved his language and the quality

of his speech to the extent that this will be the first year he will not have an interpreter in the classroom.

Our daughter speaks in sentences and understands most of what is said even by strangers. She sings and is ahead of her grade in reading.

Our son picks up things and sayings from hearing them, not by us drilling them into him.... He still has a way to go, but we can't believe the progress he's made in just 11 months post-implantation.

[Our son's] language acquisition took off after implantation, and he is now fully mainstreamed in a public-school kindergarten class with no assistance from an aide. His vocabulary is at or above his peers.

Our son has increased his vocabulary and extended the length of his sentences.

Prior to the implant our daughter had no vocabulary and never vocalized. She had only a few simple gestures. Since her implant [at age 2.4] and one year of training, she now has a vocabulary of over 500 words, follows two-step commands (auditory only), is emerging into two-word utterances and is consistent in identifying information given only by auditory means in closed sets of up to four words.

In one year since implantation, our daughter has gone from having a language age of 6 years–7 months to between 8 years–10 months and 9 years–11 months.

Our son's language is [now] average or above for his age. We carry on normal conversations like you would with any child his age.

Before the implant our son knew 20 words. Now, two years after the implant, he knows 2,000-plus words.

In the first six months of activation, our daughter gained eight months of vocal language as measured by testing. She learns more indirectly than she did before. She eavesdrops continually.

[The cochlear implant has had an] unbelievable effect [on our son's language]. [At 8 years old] our son is just nine months behind his peers in language, reading, and writing at school.

Our daughter started with 50 words before her implant six months ago, and now she understands and expresses 220 words and she can understand and follow around 80 percent of what is said.

Our daughter's first year of post-implant testing indicated a vocabulary level of 2–4 years of age. Recent testing showed a jump to 6–8 years, and this is only her third implant year. Reading comprehension has jumped from 1.1 grade level to 3.0 grade level.

Our son's school reported that he knew under 50 words at age 3.3. After the implant he made rapid progress. [At 4.9 years he] had a preschool language scales test and scored age equivalent 5.8 on comprehension and 4.10 on expressive language.

Receptively, our son is able to understand a tremendous amount of information. He is 3 years–10 months (and has had the implant for ten months). He has tested from 3.4 years to 6.8 years on a number of language tests.

Our son tests in the 99th percentile for vocabulary and language comprehension when tested against hearing children of the same age.

In the eighteen months since receiving his implant our son has developed language skills comparable to a hearing child 30–32 months old [he is 3.6 years old].

Our daughter has only had her implant for two and one-half years and is now 5 years old. After recent evaluation she was found to have the receptive language of a 7-year-old.

Our son has more than tripled his vocabulary in six months since his implant was activated.

Before receiving his implant [at 5 years] our son had less than 50 words and no sentences or connector words. Now, in the third grade, he is able to communicate with words and sentences the same as any 6-year-old hearing child.

Problems/Complaints

Parents reported problems and complaints similar to those noted by the adult cochlear implant recipients. In addition, parents complained that the equipment is big and bulky for small children, that equipment parts break too frequently, and that, because of problems with static electricity, children with implants cannot use plastic play equipment.

NOTES

1. Note that the author had no control over which individuals elected to respond to the questionnaire. Thus, it is possible that some "unhappy" implant recipients (as well as other "happy" recipients) chose not to respond to the survey.

2. Both Cochlear Corporation and Advanced Bionics (makers of the Clarion devices) informed the author that only a small percentage of *adult* recipients of their implants in the United States were prelingually deaf or deafened.

3. In instances in which a recipient responded with a range wider than 10 percentage points, the average percentage was calculated for data-entry purposes (i.e., 30–50% = 40%).

4. The many people perceiving less open-speech discrimination than shown in test scores may be due to differences between the real, noisy world and the sound-deadened test booth.

In a few cases (less than five) the reverse was true. Thus, for example, the test scores of one individual who perceived having 90% open-speech discrimination showed that individual as having 80% open-speech discrimination; the test scores of one individual who perceived having 90% open-speech discrimination showed that individual as having 70% open-speech discrimination.

5. The remainder of the respondents who were profoundly deaf for 1–10 years before implantation reported perceiving between 0% to 70% open-speech discrimination post-implantation, with approximately 8% of the respondents perceiving the ability to discriminate open-speech along each increment of 10% on the scale of open

speech discrimination (i.e., 0–10%, 11–20%, 21–30%, etc., open speech discrimination). (Seven percent of the respondents in this group did not answer this question.)

6. Fourteen percent of the respondents in this group (3 individuals) did not answer this question.

7. One individual in this group did not answer this question.

8. In instances in which a parent responded with a range wider than 10 percentage points, the average percentage was calculated for data-entry purposes (i.e., 30–50% = 40%).

Chapter 6

The Auditory-Verbal Approach: The Voices of Experience

The following excerpts were written by some of the foremost clinicians in the field of cochlear implants in the United States and Canada: seven auditory-verbal specialists and one medical doctor, a surgeon who specializes in providing children with cochlear implants. Each of these individuals discusses the issue of cochlear implants, particularly with respect to children, from a somewhat different perspective. Together, they offer a wealth of information about such significant issues as criteria for candidates for implantation, expectations for use of and results from the implant, and effective training and testing post-implantation. Each author discusses fascinating and illuminating case studies and true-life stories.

These are the voices of experience. It is in large part through the insights and stories of these (and other) experts that a true picture of the potential or actual effectiveness of cochlear implants emerges.

Cochlear Implants for Children from Auditory-Verbal and Speech-Language Pathology Perspectives

Carol Flexer, Ph.D., CCC-A, FAAA, Cert. AVT
and Denise Wray, Ph.D., Cert. AVT

Carol Flexer received a Ph.D. in Audiology from Kent State University in 1982. She is Professor of Audiology in the School of Speech-Language Pathology and Audiology at the University of Akron.

Denise Wray received her M.A. in Speech-Language Pathology and her Ph.D. in Elementary Education from the University of Akron, where she has taught for seventeen years.

Dr. Flexer and Dr. Wray cosupervise children with hearing loss in an early-intervention auditory-verbal clinic at the University of Akron.

An Auditory-Verbal Perspective, by Carol Flexer

Cochlear implants for children should be examined in the context of the pivotal role that hearing plays in a child's language, reading, and social development. A cochlear implant can enable the attainment of the desired outcomes of spoken language, literacy, academic performance, and incidental learning in a mainstreamed setting for children with profound hearing loss ... *if* the child's attention is focused on auditory information. A cochlear implant, if received when the child is very young and if used with an emphasis on auditory learning, can enable a child who is profoundly or severely deaf to function like a child who is hard-of-hearing.

Hearing Loss

Hearing impairments in children are caused by damage or disease in the auditory system. Based on the location of the damage, called the "site of lesion," there are three general types of hearing impairments: conductive, sensorineural, and mixed.

A *conductive hearing loss* occurs when the damage is located in the outer or middle ear. The most common conductive-type hearing losses in young children are caused by otitis media or ear infections. Conductive hearing losses often can be "fixed" by medical or surgical intervention.

A *sensorineural hearing loss* occurs in the tiny, intricate inner ear called the cochlea. Most often, the delicate hair cells (sensory receptor cells) are affected, and sometimes the auditory cranial nerve is also affected. The inner ear may not have developed fully in the first place, or it may have been damaged by disease, lack of oxygen, noise, or medications. Sensorineural hearing losses cannot be fixed by medicine or surgery.

A cochlear implant actually bypasses or "replaces" the absent or damaged hair cells in the cochlea. Coded electrical signals stimulate different hearing nerve fibers, which then send information to the brain. A cochlear implant, therefore, is a "treatment" for severe to profound sensorineural hearing impairment.

Time of Onset of Hearing Impairment

Hearing impairments in children can be classified into congenital and acquired hearing loses relative to when in the child's life the hearing impairment first occurs. *Congenital hearing impairments* typically occur before, at or shortly after birth but before the learning of speech and language—usually before the age of three. In contrast, *acquired hearing impairments* occur after speech and language have developed. The negative effects of an acquired hearing impairment tend to be less severe relative to overall child development than those of a congenital hearing impairment because, in the latter case, the auditory system already has been programmed for language and spoken communication.

Severity or Degree of Hearing Impairment

In addition to being classified by type and by time of onset, hearing impairment also can be categorized by severity, that is, by how much the hearing impairment blocks an infant's sound reception.

Children with normal hearing sensitivity are able to detect sound intensities at 15 dB HL[1] or less in a quiet room. A minimal or slight hearing impairment for children occurs from 16 to 25 dB HL. A child with a minimal hearing impairment may experience problems hearing faint or distant speech, detecting subtle conversational cues, keeping up with fast-paced communicative interactions, and hearing the word-sound distinctions that compose the meaning for tense, plurality, possessives, and so on.

A mild hearing impairment is one between 26 and 40 dB HL. Without audiologic management, a child who experiences a 30 dB hearing impairment can miss 25 to 40 percent of the speech signal depending on the noise level in the room and the distance from the speaker. Without the use of hearing technology, the child who has a 35 to 40 dB hearing impairment can miss up to 50 percent of class discussions.

A moderate hearing impairment is one between 41 and 55 dB HL. Before effective hearing management, a child with a moderate hearing impairment might understand face-to-face conversational speech at a distance of three to five feet if content, topic, and vocabulary are known; 50 to 75 percent of the speech signal can be missed with a 40 to 45 dB hearing impairment, and 80 to 100 percent might be missed with a 50 dB hearing impairment. Without amplification and intervention, the child is likely to have a limited vocabulary and imperfect speech production.

A moderate-severe hearing impairment is one between 56 and 70 dB HL. If amplification technologies are not used, spoken communication must be very loud and very close to be minimally understood.

A severe hearing impairment occurs from 71 to 90 dB HL and will prevent a child from hearing conversational-level speech without amplification. With early and appropriate amplification (hearing aids and FM systems), that child should be able to detect all speech sounds as well as environmental sounds—but not at great distances. And the child must have therapy and intervention to learn the meaning of incoming sounds.

A profound hearing impairment means that the hearing loss is 91 dB HL or worse. A person with a profound hearing loss cannot hear any sound without amplification. However, very few people have absolutely no residual or remaining hearing. The vast majority of people with profound hearing impairments do have some residual hearing.

The degree of hearing loss alone does not determine communicative function. Many children with profound hearing losses are finding excellent auditory opportunities via use of cochlear implants.

Acoustic Filter Effect of Hearing Impairment

Any type or degree of hearing loss that occurs in infancy or childhood can interfere with the development of a child's spoken language, reading and writing skills, and academic performance. That is, hearing loss can be described as an *invisible acoustic filter* that distorts, smears, or eliminates incoming sounds, especially sounds from a distance—even a short distance. The negative effects of a hearing loss may be apparent, but the hearing loss itself is invisible and easily ignored or underestimated.

It is critical to note that as human beings, we are neurologically "wired" to develop spoken language (speech) and reading skills through the central *auditory* system. Most people think that reading is a visual skill, but recent research on brain mapping shows that the primary reading centers of the brain are located in the auditory cortex—in the auditory portions of the brain. That's why children who are born with hearing loss, who do not have access to auditory input when they are very young (through amplification and auditory training), tend to have a great deal of difficulty reading even though their vision is fine. Therefore, the earlier and more efficiently we can allow a child access to meaningful sound with subsequent direction of the child's attention to sound, the better opportunity that child will have to develop spoken language, literacy, and academic skills. A child with a hearing loss and a normal-hearing child *can* have the same opportunity to develop spoken language, reading, and academic skills.

Distance Hearing

Children with hearing losses, even minimal ones, cannot receive intelligible speech well over distances. This reduction in "earshot" has tremendous consequences for life and classroom performance because distance hearing is linked to passive, casual, and incidental listening and learning. Research in the field of developmental psychology tells us that about 90 percent of what very young children know about language and the world is learned incidentally. That is, young children learn a great deal of information unintentionally because they overhear conversations that occur at distances. Thus, any type and any degree of hearing loss can present a significant barrier to an infant or child's ability to receive information from the environment.

Because of the reduction in acoustic signal intensity and integrity with distance, a child with a hearing problem has limited range or distance hearing. Accordingly, that child may need to be taught directly many language, thinking, conversational, and social skills that other children learn incidentally.

One of the advantages of a cochlear implant over hearing aids for a child with a profound or severe hearing loss is that cochlear implants increase distance hearing. Most children with cochlear implants have indoor-distance hearing that is greater than thirty-two feet, even for the "s" sound. Children with severe to profound hearing losses who wear hearing aids, to the contrary, either have no sound detection available for the "sh" and "s" sounds or have distance hearing of only a few feet.

Audibility/Intelligibility Distinctions

There is a big difference between an "audible" signal and an "intelligible" signal. Speech is audible if the person is able simply to detect its presence. For speech to be intelligible, however, the person must be able to discriminate the word-sound distinctions of individual phonemes or speech sounds. Speech might be very *audible* but not consistently *intelligible* to a child with even a minimal hearing loss, causing the child to hear, for example, words such as "walked," "walking," "walker," and "walks," all as "ah."

Vowel sounds (such as "o," "u," "ee") are low-frequency sounds and the most powerful sounds in English; they cause speech to be audible. Consonant sounds (like "sh" and "s") are high-frequency sounds and are much weaker; consonants allow speech to be intelligible. For speech to be heard clearly, both vowels and consonants must be acoustically available. People with hearing losses typically have the most difficulty hearing the weak, high-frequency consonant sounds. Cochlear implants can provide wonderful access to those high frequency consonant sounds in cases in which hearing aids cannot.

"Computer Analogy" and Amplification Technology

One way to illustrate the potentially negative effects that any type and degree of hearing impairment has on a child's language and overall development, and to explain the role of amplification technology, is to use a computer analogy. The primary concept is that *data input precedes data processing*.

An infant or toddler (or anyone) must have information-data in order to learn. A primary avenue for entering information into the brain is through the ears, via hearing. So, the ears can be thought of as analogous to a computer keyboard, and the brain can be compared to a computer hard drive. Remember, as human beings, we are neurologically wired to code and hence to develop spoken language and reading skills through the auditory centers of the brain: the hard drive. Therefore, auditory data input is critical, and every effort must be taken to access auditory information. If data are entered inaccurately, incompletely, or inconsistently, analogous to using a malfunctioning computer keyboard or to having one's fingers on the wrong keys of a computer keyboard, the child's brain—the hard drive—will have incorrect or incomplete information to process. How can a child be expected to learn when the information that reaches his or her brain is deficient? Amplification technology such as hearing aids, personal FM systems, sound-field FM systems, and biomedical devices such as cochlear implants all can be thought of as keyboards ... as means of entering acoustic information into the child's hard drive.

So, technology is really just a more efficient keyboard. Unfortunately, technology is not a perfect keyboard, and it does not have a life of its own, any more than a car has a life of its own. Technology is only as effective as the use to which it is put and is only as efficient as the people who use it. Conversely, without the technology, without acoustic data input, auditory access is not possible for people with hearing impairments.

To continue the computer analogy, once the keyboard is repaired or the figurative fingers are placed on the correct keys of the keyboard allowing data to be entered accurately, analogous to using amplification technology that enables a child to detect word-sound distinctions, what happens to all of the previously entered inaccurate and incomplete information? Is there a magic button that automatically converts inaccurate data to complete and correct information? Unfortunately, all of the corrected data must be reentered. Thus, the longer a child's hearing problem remains unrecognized and unmanaged, the more destructive and far-reaching are the snowballing effects of hearing impairment. Early intervention is critical—the earlier the better!

Hearing is only the *first* step in the chain of intervention. Once hearing has been accessed as much as possible through appropriate amplification or biomedical technology, the child will have an opportunity to discriminate word-sound distinctions as a basis for learning language, which in turn provides the child with an opportunity to communicate and acquire knowledge of the world. All levels of the acoustic filter effect of hearing impairment discussed previously need to be understood and managed.

The longer a child's data entry is inaccurate, the more damaging the snowballing acoustic filter effects will be on the child's overall life development. Conversely, the more intelligible and complete the data entered are, the better opportunity the infant or toddler will have to learn language that serves as a foundation for later reading and academic skills. It can't be said often enough: early intervention is critical!

From the inception of early-intervention programming, for a child of any age with any type of hearing or listening difficulty to have an opportunity to learn, comprehensive audiologic and hearing management is an absolutely necessary first step. A critical caveat is that although amplification technology can provide a better "keyboard," a more efficient and consistent route of data entry, that keyboard will not be perfect. Thus, listening and learning strategies also need to be implemented. The exciting news is that a cochlear implant can provide a much more complete and efficient keyboard than can hearing aids for a child with a profound hearing loss, even if that child is obtaining some benefit from hearing aids and FM systems.

Candidacy for Implantation

My audiologic criteria for cochlear implant eligibility include the following: (i) a desired outcome for that child of spoken language and reading and academic skills consistent with hearing peers; (ii) mainstream placement; (iii) unaided thresholds of 90 dB or worse from 750 Hz through 8,000 Hz[2]; (iv) aided distance hearing less than ten feet for "s" and less than twenty feet for "sh"; (v) some difficulty following an open-set communicative exchange between two people; and (vi) an aided Speech Recognition Threshold (the softest level at which known speech material can just barely be recognized using a closed-set task) of 35 dB HL or worse. If children who have been receiving auditory-verbal communication intervention meet these criteria, I refer them for a cochlear implant evaluation even though they are receiving benefit from their hearing aids and are using their amplified hearing in a functional and productive way.

Some professionals ask why we should recommend cochlear implants for children who are receiving benefit from amplification. The answer is simple: because such children could receive greater and easier acoustic access with a cochlear implant than they receive with hearing aids. Why should auditory-verbal children be denied a better technology (cochlear implants) just because they have had extensive therapy and have learned to use the more limited auditory cues provided by their hearing aids?

The cochlea of an auditory-verbally taught child with a profound hearing loss is not more intact than the cochlea of a visually taught child with a profound hearing loss. The auditory advantage for the auditory-verbal child is in the high expectation of the ability to use hearing, extensive use of technology, and auditory-based rather than visually based teaching. In fact, the more the child benefits from hearing aids and the more auditory focus and experience a child has had with hearing aids before receiving a cochlear implant, the faster and more efficiently that child can progress after receiving the implant because the child's brain has already been "programmed" with auditory information. Using the computer analogy, the child's hard drive is available to receive the more complete auditory information provided through the keyboard of a cochlear implant.

In a child who has already been receiving auditory-verbal therapy and for whom an auditory-verbal commitment has been made by the family, very high expectations are encouraged. Because a cochlear implant is a more effective and efficient keyboard, it enables potentially easier and faster access to the desired outcomes previously specified by the family. Those desired outcomes include being functionally hard-of-hearing (auditorally focused rather than visually focused); being able to detect all speech sounds, including consonants such as "s" and "sh" at distances of thirty feet or greater; being able to recognize known speech material at 15–20 dB HL; having access to the entire speech spectrum in the normal to mild hearing-loss range; and being able to overhear the conversation of others.

A Speech-Language Pathology Perspective, by Denise Wray

One of the major distinctions between desired long-range outcomes established for children using an auditory-verbal approach and desired outcomes from using other educational methodologies lies with expectations. The outcomes (including independence and integration in hearing society as a contributing citizen) mandate that the child be compared with and compete with hearing peers from the outset. A natural developmental speech-language model is used as the measure in ongoing diagnosis and assessment of the child's communication gains. The goal is for communication development that involves literacy skills that go far beyond the "three R's of reading, writing and 'rithmetic." Literacy equates with at least a high school level of reading (70 percent of the reading material in a cross section of jobs nationally is written on *at least* a ninth-grade reading level), adequate listening and writing skills, effective oral communication, problem solving abilities, engaging in high-level communicative functions such as negotiating, compromising, and persuading, and literacy in computer and telecommunicative technology.

To achieve this end, an intervention plan for a child with a cochlear implant must be multifaceted and include objectives that target the following areas: (1) audition, (2) language, (3) speech, (4) cognition, (5) pragmatics, and most important (6) parent training.

A critical concept that pertains to the attainment of targeted objectives is the notion of hearing or listening age. A child's auditory and language development begins when amplification technology is employed; in this case, a child's listening and learning begins when the child's implant is first activated and mapped. For example, if a child is 3 years old chronologically when he or she receives the implant and the implant is activated, that child has a hearing age of *one day old*. When that same child reaches age 4 years chronologically, he or she now has a listening or hearing age of 1 year. That is, this child has had one year's worth of experience hearing spoken language and receiving auditory information from the environment. Therefore, we would expect this child to have spoken language skills closer to those of a 1-year-old than to those of a 4-year-old. Furthermore, the more auditory experience a child has had pre-implant (through the use of hearing aids), the faster progress that child is able to achieve post-implant. With active and thoughtful auditory-verbal intervention, this gap between hearing age and chronological age is expected to diminish. The younger a child is when he or she receives an implant, of course, the less time gap between hearing age and chronological age will exist.

Goals for Intervention Plan

Audition

This is the most crucial feature of intervention following an implant. A genuine commitment to auditory skills must proceed with simultaneous attention to both the suprasegmental aspects of speech, which include the features of duration, intonation, intensity, and stress, and the segmental aspects of speech, which include the perception of vowels and consonants. With cochlear implants, sounds that cover the speech spectrum are enhanced, and it becomes possible to detect and identify those sounds at a distance and in the presence of varying degrees of noise. Cochlear implant technology has permitted access to sound and linguistic information far beyond the capabilities of traditional hearing aids and at distances never before dreamed possible.

Auditory skills are taught by therapists and parents in both structured sessions and in the context of natural routines that permeate everyday living. Listening is expected and integrated into the child's "personality." Listening to the colorful world of sound becomes a way of life.

Language

Teaching language includes instruction in both understanding and expressing oneself. One of the most striking contrasts to language development involving hearing aids is the capacity of the child to learn grammatic inflections, or endings, of words and syllables, possibly within the first year following the implant. The understanding of contractions, plurals, possessives, verb tense endings, gender, and auxiliaries (all involving high-frequency, low-energy sounds) often surfaces without having been taught directly. In other words, children acquire these crucial grammatical endings incidentally, in a manner similar to the acquisition by children with normal hearing. These meaningful function words and segments add significant sophistication to the child's language, thereby advancing intelligibility for the listener. And due to the facilitation of speech perception and production from the implant, more time can be devoted to the enhancement of language skills that lay the foundation for subsequent reading and writing growth.

Speech

Promoting imitation of the speech sounds in the child's native tongue, in the course of natural play, is a first step in speech development. Phonetic perception precedes speech production. While the interventionist is fostering perception of the melody, the intensity, and the stress of speech, he or she is targeting early-developing sounds that bombard the child meaningfully in the context of play. A natural developmental hierarchy is followed, using many strategies garnered from studies conducted on "parentese," the language that parents use as they facilitate the development of language and speech in children with normal hearing. Parents are taught that all physical movements and toys are accompanied by a sound.

Research on children with implants suggests that one may expect perception of suprasegmentals (duration, intensity, stress) early on in the program. This is followed by vowel, diphthong, and early-developing consonant perception involving consonants that differ first in manner (a long sound versus a short, fast sound), followed by voice (a sound that vibrates the vocal cords when phonating versus a sound that does not), and then place (a sound made with the lips versus one made with the tongue). A pivotal point to make is the importance of baselining and collecting of speech data soon after the implant. This information can be most helpful to the audiologist, who may be frequently mapping the child's speech processor, particularly during the first six months. Both concerns for effective maps can be revealed through carefully monitoring and reporting to the audiologist the child's spontaneous and imitative speech productions.

Cognition

Cognitive skills closely parallel language and intelligence development. This aspect of the intervention program may be traditionally assigned to the teacher but also should be a part of the speech-language plan. It includes teaching the concepts of sorting by categories (e.g., colors, function, attributes) and sorting based on similarities and differences, counting, shapes, texture, comparisons of any type (e.g., color, texture, shape, function), sequencing, analogies, opposites, inferences, and problem-solving strategies. These skills are generally coordinated with the language activities of daily living and structured teaching and can often reveal the inclination of the child to learn new concepts.

Pragmatics

Pragmatics compose one of the most important parameters of language learning. Pragmatics involve the social use of language: how can the child integrate all he or she hears and use it to effectively manipulate the environment? The child must be taught the various functions of language. For example, one uses language to request, deny, greet, depart, reject, inquire, comment, persuade, recount events, explain, compare and contrast, interrupt, repair breakdowns, negotiate, etc. It is this aspect of language that transforms the child into a socially acceptable member of hearing society. This variety of skill training begins immediately after the child has gained ample access to sound. The implant permits the interventionist to expect appropriate social use of language early on in the program, particularly because many of these communicative functions are conveyed through intonation, stress, and intensity (e.g., anger, pleading, social amenities, happiness).

Parent Training

A professional's responsibility is to teach the family how to nurture the development of language. Parents who are successfully empowered to teach language are more likely to raise children displaying greater expertise with spoken communication.

Case Study: Sara

Once told of their 1-year-old child's profound hearing loss, Bob and Karen began the process of determining whether their daughter, "Sara," was a candidate for a cochlear implant. The FDA had approved the implantation of children as young as two years, but their surgeon gained special permission for Sara to receive an implant as early as 18 months, making Sara one of the youngest toddlers implanted at this center, in October 1994. We were about to find out if, in fact, "sooner was better."

Within a month after her implant was activated, everyone agreed that Sara's performance with the implant was comparable to her performance with hearing aids pre-implantation. At this same time, however, impressive distance hearing began to emerge. Sara's father yelled Sara's name from ten feet outside the bathroom after discovering she was drinking the toilet water. Rather than simply looking up, Sara actually startled to her father's reprimand. Suprasegmental features of speech also emerged. In addition to imitating intentional patterns well, Sara understood many of the common directives that were accompanied by predictable inflectional patters (e.g., thank you; uh-oh!; all gone!). Early-developing sounds began to rapidly emerge. Sara could hear sounds such as "t," "d," and even "s"; shortly thereafter she could hear "g" sounds. About two months post-activation, reduplication of syllables surfaced. This was significant because it set the stage for common two-syllable words that children begin using at age 1 year to 18 months (wa-wa for water; ma-ma for mommy; daw-daw for doggy), and using two-syllable words lays the foundation for combining words into sentences. Further, Sara began alternating vowels in two-syllable words, such as "eyo" for "yellow." On Christmas Eve, exactly two months after Sara received her first mapping, I was in the midst of entertaining a large family gathering in my home when the phone rang. It was Sara's mother, who had called to say that for the first time, Sara had said "a-e" for "Daddy" and understood its meaning. Karen was ecstatic and in tears. I put down the phone and thought ... Happy Holidays.

A month later Sara was imitating sounds such as "ch," "sh," and "s" with ease. She began using her name, which contained the challenging "s." And her receptive skills began to show significant strides. Sara seemed to soak up as much as we poured into her auditory system. She perfectly imitated everything she heard. At ten months post-activation, she began to use blends consistently in words, such as "ple" for "please." More important, she used final sounds, even those that were late developing, such as "ch" and "r" in words such as "ouch" and "more." This use of final consonants enormously improved Sara's speech intelligibility. One and a half years post-activation, Sara had a wide repertoire of over one hundred words and thirty-five statements, and she used pronouns, negatives, and questions (all of which could be understood by the unfamiliar listener).

Formal and standardized testing revealed a steady pattern of progress. For instance, a single-word vocabulary test of reception (Receptive One-Word Picture Vocabulary Test, Gardner, 1985) initially placed Sara in the eighteenth percentile, slightly more than one standard deviation below the mean, when she was chronologically 3 years old and a year and a half post-implantation. Since this was Sara's first attempt at a standardized picture-vocabulary test, we were encouraged. We felt cause for celebration when, following three administrations of the Early Language Milestone Scale-2 test (Coplan, 1993), Sara achieved an age equivalency score of 30 months, in comparison with her chronological age of 37 months.

One year later and two and a half years post-implantation, progress continues at a steady and sometimes rapid pace. In terms of vocabulary comprehension, Sara made it into the "average range" on the Receptive One-Word Picture Vocabulary Test, moving up into the forty-fifth percentile from the last year's eighteenth. In an informal, nonstandardized single-syllable word (consonant-vowel-consonant combinations) repetition task, through audition alone Sara achieved 60 percent perfect approximation. She also received 100 percent perfect vowel production, 88 percent perfect initial consonant production, and amazingly, 68 percent perfect final consonant production. This is a respectable performance by even a hearing child having a chronological age of 3.10 years. In terms of distance hearing, a recent test revealed that Sara could perfectly repeat all six Ling sounds[3] with 100 percent accuracy at a distance of thirty-five feet (through audition alone)!

Now that Sara's speech production is progressing well, we are honing in on conversational competence and developing communicative acts that will enable Sara to relate events, inquire, compare-contrast, comment, negotiate with classmates, request assistance from peers and teachers, and adequately survive in this auditory-verbal society. There is no doubt that her young but astute parents made the right choice when they elected to give Sara the gift of a cochlear implant!

Case Study: Kim

Due to hearing loss in the family, baby Kim's hearing was tested shortly after birth. A profound hearing loss was suspected almost immediately. Kim was fitted with two hearing aids at age four months. Intense auditory-verbal therapy followed, with slow but steady progress. Hearing aids provided hearing in the moderate range up through 1,000 Hz but little benefit for conversational speech.

Kim received a cochlear implant at 2.10 years of age; her implant was activated in early February 1997. Her speech perception immediately improved, and speech production gains quickly followed. Interestingly, there appeared to be little, if any, transition period between Kim's use of hearing aids to her use of the implant. The implant seemed to simply substitute for the aids.

Three months post-implantation, Kim's vowel perception and production was 100 percent correct, and she had mastered the "sh" and "s" sounds. Sound was slightly distorted but contained the necessary stridency feature. Her spontaneous productions showed differing semantic relations. To the question "Where's Mommy?" Kim responded "Dat Mommy!" and pointed to her mother. Later that same session, when I had accidentally picked up the scissors that her mother had been using during our craft activity, Kim indignantly reprimanded, "Dat Mommy!" Clearly, Kim was not simply labeling her mother once again but was demonstrating her comprehension and use of the semantic relation of possession.

Word endings, crucial for improving intelligibility, began to emerge three months post-implantation, even those late-developing sounds, particularly "sh." Kim was uttering two-word sentences, frequently accompanied by appropriate prosody (i.e., intensity, stress, intonation). Several three-word sentences spontaneously surfaced, such as "It my turn," and "Mom, McDonald cookies." Kim's two older brothers provide ample opportunity for developing the communicative acts of refusing, requesting, denying, and tattling. At this point, five months post-implantation, Kim demonstrates detection of all six Ling sounds at a distance of twelve feet. Her family is enormously impressed with the ease with which they can communicate with Kim, even in the presence of noise.

NOTES

1. Decibel (dB) is the unit of measurement of intensity used in acoustics and in audiometers. The "bel" is named after Alexander Graham Bell, and "deci" means one-tenth of a bel. There are five unique and distinguishing aspects of the decibel: (1) it is a relative unit of measure; (2) it therefore involves a ratio; (3) it involves a logarithm; (4) it therefore is nonlinear; and (5) it is expressed in terms of various reference levels that must be specified—one of which is HL, or Hearing Level.

Hearing Level (HL) means that the decibel is referenced to normal hearing. Thus, the lowest or softest sound intensity that stimulates normal hearing has been termed 0 dB HL. Because there is a range for "normal" function, a child is considered to have normal hearing sensitivity if the softest sounds that he or she can just barely detect (thresholds) fall between 0 and 15 dB HL.

2. Hertz (Hz), adopted to honor the nineteenth century German physicist Heinrich Hertz, means cycles per second (cps) and is a measure of the frequency (heard as pitch) of a tone. The mid-high speech frequencies of 750 Hz through 8,000 Hz carry 90 percent of the intelligibility of speech in the form of consonant sounds. For a child with a profound hearing loss, a hearing aid will have difficulty providing sufficient amplification to make these soft yet critical speech sounds audible, even at a very close range. A cochlear implant, on the other hand, potentially can make these mid- and high-frequency consonant speech sounds audible even at great distances.

3. In the Ling six-sound test children are asked to respond to speech sounds "m," "oo," "ah," "ee," "sh," and "s." These sounds range from low to high frequencies and assess how much of the speech range a child can hear.

Evolving Views of Cochlear Implants in Children

Elizabeth Fitzpatrick, M.S., AUD(C), Cert. AVT

Elizabeth Fitzpatrick received an M.S. in Audiology and Rehabilitation of the Hearing Impaired from McGill University, Montreal, Canada. She is coordinator of the Cochlear Implant Program in the Audiology Clinic at Children's Hospital of Eastern Ontario in Ottawa, Canada.

Which Children Can Benefit from Implants?

Expectations for children who use cochlear implants have changed rapidly in the past ten years as technology has evolved and clinical knowledge has grown. In the pre–cochlear implant era, auditory-verbal therapy and oral programs demonstrated that most children with profound hearing impairment have minimal residual hearing that can be developed to achieve spoken language communication. Cochlear implant technology now makes spoken communication and mainstreaming a viable possibility for children who previously were considered to have insufficient residual hearing to benefit greatly from hearing aids. *Cochlear implants may thus be recommended for the majority of children who are categorized audiologically as having a severe to profound hearing loss.*

Children diagnosed with hearing impairments should all receive intensive audiological management and diagnostic therapy. Cochlear implants are a natural evolution in a comprehensive management approach for children. The children who are candidates for implants fall into three basic categories, as outlined below.

Category 1

The first category includes children who have insufficient residual hearing to develop spoken language without an implant. This category consists primarily of preschool children. In the pre–cochlear implant era, following a period of intensive audiological management and auditory-verbal therapy, we referred these preschool children with no measurable (for all practical purposes) hearing to a total-communication program. They were educated in a special classroom for children who are deaf or hard-of-hearing or in a special school for the deaf. When implanted at early ages, these children can develop good speech and language skills. The following is a "typical" case study.

Case 1. J.C. was diagnosed at the age of 10 months as having a profound hearing loss. She was fit with powerful amplification and was enrolled in the diagnostic auditory-verbal therapy program, where the parents attended weekly parent-guidance sessions. During this period it was determined that she had no measurable hearing. At age 2, she was fit with a tactile aid in addition to her hearing aids and continued to be followed in therapy. At age 2 years, 6 months, she was referred to a preschool total-communication program; shortly thereafter, the parents began exploring the option of a cochlear implant. J.C. received a cochlear implant at 3.3 years of age. J.C. continued to attend a total-communication class post-implantation and also received intensive auditory-verbal intervention. One year post-implant, she was integrated into a kindergarten class with specialized support services. Six years post-implant, she has very intelligible speech, communicates effectively with unfamiliar talkers, and successfully talks on the telephone. On speech perception testing when presented an audiotaped version of the CID Everyday Sentences, she identified correctly 87 percent of the key words in sentences. On the Test of Language Development-Intermediate, administered at school, she obtained a Spoken

Language Quotient of 100, suggesting that her overall language abilities fall within the average range. At a chronological age of 9 years, 8 months, her receptive vocabulary score on the Peabody Picture Vocabulary Test was 8 years, 3 months; on expressive vocabulary testing, as measured by the Expressive One-Word Picture Vocabulary Test, she placed in the seventy-ninth percentile rank for her age. She is now completing a regular grade-six program in her neighborhood school and receives support services from an itinerant teacher of the hearing impaired.

This category also includes children for whom implants and oral communication were not an option during their preschool years but who have received implants during their elementary or high school years. Before receiving implants, these children had established gestural systems and were acquiring academics in a total-communication or bilingual/bicultural (American Sign Language) environment. Due in large part to their late age of implantation, these children may not achieve sufficient spoken language to be included in classrooms with children who hear normally. This does not, however, mean that they receive no benefit from the implant. In most cases, they detect sound and may learn to process closed-set information auditorally (i.e., information related to pictures or other materials, such as toys, where there are a small number of choices). They may use the implant to assist in speechreading and overall understanding of spoken language. Parents may feel that by increasing awareness of sounds in the environment, the implant is contributing to the safety of the child. An example of one such child is shown in Case 2.

Case 2. D.D. was diagnosed with a profound hearing loss at the age of 2 years. She was fit with powerful amplification and was enrolled in the auditory-verbal therapy program. After one year she was referred to the total-communication classroom program, where she developed communication and academic skills through sign language. After five years in this program, her parents decided to give D.D. a cochlear implant. D.D. was implanted at 7.7 years of age. Although D.D. continues to wear her cochlear implant and receives hearing benefit, she has not been able to develop spoken communication. She continues to use sign language as her primary communication mode and attends a self-contained total-communication classroom. After three years of implant use, she is able to identify, based on the number of syllables, very familiar vocabulary when a small number of choices are presented.

Category 2

The second category consists of children for whom it is felt that a cochlear implant will provide more auditory information than can be provided by hearing aids.

Most children who are deaf have some residual hearing that, when amplified, can be developed to achieve spoken communication—particularly if the child's hearing loss is identified and managed early. Near age-appropriate language skills can be developed, and the child's spoken language can be intelligible, although sometimes difficult to understand for the unfamiliar listener. Many of these children are fully integrated with their hearing peers and receive various levels of specialized educational services depending on academic, speech, language, and psychosocial needs as well as on simple geographical location and availability of programs. There is a growing awareness that a cochlear implant will provide access to a greater quantity and quality of sound than these children (whether of preschool age or school age) can access with current hearing-aid technology. The following two cases exemplify "typical" children who may be included in this category.

Case 3. D.H. was diagnosed at the age of 2 with a severe to profound hearing loss. He was learning to use his limited residual hearing in the auditory-verbal therapy program and demonstrated the ability to understand closed-set simple communication in therapy and in more formal speech-perception testing. Expressively, he used short phrases of two to four words and was considered to be very communicative. Although it is believed that D.H. would have continued to progress with hearing aids, after two years of therapy the therapist began discussing a cochlear implant with the family. D.H. was implanted at the age of 5. D.H. appears to be developing spoken language faster with the cochlear implant than he did with hearing aids. At eighteen months post-implant, language testing indicated that he was about two years behind his hearing peers in vocabulary and expressive language development. His language delays are steadily being reduced, however. Testing at eighteen months post-implant indicated significant improvements in vocabulary development, showing an increase from an age equivalent score of 2 years, 4 months pre-implant to a score of 4 years on the Expressive One-Word Picture Vocabulary Test. His speech is fairly intelligible, with about 78 percent of words understood by a familiar listener. He is able to process through listening alone about 70 percent of familiar vocabulary and sentences presented using audiotaped sentences from the Glendonald Auditory Screening Procedure. He attends a grade-one classroom with hearing children, and his language skills are gradually improving.

Case 4. N.N. was diagnosed at the age of 3 months with a severe to profound hearing loss. She attended the auditory-verbal therapy program for five years and was integrated with hearing peers in a regular nursery school and school. She demonstrated the ability to identify 46 percent of key words presented in the auditory mode only on a commonly used open-set speech perception test (i.e., she was able to understand sentences presented out of context through audition alone). She functioned fully in the hearing world, with age-appropriate or above-age-appropriate language, vocabulary, and academic skills. She received itinerant services throughout the school years but no other special-education support services. She was considered a successful auditory-verbal child. N.N. received a cochlear implant at the age of 15.7 years. Although N.N. had some difficulty adapting to the new sound in the first month of implant use, by three months post-implant she was showing significant gains in processing speech, including unfamiliar information through listening alone. She quickly discontinued hearing aid use, since she felt that the information received through the implant was overwhelming compared with the hearing aids. She reports that she is able to understand speech via her implant with greater ease than when using hearing aids. Three-month speech-perception scores on the Glendonald Auditory Screening Procedure corroborate these comments: N.N. scored 90 percent on sentences, compared with 50 percent pre-implant. On the CID Everyday Sentences, she identified 64 percent of key words in sentences, compared with 46 percent during pre-implant testing. Since N.N.'s language and academic skills were age appropriate at the time of implantation, the goal of an implant for N.N. and her family was not to develop language abilities but rather to facilitate spoken communication and overall inclusion with hearing peers.

Category 3

There is also a smaller, third category of children who are candidates for cochlear implants—children with post-lingual deafness (such as children who became deafened due to meningitis). Children in this group tend to be excellent performers with cochlear implants. The following is a case exemplifying a "typical" child in this category.

Case 5. S.A. was first diagnosed with a unilateral hearing loss at age 3 years, 6 months, and was monitored audiologically. At age 5, her hearing thresholds in the impaired ear decreased to a profound level. At age 6, she experienced a decrease in hearing in the other ear, and test results showed a profound bilateral hearing loss. She was aggressively managed medically, with no improvement in hearing levels. After six months of medical management and habilitation using a hearing aid, a cochlear implant was recommended. S.A. received an implant at age 6.9 years. S.A. has been using her implant for only two weeks and already is processing, through listening alone, familiar language used out of context. She quickly adapted to the new acoustic signal, and the first day she wanted to sleep with her speech processor. It is expected that she will receive excellent benefit from her cochlear implant.

Factors Affecting Learning with an Implant

The ability of a child to develop spoken communication is influenced not only by the amount of residual hearing but by a myriad of other variables, including age of detection of hearing loss, audiological management, the quality of parental input, the type and nature of the habilitation program, the child's environment (both at home and at school), and the presence (or absence) of other neurological and cognitive deficits. It is likely that these factors are inter-related. For example, the therapy program may influence the quantity and quality of parental input and perhaps even a child's ability to learn language despite other developmental difficulties.

Most factors affecting learning with a cochlear implant are the same as those affecting spoken language acquisition through a hearing aid. In addition, however, auditory functioning with the implant may be affected by physiological factors that cannot be measured pre-implant, factors such as the quantity and location of auditory nerve fibers available for electrical stimulation.

The variables affecting a child's ability to develop spoken communication are not always easily measured or quantified and will be assigned relative importance depending on the expectations and experiences of the professionals assessing the child. To date, no preselection process has been identified to determine which children with profound hearing losses will most likely benefit from therapy that emphasizes spoken communication. Thus, auditory-verbal therapists have advocated a diagnostic therapy period in which the therapist and family work together to develop the child's hearing potential. In a survey conducted by this author, therapists and parents identified expectations for spoken language and mainstreaming as a major difference between auditory-verbal therapy and other therapy programs.

The ability to predict preoperatively the "hearing potential" of a child is highly desirable. Cochlear implant candidates are typically selected on the basis of medical, audiologic, and other criteria, following approval of such criteria by appropriate governing agencies. These criteria provide only general guidelines, and criteria such as "receiving little or no benefit from amplification" and "family commitment and expectations" are open to interpretation. Different centers have developed their own criteria. Thus, for example, the Manhattan Eye Ear and Throat Institute proposes a systematic evaluation of ten specific criteria.[1] Expectations and past experiences of professionals and parents have influenced the growth and content of therapy programs, and expectations are probably the single largest determiner of who is referred and who is accepted as an implant candidate. This can cause confusion for parents or even professionals, since a child referred for a cochlear implant assessment may be accepted by one team and not by another for the same device and the same treatment.

The factors that lead to a recommendation for a cochlear implant and that have been observed to affect the child's ability to acquire spoken communication are discussed below.

Hearing Potential

In an auditory-verbal program, hearing potential is evaluated on an ongoing basis. A therapist's concerns about the child's ability or slow progress in developing spoken communication is often the first indication that a cochlear implant should be considered. Once an accurate diagnosis of the hearing loss has been obtained, and once the possibilities offered through hearing aids have been evaluated through therapy, the cochlear implant is the next step in a comprehensive process to provide a child with the best possible access to sound. The question is very simple: Can one expect that the child will have an opportunity for an increase in the quality and quantity of sound input with a cochlear implant?

Results from our own and other programs indicate that children who use implants can learn to process meaningful auditory information, which in turn leads to intelligible speech production and spoken language. These conclusions are leading us to begin discussing, with the family of any child for whom audiological results coupled with therapy indicate a severe to profound hearing impairment, the option of a cochlear implant.

Observations suggest that children who have some residual hearing and verbal language pre-implant may adapt more quickly to the new sounds heard via the implant. Thus, we work on developing this small remnant of hearing during the pre-implant stage when audiological information is still being collected and the child is undergoing a pre-implant evaluation. In addition, the programming of the speech processor may be easier and faster with children who have some awareness of sound. Furthermore, children who have some auditory abilities with their hearing aids seem to be able to transfer this processing ability quite quickly (within a few weeks or even days) to listening through a cochlear implant. Sign language is not usually introduced formally in the pre-implant stage if a cochlear implant is being considered, although natural gestures are used extensively in communicating with young children.

Some preschool children receive a cochlear implant after a period of sign language use either because an implant was not initially an option or because they began therapy in a total-communication program. Our experiences to date suggest that if children receive implants before age 3 or 4 and follow an auditory-verbal program, there is no indication that having used sign language pre-implant interferes with their ability to develop spoken language, assuming that they are now in a non–sign language environment. However, therapists have remarked that children who have learned to use their residual hearing seem to "tune in" to the new sounds more quickly.

Many programs appear to place a significant emphasis on assessing the child's functional hearing through various closed- and open-set speech-perception tests to determine implant candidacy. In our program, speech-perception testing is completed using assessment tools commonly used in cochlear implant centers, to establish baseline information. Since most of our children are already enrolled in an auditory program, these results rarely determine whether the child will receive an implant. Children who are referred from other clinics have their auditory abilities assessed through intensive therapy sessions in conjunction with more standard speech-language tests. A skilled therapist who has worked with a variety of children with severe to profound losses who use hearing aids or cochlear implants is perhaps the best assessment tool on the market, particularly when "borderline" candidates are being considered.

It is a well-established fact that cochlear implants increase the hearing potential for children with severe to profound losses. The very dramatic effect of providing access to high-frequency sounds such as "s" and "sh" is often one of the first "rewards," along with the overall improved detection levels across the range of speech sounds that are important for the understanding of speech. Other advantages over the hearing aid include the improved understanding over distance and in noisy environments and the ability of the listening child to "overhear" conversation. As one mother said, "We get bonus words that I haven't had to teach." Many therapists and parents comment that there is an overall ease of hearing and that listening is not a struggle anymore. An unplanned bonus, particularly for the young child, is the absence of the acoustic feedback so common and so annoying with powerful hearing aids. One can only assume that new cochlear implant technology will provide even greater benefits.

Age

There is a growing body of literature suggesting that the age of onset of deafness and the duration of deafness affect performance with implants. Adults with congenital deafness who have not been successful hearing aid users are, as a group, not considered good candidates, since they have not demonstrated high levels of auditory performance. Researchers have reported that children who are pre-lingually deaf perform better if they receive implants before 6 years of age (or earlier).

Early identification and early intervention with children who have hearing impairments are considered to be critical factors in the development of spoken language. Therefore, the sooner after diagnosis that amplification and implantation (when indicated) can occur, the greater would appear to be the opportunity for spoken language. The central nervous system of a young child is believed to be capable of organizing itself around the stimulation it receives. Auditory deprivation, rather than age of onset and duration of deafness, may indeed have the greatest impact on potential outcome with an implant. Children who have learned to use even minimal residual hearing to develop verbal communication can be expected to benefit more than children of the same age who have been in total-communication or other signing programs.

Communication Competence

There are different opinions regarding the competency level a child should have before receiving an implant. Some centers feel that a child should be able to communicate through sign language and or speechreading in order to complete the programming of the device and start the habilitation program. These centers may even recommend that there be a pretrial period in which the young child learns these skills before the pre-implant assessment continues. In an auditory-verbal program, in which the cochlear implant is viewed as a hearing device that will likely facilitate the development of communication, the emphasis is on implanting as soon as possible, that is, as soon as the audiological and therapy results confirm that the child will likely benefit more from an implant than from a hearing aid. There is no indication that children who are competent sign-language communicators adjust or progress more rapidly with a cochlear implant, and thus in auditory-verbal programs the implant process is not delayed in order to develop manual communication.

Our experience with young children with profound deafness leads us to expect that most will attempt to communicate using a combination of signs, natural gestures, and vocalizations. Accordingly, communicative intent is seriously considered during the pre-implant stage. A child who is not attempting to communicate through even natural gestures presents a concern. It is important to differentiate between lack of communication due to deafness and lack of communication due to other learning and language disabilities that may interfere with the development of spoken language if more hearing is available with an implant. Children who present concerns are evaluated by child-development specialists so that the parents can be more appropriately counseled regarding expectations.

Behavioral issues are not uncommon with children who have limited communication skills. Although these issues must be addressed and guidance must be provided as part of the habilitation service, difficult behaviors are not considered a reason to delay the implant. In fact, access to sound and communication for the child and a new focus and new hope for the parents may help alleviate some of the frustration. Difficult behavior will likely interfere with the child's attention and ability to focus and therefore will hinder the learning process with the implant. However, the fitting of a hearing aid would not be delayed because of behavior that is challenging to manage and neither should a cochlear implant, except perhaps in the unusual case where experts in the psychosocial field view the situation as so serious that implant surgery or the introduction of a new device may be harmful to the family's efforts to manage the behavior.

For children with longer durations of hearing loss, communicative competence (which is often but not necessarily linked to the amount of residual hearing) appears to be a key factor affecting language processing with an implant. The ability to communicate orally is a major factor in considering children beyond age 5 or 6. In our experience, most children who receive implants and who have already established gestural communication systems will not use the device to attain spoken communication. When the goal of the implant is to provide more hearing in order to develop oral competency, the child and parents are expected to start a new beginning in communication. Although some hearing and spoken communication can be developed, these benefits must be weighed against introducing new expectations that may affect the child's social functioning and even self-esteem. Signed communication modes, rather than simply duration of deafness, appear to impact negatively on a school-age child's ability to become a proficient oral communicator.

Experience with older children who communicate orally is perhaps more limited than with any other group of children. Our experience with a limited group of three adolescents who fall in this category has been very positive. The adolescents themselves must, of course, want the implant and be fully involved in the decision-making and assessment process. The adolescents are reporting that they obtain significant benefit from their implants, and this is corroborated by speech-perception test results. Thus children who are competent oral communicators appear to be good cochlear implant candidates; indeed, with solid linguistic functions, these children may function more like post-lingually deafened children. As one 15-year-old adolescent who recently received an implant said, "I didn't realize what I was missing."

Family Input and Commitment

Most programs involved in the habilitation of children with hearing impairments identify the importance of parents as partners. In auditory-verbal therapy programs, parents or significant caregivers must take on the responsibility for teaching their children. Our observations in an auditory-verbal program over more than twenty years indicate that regardless of whether a child is using hearing aids or cochlear implants, the more auditory, speech, and language input a child receives, the faster will be the progress. Although many other factors undoubtedly contribute to the child's overall successful development of language, this may be the single most important factor differentiating the performance levels of children with cochlear implants. Just as computer technology has facilitated certain services but has not replaced the human dimension, cochlear implant technology cannot replace good old-fashioned teaching and nurturing. The therapist's primary role is to guide the parent in developing spoken-language communication and in enriching the auditory-verbal communication environment outside the clinic.

Families who are enrolled in auditory-verbal therapy or similar parent-taught programs when they begin the implant process often view the implant as a final opportunity for their children to develop spoken communication and be included in hearing classrooms. Expectations and the realities of costs, equipment breakdowns medical risks, and the possibility that the implant will not provide better hearing all need to be explored with the family. The decision to implant a child is a difficult one for many families; for some, the realization that noninvasive technology is insufficient constitutes another critical stage in the grieving process. Not all families have equal resources, and even in a public health-care system such as Canada's, where implants and services are provided without fees, the day-to-day financial realities related to travel, babysitting, and replacement of equipment can cause anxiety. Some immigrant families may be learning the language of instruction as their child is being taught. A social worker is an invaluable member of the cochlear implant team in assisting with families and directing them to community resources to deal with these issues.

Families who come to the implant process not having had previous experience in a therapy program in which parents are the primary teachers may have a different understanding of the post-implant process. Families are being interviewed at a difficult and anxious time, and they may not always verbalize concerns related to their ability to teach their child, since they may fear that this will interfere with the child's acceptance for an implant. In some cases, we have required that families enroll in the auditory-verbal program during the pre-implant stage, primarily to help them realize the expectations and the reality of what is involved in assuming the responsibility of starting over with their child.

As professionals, we cannot advise parents to interrupt a career to teach their child. However, we have a responsibility to inform the families of the required commitment and advise them that the success of treatment (output) is dependent on the teaching (input). This is perhaps best demonstrated by having families become involved in "doing" what is required in the pre-implant stage.

Other Learning Problems

Cognitive, neurological, and developmental problems may affect the development of spoken communication for a child with hearing aids or a cochlear implant. The implant team psychologist completes a cognitive assessment with all children considered for an implant and conducts a parent interview. Other developmental specialists should be consulted and involved in the assessment and management if concerns regarding overall development are expressed by the parents or therapist.

Therapists are typically the first to notice that there may be something "different" about a particular child's learning style or behavior. Every child diagnosed with a hearing loss in our clinic is offered hearing aids and diagnostic therapy and is referred to another service only if an auditory-verbal option is considered to be inappropriate. Since a cochlear implant is more permanent than hearing aids, every attempt is made to be thorough in investigating suspected difficulties so that parents can be appropriately counseled regarding the possible impact on language learning. Unfortunately, it is often difficult to discern some of the more subtle neurological and cognitive deficits in young children, and we are faced with the decision of waiting until the child is older or maximizing the opportunity for learning language by implanting at a younger age. For example, a young child who has meningitis might be implanted earlier than usual due to medical concerns, but learning problems may not always be evident at this stage.

Cognitive delays are not necessarily viewed as a barrier to receiving a cochlear implant. One mother of a child who has been diagnosed with a cognitive deficit frankly and simply stated her feelings: "You would give my child glasses, you have given him a hearing aid, he deserves another opportunity with a cochlear implant." It is important that parents be fully informed and that they understand that the programming of the device and the development of spoken communication may be slower and more challenging for these children than for other children of a similar age but different developmental stage.

Management of Children with Cochlear Implants

Although all cochlear implant programs recommend post-implant habilitation that includes an auditory component, each program has its own definition of the term "auditory component." If the expectation is that a cochlear implant will provide the child with sound information, an auditory-based program such as auditory-verbal therapy would appear to provide the best opportunity for maximizing this opportunity. If the expectation is that the implant will provide access to environmental sounds and will improve speechreading while the primary communication mode will continue to be sign language, other approaches would appear to be more suitable.

The basic premise of the auditory-verbal approach is very simple: children with implants (or hearing aids, as the case may be) will learn to communicate orally so that they can attend schools and participate in community activities with children who have normal hearing. A full description of auditory-verbal principles and techniques practiced in various clinics is presented in a "Special Focus Section" of the *Volta Review*.[2]

Habilitation post-implant may be complicated by the fact that children who are already enrolled in the school system when they receive their implants, or who live at a considerable distance from an implant center, likely also benefit from the services of other professionals in the education of children who are deaf or hard-of-hearing. It is imperative that the various professionals communicate and collaborate to ensure continuity and consistency of care and objectives.

Children who are in total-communication programs when they receive their implants sometimes continue in these program while receiving auditory-verbal therapy in a clinic or school setting. This transition period of six months to a year may exist because parents and professionals are reluctant to entirely remove manual communication from a child before some oral communication has developed; the transition program may also exist simply because of the logistics of transferring a child from one school setting to another and finding appropriate support services during the academic year. When the auditory program and the total-communication program are truly working in partnership to develop an auditory focus, and when high-quality input exists at home, this "weaning" period does not appear to interfere with the longer-term acquisition of spoken language.

Although chapters have been written on how to habilitate children with cochlear implants (as if they were a group separate from other children who have hearing impairments), most auditory-verbal therapists report applying the auditory and language teaching techniques they use with any child with a significant hearing loss. Parents may need specific guidance and encouragement in this "new beginning" phase with their child, since they have already had experience teaching a child who has had less access to sound. Some parents may need to change old habits of communicating visually rather than auditorally. Parents need to understand that the "switch on" does not necessarily mean that hearing is suddenly activated; programming the speech processor and tuning in to meaningful sound can be a lengthy process.

This new beginning with children who communicate primarily through sign language presents some special challenges. Likewise, teaching older children who communicate orally to hear with a new device with sound patterns that differ from those heard with a hearing aid can be both frustrating and rewarding in the early stages depending on how quickly the child can learn to process the new auditory information. The task of developing simple-level auditory skills with children who are cognitively and linguistically advanced can challenge even the skilled therapist and parent.

Therapy sessions can provide critical information for the programming of the speech processor. The therapist working with the parent and the child can determine where the child is having difficulty hearing (i.e., in what frequency range) or whether the detection levels are appropriate, and immediate changes can be made to the speech processor program. This is particularly valuable when working with young children who cannot give reliable conditioned responses to sound during the programming sessions of the processor. A comprehensive implant program in which therapist and audiologist work together maximizes the auditory potential of the child.

A comprehensive habilitation program should also be sensitive to and, when appropriate, should attend to the psychosocial needs of the child and family. The team psychologist and the social worker, as well as classroom teachers and other school personnel, may all play a role in this aspect of managing the child with hearing loss. Indeed, social integration concerns may be more evident and more appropriately addressed in the school environment than in the one-to-one therapy sessions in the clinic. Referrals may also be made to appropriate community agencies and services.

Conclusions

The majority of severely or profoundly deaf children who receive cochlear implants in the first two to three years of life and perhaps up to 5 or 6 years of age can be expected to develop spoken communication enabling them to be educated alongside their hearing peers. Specialized services from school therapists who support the concept of spoken language will be important in maintaining and continuing language development, since many children will enter school with a "hearing age" or listening experience of only two or three years. Children should also have the benefit of other available technology, such as personal FM systems, to improve the signal-to-noise ratio (i.e., the ratio between the speech sound being transmitted and the sound from background noise) in the classroom.

A small number of children, even when receiving an implant at a young age, may not be able to utilize sufficiently the information to process spoken language and after a diagnostic period may require sign language. This may be due to the lack of neural survival, which we are unfortunately unable to measure pre-implant. Other children may progress slowly due to language-processing, learning, or neurological problems that we are not always able to identify in the very young child. Even when a learning difficulty is recognized, it is difficult to evaluate the effect on language or predict the outcome with an implant. Other children may simply not be in a learning environment where they can receive the required input.

The results with elementary and high-school children who are competent oral communicators, and who did not have the opportunity to benefit from an implant during the preschool years, suggest that benefit can be obtained in terms of auditory processing, speech intelligibility, and overall ease of communication.

School-age children who communicate primarily through sign language receive some benefit from implantation, such as awareness of environmental sounds, speech detection, speechreading enhancement, and even some auditory comprehension. However, it is unlikely that they will acquire a level of spoken communication permitting them to be included in hearing classrooms. An important consideration is whether emphasizing hearing and spoken communication at this late stage will interfere with social development and self-concept. All children who have an adequate level of understanding and maturity should be included in the decision-making process.

Parents are ultimately responsible for their children's well-being and must make the best decisions for their children. The very large majority of parents of children who are deaf would like to give their children the opportunity to develop spoken-language communication and the choice to integrate into hearing society. It is important to recognize and accept that all children and families have different potential and resources. Professionals have a responsibility to help parents make an informed decision by providing them with the most complete and accurate information based on scientific data and clinical experience. To date, unfortunately, the collection of scientific data lags behind clinical experience.

NOTES

1. M. E. Nevins, P. M. Chute, *Children with Cochlear Implants in Educational Settings* (San Diego: Singular Publishing Group, 1996).
2. D. Goldberg, "Auditory-verbal Philosophy: A Tutorial" ["Special Focus Section"], *Volta Review* 95, no. 3 (1993): 181–263.

Experience with Cochlear Implants: Case Studies

Linda Daniel, M.A., M.S., Cert. AVT

Linda Daniel received an B.S. in Speech and Hearing Sciences at the University of Iowa, an M.A. in Audiology from the University of Denver, and an M.S. in Communications Disorders from the University of Wisconsin. Since 1993 she has operated a private practice called "HEAR in Dallas."

Daniel currently works with twenty children, from 2.5 to 11 years of age, who have received multichannel cochlear implants. In addition to profound deafness, many of these children have multiple disabilities, including pervasive developmental delay, language and learning disabilities, dyspraxias ranging from moderate to very severe, attention deficit disorder with hyperactivity, and neurological disorders.

Case Studies

Lily

I met Lily when she was 12 months old. She had ear-level hearing aids, but after a few weeks of therapy I saw no evidence that she could hear. She was then fit with a very powerful frequency-transposition hearing aid that shifted the high frequencies of speech down to the lower frequencies, where she had a little residual hearing. Shortly after this change in amplification, her mother and I began to see Lily develop responses to sound. Lily's parents committed themselves to the auditory-verbal program. As therapy continued, it was obvious that Lily heard very little but did hear something. She began babbling "mum-mum-mum" and produced a few "buh-buh" sounds. Nearing her second birthday, she was saying a few words spontaneously such as "ow," "more," "no," "uh-oh," and "bye-bye." But new sounds and words came slowly.

On her second birthday, Lily underwent surgery for a cochlear implant. She responded to it instantly and asked to wear it in the days following her hookup. In the months to follow, Lily exploded with hearing, speech, and oral language. At this time, Lily has been hearing with the implant for eight months. She uses over seventy words spontaneously and is beginning to use two word phrases such as "where shoes?" and "see horsie." Her speech and voice quality sound normal, and she loves to hum with a pretty melody. In just eight months, Lily has acquired the oral language capabilities typically seen in normally hearing children at 20–24 months of age.

Travis

I met Travis in March of 1996. He had been implanted in January at the age of 2 years, 4 months, and had been using sign language for over a year. He had no speech and no natural babbling sounds. I knew that he could hear both the voiced and the whispered sounds I made, however, because he consistently imitated me with a series of smacks that mimicked the timing pattern of what I said. For example, if I ran the train across the table and whispered, "ch-ch-ch," Travis would produce three smacks at the same rate that I spoke. I knew he was hearing, but he had never gone through the normal stages of speech development, most likely due to his heavy use of sign language at the public preschool and at home. His early communication had been visually trained, and he had no concept of sound and little use of his hearing.

Travis has now been in auditory-verbal therapy twice a week for thirteen months and attends a regular preschool two mornings a week. His listening skills are remarkable, but in comparison, his speaking skills are considerably delayed. His comprehension of spoken language has steadily grown over the past year. It has taken him a year to drop the smacking pattern, but he is now beginning to progress through the normal stages of babbling. His parents report that he understands most of what they say in daily conversations with him and that he continues to surprise them with things he understands and overhears. Recently they were planting flowers outside, and Travis's older brother was asking his father what doctors do in their work. Travis was digging in the flower bed about five feet away as this conversation unfolded. After Travis's father recapped his wife's recent trip to the doctor and how she had had her "tummy cut" in the hospital, Travis scurried over to his mom, lifted up her T-shirt, and pointed to her scar. Travis's parents were shocked that he understood his father's description and especially that he had overheard a conversation that was not directed at him while he was playing in the dirt.

Travis's mother notes:

> I could write a book on how the implant has changed our lives! Travis wears his implant from morning until the minute he falls asleep. It is special to him, and he tries to take good care of it (even though he is only three). He has changed so much—he is much happier, and that makes me happy! He laughs all the time! Before the implant, he was so quiet, and it was difficult to get him to vocalize; now he makes noise all the time— he sings with the radio and makes all the right sound effects for airplanes, boats, and monsters. He is learning to talk and uses lots of words and sometimes puts two words together. He can keep up with playing with the little boys in the neighborhood! He can hear birds singing, airplanes overhead, and water running. We can call him from another room in the house and here he comes. Many times I have said a little prayer of thanks to God for Travis's hearing. I have stopped him from running into the street, burning himself, and other dangerous situations by yelling "Travis, stop!"—that by itself is such a gift.

Andrea

When I met Andrea she was almost 4 years old. She had no intelligible speech and communicated in babbling, whining, gestures, and signs. Andrea's deafness was caused by a viral infection. I could tell by the beautiful quality of her babbling that she was hearing quite a bit with the implant and she did not seem to be multiply impaired except for a visual problem, which was partially corrected with glasses. In early summer 1996 Andrea's parents committed themselves to the auditory-verbal approach, and she was removed from her deaf-education class. I did not suggest that they stop signing at home because that was their primary form of communication. However, I did recommend that they come to therapy twice a week and begin working with Andrea daily to develop her auditory comprehension for spoken language and her speaking skills.

Andrea progressed quickly in therapy. As her parents saw her comprehension and speech-imitation skills growing, they naturally began using less and less sign language with her. Likewise, Andrea gradually replaced signs with speaking as her vocabulary and sentence-building skills grew.

Andrea just turned 5 years old and has acquired about two and one-half to three years of oral-language skills in the one year she has been in therapy. She talks freely to her family, therapist, friends, cousins, grandparents, and teachers at school. Her sentences are telegraphic in nature, but she usually gets her point across. An example of her spoken language is a sentence stating,

"Mommy, Daddy, Matthew, Andrea pizza!" To announce the birth of her dog's babies, she said, "Slinky two baby." And the other day she said, "Sean school time out ... five," telling me about a little boy who got in trouble in school and had to sit in time-out for five minutes. Andrea now attends an oral preschool program in the public schools and will be partially mainstreamed into regular kindergarten next fall.

Andrea's mother reports: "Andrea wears her implant all the time. She even falls asleep with it at night because she doesn't want to miss anything. She loves it, we love it, it is a miracle. Andrea talks! I never imagined it would bring us this far, and she's only five years old."

Keely

Keely came into my office at 11 months of age. She wore two ear-level hearings aids and was accompanied by her parents. Her audiological records showed a profound loss in both ears and little benefit from hearing aids. I suggested she wear an FM system at all times so that either her mother's or her father's voice was directed into her hearing aids throughout her days.

We began doing therapy twice a week: mom, dad, baby, and I were on the floor in my office making choo-choo sounds, barking like puppy dogs, and doing whatever we could to teach Keely to hear and associate sounds with toys, people, and things in her environment. Ever so slowly, but equally surely, Keely began to show some responses to sound. The excitement continued as she attempted her first sound imitation by blowing raspberries.

Throughout the first year of listening, Keely's mother and father split the work at home: her dad did the more structured listening and talking games he'd learned in therapy, and her mom did the natural speech and language stimulation throughout her daily routines with her little daughter. Whoever was with Keely wore the FM transmitter. Keely began to say the same first words as any toddler—"bye-bye," "more," "no," "mama," "dada"—as the year passed. By 2 years of age she was beginning to put two words together, at the same age as her hearing peers. One day in therapy, she pointed to a doll that was barefoot and said to me, "not shoe!" Eight months later, three months before she turned 3, Keely received a cochlear implant. I immediately noticed the difference between her hearing abilities pre- and post-implantation. Her language took off like wildfire after several months of therapy; we couldn't keep up with her language development.

Keely is now 6 years, 6 months old. Three weeks ago she made her dancing debut with the "HEAR to Dance Kids" in downtown Dallas and did a little solo on stage for all to see. The remarkable thing about this is that she danced to her own speech, taped ahead of time for the production. The audience heard, in perfect speech: "My name is Keely. I'm six years old. My birthday is November 18th. My favorite kind of ice cream is chocolate!"

Keely is finishing regular kindergarten in her neighborhood school, where she is already learning to read and write. She will go on to regular first grade next year. She can understand speech over the television and acquires new words and silly phrases when she watches her favorite videos. She enjoys talking on the telephone to family members and familiar people. Keely is a 6-year-old chatterbox and exhausts her parents with her endless questions and perceptions of the world.

Veronica

Veronica was born in Romania and was living in an orphanage when she captured the loving eyes of a U.S. couple who had already picked up the little girl they had come to adopt. Totally taken by this eight-pound, 6-month-old baby girl, the couple left the orphanage with not one but two new daughters. On returning to the United States, her parents nurtured her to health and discovered her deafness at 1 year of age. She was fit with hearing aids and, at the age of 18 months, began auditory-verbal therapy.

Veronica's progress was slow. In addition to her severe hearing loss, she had almost continuous ear infections, which rendered the hearing aids of little benefit most of the time (though her hearing aid dispenser obtained quite good aided responses when Veronica's ears were clear). Veronica made progress, but everything seemed like such a struggle. Her language acquisition advanced at a snail's pace. We often said that we wished her loss were profound rather than severe so that she could have an implant.

I was beginning to worry that Veronica had cognitive delays, language-learning difficulties, or learning disabilities. As her mother's questions about the cochlear implant became more persistent, I decided to fit Veronica with a very powerful frequency-transposition hearing aid to see if more sound would hasten her language acquisition. At this point, almost overnight Veronica began learning new words. Every week her mother brought in a list of words Veronica had said for the first time. I realized, therefore, that there probably was nothing else complicating Veronica's development other than the fact that she was not hearing enough to learn to talk. I referred the family to a physician to begin the evaluation process to determine her candidacy for the cochlear implant.

When she was 4 years, 6 months old, Veronica received an implant. What a difference that implant made! Now, a year and a half later, she is 6 years old and finishing kindergarten, absolutely loves to read, and always has more to say than anyone has time for. Her mother reports:

> Veronica is speaking more clearly every day. She calls her implant her "battery" and won't let anyone touch it. Her language has exploded, and with the big growth in language, all of us — parents, teachers, therapists — have come to realize how smart she really is. The implant is wonderful. She comes home from school learning new words all on her own.

Kerry

At 3 years, 6 months, cute little Kerry was profoundly deaf and wore ear-level hearing aids. His mother suspects that he lost his hearing at about 15 months of age after having his DPT shot. He was extremely irritable, had several health problems, and would not sit and play at the table. Instead, he would begin to cry and writhe on the carpet as if something was bothering him from the inside out. He had sensory integration dysfunction and was receiving therapy with an occupational therapist. Therapy sessions were difficult, to say the least. We persevered, and he began to show signs of progress. Progress was very slow, however, and he seemed to be losing the little hearing he had initially possessed. As Kerry grew older, most of these early problems were resolved, but his deafness was becoming worse.

Kerry was implanted at age 4. His first year with the implant was filled with lost and broken parts and inconsistent attendance in therapy. The next several years got better, his behavior improved, and he began to learn to listen and talk. I had to be quite creative in therapy, however, because he had only one interest: cars, trucks, and crashes. So I began teaching him to produce vocal play sounds that went with the different vehicles. Then we moved on to his first words: "car," "truck," "van," "airplane," and "crash!" You can imagine his first efforts at word combining: "car fast," "crash van." From then we went to three- and four-word sentences: "car crash truck" and "blue car go fast." We began drawing story books about vehicles, people going fast, policemen stopping them and taking them to jail, accidents, ambulances, and all that goes with these topics. From picture books, Kerry learned to read and write. Over a four-year period we went from babbling to reading, all within the topic of his choice! To this day, Kerry comes to therapy and tells me the details of the traffic between his house and my office.

Kerry's school did not offer any program except sign language for the hearing-impaired children in his district. Consequently, he is learning two language forms: he signs at school, where most of the children sign without talking, and he uses a combination of speech and sign at home. He actually has quite good speaking and listening skills considering the amount of time he is communicating in sign language each day. He enjoys doing listening activities over the telephone in therapy. His speech is somewhat labored and lacks the fluency of the children who are in environments that encourage talking and listening all day. He has to think as he talks to select the words and articulation skills in order to be understood. His parents hope to place him in an oral program next year, since he is 8 years old and they fear his verbal skills will not improve substantially until he is in a constant verbal environment.

Kerry's parents are thrilled with the implant. Kerry's mother comments: "[Kerry] uses words that he picks up from the neighborhood kids and his brothers and sisters ... like 'dumb,' 'stupid,' 'pea-brain,' 'shut up,' and when

he's mad at me he says, 'I love you … not!' The most incredible thing is that
he has a Texas accent!"

Leana

At 3 years of age, Leana was a gorgeous child. Profoundly deaf, she did
not speak; she communicated with her parents through signs. As I began to
work with her I became very concerned that she was unable to imitate any
mouth movements. She was diagnosed as having oral dyspraxia, a neurological impairment that makes it very difficult to imitate speech movements with
the muscles in her mouth. In addition, it was difficult for her to maintain eye
contact and focus her attention. I could not predict what level of verbal communication Leana would achieve, but her parents and I wanted to give her every
opportunity to hear and speak. Throughout the following six months, Leana
began to show signs of progress with her hearing aids. When she was 4 years
old, she received a cochlear implant.

Leana is now 9 years old and loves to talk more than anything else. She
has a beautiful voice quality and a delightful and very endearing personality,
and she is always a joy to be with. She wants to know everything about everyone. The dyspraxia still makes it hard for her to pronounce some words. She
loves to dance and is in the dance program for children with cochlear implants
as well as jazz and tap classes she takes in her community. She is a natural on
stage and loves the glittery costumes. She attends an oral class in the public
school-system and is learning to read and write. Leana talks on the phone to
familiar individuals, and her mother helps her when she can't understand over
the phone.

Leana's parents report:

> The implant has given Leana more hearing than we were led to expect it
> would. Leana can hear things she never could before. The first sound I
> noticed her hearing after the implant was the microwave. This was fol-
> lowed by birds singing, whistling, singing in high octaves, etc. Also, it is
> now possible to talk to her through closed doors! She still is shy when
> faced with a group situation, but one on one she does very well. The
> implant and therapy go hand in hand. We now have a hard-of-hearing
> child who can talk and hear instead of a deaf child who can do neither.

Matthew

Matthew was diagnosed as profoundly deaf at 15 months of age and was
fit with hearing aids at 17 months. At that time he started in the auditory-verbal program twice a week. Fifteen months later, Matthew had acquired seventy-six words. His parents then scheduled surgery to give him a cochlear
implant.

It took Matthew a few weeks to adjust to the implant; after he adjusted, his progress was noticeably more rapid. He moved into word combinations and over the next five years acquired very clear speech and sophisticated language. He is now 8 years old, attends regular second grade where he earns "A's" and "B's," talks on the phone with familiar people, and is one of the leaders in our dance program. He is a delightful child with unusual poise. People who meet him are shocked to know that without his implant, he is profoundly deaf.

Mathew's parents report:

> Matthew puts his implant on first thing in the morning and takes it off as he is climbing into bed. He is fully mainstreamed in public school and uses an auditory trainer (FM system) when he needs more auditory support at school. He converses on the telephone with family members. He enjoys music and has recently started to collect CDs to play on his boombox. I never dreamed that Matthew would hear birds singing, enjoy music, talk on the phone, or even order his favorite treat from the snack counter by saying, "A small cherry icy please."

Ali

Ali arrived in Dallas one December day after having her implant hooked up. She was 5 years, 6 months old, communicated in sign language, and had just finished her first semester of kindergarten in a deaf-education class where sign language was used for instruction and communication. She impressed me from the first five minutes of the evaluation: she readily imitated all of the vowels and vocal play sounds I made. Her voice was clear, her eyes were bright, and she was an extremely attentive child. She intently watched as I and her family members jumped right into the therapy activities. I recommended that Ali enroll in the regular kindergarten class for the second semester and repeat kindergarten the following fall to give her an extra year to learn to talk. Since her mother and father worked full time, a full-day school program was the only option for her.

Ali's grandmother brought her to Dallas each week for a two-hour session of therapy. Ali was the hardest-working child I had ever seen. She even insisted on making the three-hour drive to Dallas when she was sick! She was determined to hear and talk. Ali has had her implant for four and a half years. Her mother's words say it all:

> Now that Ali has the implant, I wish we had done it sooner. She did not respond with her hearing aids ... with the implant she wants us to talk, talk, talk! She does not like sign language anymore....
>
> Ali now is in third grade and reads on a sixth-grade level. She goes to regular school (where she is an "A" student), hears the phone ringing, talks on the phone, and can hear cars, dogs barking, rain, and birds. She is very

verbal and has no problem understanding. She reads well, speaks well, understands well, and has surpassed all our wildest dreams.

What Do the Children Think?

Here's what these children have to say about what they hear with their implants:

LEANA

I like to hear:

I like to talk to my friend Kelly a long time on the telephone. I like to learn how to sing songs ... I love the song "Tomorrow." I like the bell choir at church. I like to hear the radio and TV singers with microphones. I like to hear my cat's meow and my dog say "woof-woof." I'm so happy I can hear.

I don't like to hear:

Loud noises, thunder and rain and tornadoes, the wind, and babies crying.

MATTHEW

I like to hear:

Birds chirping, music—especially the Hallelujah Hop and the River Dance CD, when people talk normal, church bells, and TV. I like the music from the movie *Fly Away Home* ... it sounds real low pitched, and it has a piano in it too, and I like the way the man sings. He sings in the sad parts and the good parts.

I don't like to hear:

The dogs barking in my neighborhood, the way some people make their cars loud, and I don't like it when people yell.

KEELY

I like to hear:

Music, popcorn popping, my dancing teacher, speech and music over the telephone, rescuers on TV, movies ... especially *101 Dalmatians*, and my mom's clown that moves his head and whistles.

I don't like to hear:

Static on TV, lions growling, and elephants (too loud).

ALI

I like to hear:

Balloons pop, cats purr, kids laughing, birds chirping, dogs squealing, fire crackling, snakes hissing, and cats meowing happily.

I don't like to hear:

The sound of the electric pencil sharpener, wind blowing, and my dog—Oreo—barking.

Cochlear Implants: The Furtherance of Auditory-Verbal Therapy

Sally Tannenbaum, M.A., M.Ed., C.E.D., Cert. AVT

Sally Tannenbaum is in private practice in Chicago, Illinois. Tannenbaum received a B.S. in Psychology from the University of California at Berkeley and a master's degree in Communication Disorders/Special Education from California State University at Los Angeles.

Principles of Auditory-Verbal Therapy

Doreen Pollack, one of the pioneers of the auditory-verbal approach, described auditory-verbal therapy as "listening as a way of life."[1] Children learn to use their cochlear implant to listen to their own voices and the voices of others in order to understand spoken language and develop meaningful conversations. A set of principles for an auditory-verbal practice was adopted by the board of directors of Auditory-Verbal International Inc.[2] These principles support and promote the following:

• Early detection and identification of hearing impairments in infants, toddlers, and children
• Aggressive audiological management
• Appropriate amplification technology to achieve maximum benefits of learning through listening
• Favorable auditory learning environments for the acquisition of spoken language, including one-to-one therapy
• Integration of listening into the child's entire being so that listening becomes a way of life
• Ongoing assessment, evaluation, and prognosis of the development of audition, speech, language, and cognition, which are integral to the auditory-verbal experience
• Integration and mainstreaming of children who are hearing impaired into regular education classes to the fullest extent possible with appropriate support services
• Affirmation of parents as primary models in helping the child learn to listen to his or her own voice, the voices of others, and the sounds of the environment
• Integration of speech, language, audition, and cognition in response to the psychological, social, and educational needs of the child and family

The cochlear implant has come of age as a rehabilitation tool for children with profound hearing impairment. With cochlear implants, each of the above

principles has been affected. Before the cochlear implant, achieving each principle was not always possible. Some children had such limited hearing that
listening as a way of life was not a reality. But now, through cochlear implant
technology, children with profound hearing impairments are able to learn to
listen and to develop spoken language. As I take a close look at each of the
principles of an auditory-verbal practice, I realize what a dramatic impact the
cochlear implant has had on my own practice and thus on the children who
are learning to learn to listen!

First, *early identification and aggressive audiological management* are
more widespread because of the cochlear implant. Because the FDA approved
the implant for children as young as 2 years of age, aggressive audiological
management is necessary to determine what the child hears in each ear and
what the child hears across the speech frequencies. In Chicago, children below
the age of 2 have been implanted because of specific medical needs. This is
possible through early identification and aggressive audiological management.

Second, *parents are taking a more active role* in the management of their
child's audiology and therapy program, in order to give critical feedback to
the implant team.

Third, the *auditory learning environment* for the acquisition of spoken
language is enhanced by the cochlear implant. The implanted children with
whom I have worked report that listening over background noise is easier with
the cochlear implant than with hearing aids. They also report that they can
hear better from a distance with the cochlear implant. I have observed this in
therapy sessions. I might ask children to listen and identify what I am saying
as I walk away from them. When these same children were listening with hearing aids, they would not be able to identify what I was saying as I increased
the distance. With the cochlear implant, however, distance was not a factor;
the children could still understand me.

Fourth, the *integration and mainstreaming* of children who are hearing
impaired into typical education classes is accomplished with less difficulty with
the cochlear implant. The two general educational goals for a child who has
a hearing impairment and who is integrated into a typical class (with hearing
children) are: (1) that the child will develop language, communication, and
social skills to the greatest extent possible, and (2) that the child will master
the same academic material as his or her hearing peers.[3] I have seen the
cochlear implant help children achieve both goals.

Many of the children I work with received their cochlear implants during the school year. Thus, the classroom teachers had a chance to work with
the children pre-implant and post-implant. All of these classroom teachers
report a major difference in the children's performance after they received
their implants. Teachers report that the children are able to hear so much better. The feeling among the classroom teachers is that the children are much

more "with it." The child with a cochlear implant not only is able to follow a class discussion but also contributes to the discussion. One teacher reported that her student Lisa, a fifth-grade student who received a cochlear implant in the middle of the school year, went from being an outsider in her class to a contributing member. Before the implant, the only contribution Lisa would make was to ask, "What time is lunch?" After the implant, the teacher reported that Lisa not only was contributing to the discussion but also was regarded as somewhat of a leader among her peers.

Lisa was able to participate with her hearing peers both because she was hearing better and because her receptive and expressive language greatly improved with the implant. Before implantation, when she was 9.8 years (chronological age), Lisa was tested on the Peabody Picture Vocabulary Test-Revised (PPVT-R) as having a vocabulary of age 5.11 years. She received a cochlear implant on her tenth birthday. At chronological age 12.4, after two years and four months with the implant, Lisa's PPVT-R score had more than doubled, to age 13.4 years (above her chronological age!). The cochlear implant enabled Lisa not only to hear language but to "overhear" language. She, and other children with implants, report that they get information from sources that did not exist for them pre-implant. Television, radio, compact discs, Walkmans, and overheard conversations are now sources providing language information to implanted children—language that these children use when communicating with others.

Sample Case Studies

Since cochlear implants became available to children with severe to profound deafness, I have seen "miracles" galore. The following are just three typical stories.

Alex

Alex, a child with congenital deafness, was fit with hearing aids at 3 months of age. He began auditory-verbal therapy immediately and was integrated into a regular preschool at 3 years of age. Alex has always attended school with hearing peers. He received a cochlear implant when he was in the first grade. A few months after he was implanted, he asked his mother if she had changed his name. When his mother asked him what he was talking about, he replied, "Is my name Al or Alex?" Before the implant, Alex had never heard the "x" ("ks") sound in his name. Soon after receiving the cochlear implant, he also started to use plurals, possessives, and tense markers in his spoken language—a very big deal for a first-grader who is integrated with hearing peers.

Pre-implant, Alex's age-equivalent score on the Expressive One-Word Picture Vocabulary Test-R was 4 years, 5 months. One year post-implant he received an age-equivalent score of 6 years, 10 months. When Alex's chronological age was 8 years, 8 months, his expressive vocabulary age score was 10 years, 6 months. Thus, within two years of being implanted, Alex achieved an expressive vocabulary age score that surpassed his chronological age.

David

David, a child with congenital deafness, was fit with hearing aids at 19 months of age. He received a cochlear implant when he was 6 years, 3 months old. A year after he was implanted, his mother shared the following story with me.

David was home sick, and his mom, talking on the phone, canceled plans that included taking David to see the movie *Space Jam* that evening. When she got off the phone, David approached her and, although he was still running a fever, pleaded his case. "Mom, I am not sick, I am much better, really, now can we go see *Space Jam*?" Gone were the days of private conversations. David's parents now have their private talks behind closed doors and out of earshot of their son!

Before David received his cochlear implant, his age-equivalent score on the Expressive One-Word Picture Vocabulary Test-R was 3 years, 4 months. Two years later (post-implant), his score was 6 years, 9 months. David thus made three years and five months of progress in just two years with his implant.

Lisa

Lisa developed meningitis at the age of 4 months and, as a result, has a bilateral, profound sensorineural hearing loss.[4] She received a cochlear implant when she was 10 years old.

After receiving the implant, Lisa stopped looking at people when they spoke to her. Her teachers were concerned that she might not be getting all the information she needed during class lectures. They also reported that she would not make eye contact during their conversations with her. When I presented her teachers' concerns to Lisa, she replied: "I don't have to watch them anymore. I can hear them now."

I couldn't believe that after spending years getting Lisa to learn to listen, I now had to talk with her about how she should look at people while they were speaking to her. I told her that she was being rude if she didn't look at the person speaking to her. Lisa saw the irony of the situation and told me; "Now that I have the cochlear implant, I don't need to learn to listen, I need to learn to look!"

Lisa's language-testing scores were reported earlier in this section.

NOTES

1. D. Pollack, *Educational Audiology for the Limited Hearing Infant and Pre-Schooler* (Springfield, Ill.: Thomas Press, 1985).
2. W. Estabrooks, *Auditory-Verbal Therapy* (Washington, D.C.: Alexander Graham Bell Association for the Deaf, 1994).
3. D. F. Moores, "Educational Programs and Services for Hearing Impaired Children: Issues and Options," in F. Powell, T. Finitzo-Hieber, S. Friel-Patti, and D. Henerson, eds., *Education of the Hearing Impaired Child* (San Diego: College-Hill Press, 1985), pp. 3–20.
4. "Bilateral, profound sensorineural hearing loss" means that the child has a hearing loss in both ears that is greater than 90 decibels.

Cochlear Implants and Children Who Are Prelingually Deaf

Judith I. Simser, O. Ont., B.Ed., Cert. AVT

For her work with children who are hearing impaired, Judith Simser received the Canada 125 Commemorative Medal in 1993, the Order of Ontario in 1992, and the 1982 Teacher of the Year Award from the International Organization of Educators of the Hearing Impaired, Alexander Graham Bell Association for the Deaf. On leave from Children's Hospital of Eastern Ontario, Ottawa, Canada, Simser is currently in Taiwan training Chinese teachers and developing three auditory-verbal centers for the Children's Hearing Foundation.

Ages 18 Months to 3 Years

It has been my experience that, given certain conditions, deaf children 18 months to 3 years old who receive cochlear implants can usually develop age-appropriate language and understandable speech within two and one-half years from commencement of auditory-verbal training. Children who are postlingually deafened adapt readily to the cochlear implant. They do not require the same amount of therapy as children who are congenitally deaf. For this reason, I will limit my discussion to *prelingually deafened* children.

Children between the ages of 18 months and 3 years are the most ideal candidates for implantation. They are usually at home with their parents or caregivers, in environments ideal for listening and language learning. Under the guidance of an effective auditory-verbal therapist, their parents can learn how to integrate—during daily activities, interactions, and experiences—specific weekly targets in listening, speech, language, cognition, and communication.

Language is developed through communication; thus, it is in a constant auditory-enriched environment that children will learn language naturally through hearing. It is neither the teacher contact hours nor the time spent in a classroom that develops the hearing potential of a cochlear implant recipient. Rather, it is the constant development of listening throughout a child's total waking hours that will result in optimum use of the implant. Parents must learn how to talk so that their children will listen and how to develop listening and language following a hierarchy of skills.

Children with cochlear implants respond across the speech range and hear all the phonemes in the Ling six-sound test without difficulty. During this test, children are asked to respond to the speech sounds "m," "oo," "ah," "ee," "sh," and "s." These phonemes range from low to high frequencies and allow the therapist to assess how many sounds within the speech range a child can hear. Children who are profoundly deaf and use hearing aids are unable to hear the higher-frequency phonemes, since hearing aids cannot provide sufficient gain at the 4,000 Hz level.

Generally speaking, given (1) the wonderful hearing potential that cochlear implants provide, (2) effective parent guidance, support, and education, and (3) an auditory-verbal approach, deaf children implanted between 18 months and 3 years have every opportunity to learn to listen and to develop natural and intelligible speech with age-appropriate language. These children should be successfully mainstreamed throughout their school years provided they continue to obtain effective support services. The following is a case study of one child, within this age group, whom I have taught and continue to teach.

Alana

At 11 months of age, Alana was diagnosed with a congenital, profound hearing impairment with no response on Electric Response Audiometry, an objective measure of hearing ability. Alana was fit with two ear-level hearing aids. After a year and a half of therapy, it was determined that she did not have sufficient hearing potential with hearings aids to enable her to develop spoken language through listening.

Alana lives with her family in Taiwan. Her mother is American, and her father is Taiwanese. Although English is the primary language spoken in the home, some Mandarin Chinese is spoken.

When Alana was 2, it was a rarity for children in Taiwan under the age of 3 to receive cochlear implants. Alana's family therefore sought the advice of a cochlear implant team in Melbourne, Australia. After extensive testing in Melbourne, it was confirmed that Alana was totally deaf and was responding only to vibrotactile sensations. Subsequently, Alana had a CT scan, which revealed severely abnormal cochleas, with a common cavity deformity on both sides. After consultations with many other centers, Alana received her cochlear implant when she was 2 years, 6 months old. Because of her deformed cochleas, only fourteen of twenty-two electrodes were implanted and only twelve were activated.

As Alana's therapist, I provided Alana and her parents with extensive auditory-verbal services for two weeks every three months, either in Canada or in Taiwan. What a challenge! Deformed cochleas and only twelve electrodes, great distances between Taiwan and Canada for therapy—and Alana had no speech or language! Nevertheless, if it was physiologically possible, Alana had many of the necessary prerequisites for the development of spoken language through listening. She was a bright, friendly, outgoing, precocious little toddler who was eager to communicate and to learn, and she had a dedicated and determined family. At the outset I stressed: "No prejudgments. We'll begin with the hierarchy of listening, speech, and language development with extensive parent participation as we would for any other beginning child cochlear implantee."

Today, two and one-half years later, those twelve electrodes are serving Alana extremely well. Alana can converse on the telephone! She is constantly asking the meaning of unfamiliar words or concepts. Recently, when she heard something that she could not understand, she said, "That must be Chinese!"

The following are results of testing performed recently, two years and two months post-implantation; when Alana had a chronological age of 4.8 years.

LANGUAGE

Zimmerman Preschool Language Scale
Auditory Comprehension: 39 points, age equivalency 4.2 years
Expressive Communication: 39 points, age equivalency 4.4 years

Test of Auditory Comprehension of Language (TACL)
Word Classes and Relations: age equivalency 4.11–5.5 years
Grammatical Morphemes: age equivalency 5.1–5.7 years
Elaborated Sentences: age equivalency 5.1–5.4 years

VOCABULARY
Peabody Picture Vocabulary Test (PPVT)
Score: 39 points, age equivalency 3.9 years

Gardner Expressive One-Word Picture Vocabulary Test
Score: 48 points, age equivalency 4.8 years

Alana attends a regular kindergarten in the Taipei American School. She is a well-adjusted, vivacious, affable, and gregarious 5-year-old. She is totally accepted by her (hearing) peers as one of them. A stranger observing her in conversation, at play, or in the classroom would not recognize her invisible disability.

Ages 4 to 6 Years

The next category of children I will describe are congenitally, profoundly deaf children who receive cochlear implants between the ages of 4 and 6. These children are often negative auditory learners because for the first four or five years of their lives they (and their families) have had little success in developing listening skills. These children will likely have developed another mode of communication, either total communication using signing or attempts to develop spoken language through speechreading.

Some of these children continue in signing or speechreading programs after implantation. It has been my experience that when children are able to acquire information through a visual approach, they will wait until they can get information visually and will not learn to use their newfound hearing potential to its fullest extent. Moreover, the natural rhythm of speech is affected when parents are in the learning stages of developing sign language, yet it is through hearing this rhythm and vowel content that a child initially begins to understand short two-to-three-word phrases. Further, since only approximately 40 percent of English phonemes are visible on the lips, it is very difficult for those children who rely primarily on speechreading to develop a natural fluency in speech.

If parents of newly implanted children are interested in an auditory-verbal approach, we discuss the available options. I stress that if we pursue an auditory-verbal approach, the goal will be to transition their children gradually from a signing mode of communication to one of listening and speaking or from a mode of reliance on speechreading to one of reliance on listening.

A hierarchy of listening skills is essential for early auditory learners. One must build on a foundation of easy-to-hear phonemes and short, expressive phrases. One must build on success in listening. There are many beginning auditory learners who become discouraged at this stage because the listening tasks they are given are far too difficult. As a result, they may claim that they receive limited benefits from the implant.

Initially, parents should encourage listening, especially when there is a situational cue to facilitate the child's understanding; for example, when preparing to go outside, parents should say to their child, "Put on your coat" or "Where's your coat?" Also, parents need to integrate easy-to-hear therapy targets throughout their daily routines and activities. If the child has begun communicating by sign language, parents should increasingly provide phrases verbally as substitutes for the child's signs; in this manner, signing will gradually be replaced by verbal communication as the child gains confidence in listening and talking. Within a period of about one and a half years, the child is usually able to transition fully to the exclusive use of hearing. Speechreading and body language will supplement audition in poor listening conditions, as it would in any communication.

The following is a case study of one child, within this age group, with whom I have worked.

Ryan

Ryan was diagnosed with a profound sensorineural hearing impairment at age 13 months. After a fourteen-month period of diagnostic therapy with effective parent participation using an auditory-verbal approach, it was determined that Ryan had very little hearing potential. The only thresholds obtained were indicative of vibrotactile responses. Since cochlear implants were not an option in Ontario at the time, both the parents and our professional team felt that Ryan and his family would benefit from a total-communication approach. It was suggested that the family be served by the local school for the deaf, which initiated a home-visiting program using total communication. When he turned 3, Ryan attended a segregated class for deaf children at a public school in his city. Ryan's parents took sign-language classes, and they and their son used sign as their primary mode of communication.

When Ryan was 4 years old, cochlear implants became available in Ontario, and Ryan was implanted. Ryan continued with the segregated program that he had attended for the previous two years.

With his implant, Ryan heard across the speech frequencies necessary for speech perception. After six months of cochlear implant use, however, Ryan's parents became concerned because Ryan continued to use sign language and only neutral vowels to communicate. They requested that Ryan rejoin the auditory-verbal program to maximize his newly acquired hearing potential.

Ryan is now 5.10 years old and two years post-implantation. Ryan converses using intelligible speech, understands conversations through listening, and is integrated into a regular class in his neighborhood school. He uses only spoken language. Results of standardized testing are as follows:

LANGUAGE

Zimmerman Preschool Language Scale
Chronological Age: 5.7 years
Auditory Comprehension: 41 points, age equivalency 4.6 years
Expressive Communication: age equivalency 4.8 years

VOCABULARY

Peabody Picture Vocabulary Test (PPVT)
Chronological Age: 5.10 years
Age Equivalency: 4.0 years
Score: 42 points

Gardner Expressive One-Word Picture Vocabulary Test
Chronological Age: 5.8 years
Age Equivalency: 5.8 years
Score: 45 points

Ryan's current language targets include refining his verb tenses, articles, and plurals and developing his vocabulary. His language skills continue to improve.

Ages 8 and Older

The third type of auditory learner includes children ages 8 and older who have congenital profound hearing losses. Very strong motivation is required for these children to learn to listen with cochlear implants, since they have well-established nonauditory modes of life. There must be a dedicated parent support team and a liaison between classroom teachers, therapists, and parents to ensure that weekly targets are consistent.

Due to the lack of early auditory stimulation, these children often find listening extremely difficult. They may become disillusioned and discouraged in using their cochlear implants. On the other hand, I have taught children ages 8 to 14 who are clearly satisfied with the benefits they receive from their implants. The implants facilitate their attending to sound and assist in their speechreading ability. It has been my experience that the more these children learn to use their hearing potential, the greater the improvement in their speech intelligibility.

The following is a case study of one child, in this age group, with whom I have worked.

Mary

Mary and her family moved to Canada when she was 9 years old. She had a bilateral profound hearing loss and very little hearing, from which she did not benefit. She communicated with her parents through speechreading, and she used one-to-two-word phrases that were not intelligible to others. Six months after moving to Canada, at an age of 9.6 years, Mary received a cochlear implant and began her journey in learning to listen. She attended a local private school, where she had a full-time resource teacher. She was integrated for many subjects but had individualized help for language-related subjects.

As can be seen by the test results below, Mary's pre-implant vocabulary and language scores were extremely low for her chronological age. She had no usable residual hearing, and learning by speechreading proved to be very difficult for her. This demonstrates the importance of a diagnostic approach with yearly standardized testing, case conferencing, and program planning.

In one year of cochlear implant use, Mary made only four months' progress in testing in vocabulary development. However, there were good gains made in language and communication skills. She achieved about one and a half years in language growth in eight months of implant use. Her sentence length increased to three to five words. Speech production improved so much that family and friends were able to understand her. Her confidence improved in communicating orally, and she became more outgoing, now initiating conversations. She followed a two-item memory task by listening alone.

Although Mary has not made gains similar to those of younger children with cochlear implants, she and her family are very satisfied with her listening ability and her gains in speech and language.

Pre-implantation

VOCABULARY

Peabody Picture Vocabulary Test (PPVT)
Chronological Age: 9.5 years
Age Equivalency: 2.7 years

Gardner Expressive One-Word Picture Vocabulary Test-R
Chronological Age: 9.5 years
Age Equivalency: 3.5 years

Six Months Post-implantation

LANGUAGE

Test of Auditory Comprehension of Language (TACL)
Word Classes: 3.0–3.1 years
Grammatical Morphemes: 2.6–2.8 years
Elaborated Sentences: 2.7–2.9 years
Total Score: 2.8–3.0 years

One Year Post-implantation

VOCABULARY

Peabody Picture Vocabulary Test (PPVT)
Chronological Age: 10.7 years
Age Equivalency: 3.1 years

Gardner Expressive One-Word Picture Vocabulary Test-R
Chronological Age: 10.7 years
Age Equivalency: 4.0 years

LANGUAGE

Test of Auditory Comprehension of Language (TACL)
Word Classes: 5.0–5.6 years
Grammatical Morphemes: 4.2–4.5 years
Elaborated Sentences: 3.1–3.4 years
Total Score: 4.2–4.8 years

Auditory-Verbal Teens and Young Adults

More recently, young adults with congenital profound hearing loss have been trained in an auditory-verbal approach since the detection of their hearing impairments as babies. Most of these young adults developed auditory association areas of the brain as young children and thus are ideal candidates for implantation. One example of such an individual is my son Scott.

Scott

Scott was born profoundly deaf. At the age of 8 months, he received binaural amplification. Scott and our family had the good fortune to be trained in the auditory-verbal approach by Dr. Agnes Phillips and Dr. Daniel Ling. Although Scott had a bilateral left-hand corner audiogram with a 108 dB hearing loss (a very minimal amount of residual hearing, without hearing in any of the higher frequencies), he developed listening skills (with his aids) to the point that he could communicate on the telephone with someone familiar to him. He was mainstreamed all his life with good support services in the regular school; he obtained an MBA degree and, more recently a degree in law.

When Scott was 6 years old he developed recruitment (an abnormal sensitivity to sound) in his left ear and was unable to be aided in that ear. In his late 20s, he developed a Tullio effect, a medical condition that caused dizziness and vomiting whenever he wore amplification; he thus became unaided— unable to wear any hearing aids. Although not considered a good candidate for a cochlear implant because of his age and congenital hearing impairment, Scott was implanted at the age of 30 in the ear that had been stimulated the longest.

The first week after switch-on Scott reported that he was unable to differentiate any sounds but that he was hearing many, many more things than he had ever heard with his hearing aids. In teaching Scott, we used the same approach that was used with any child receiving a cochlear implant (regardless of age). Because Scott had full command of the English language, it was his auditory skills, rather than language skills, that had to be developed. The beginning skills of developing perception of phonemes and short common phrases came quickly. By three weeks post-implantation, Scott was able to follow a conversation on a known topic and even understood some open-set sentences and words. Six months post-implant, Scott could understand open-set sentences spoken slowly and clearly. Nine months post-implant, Scott began to use the telephone with some people. The implant had already begun to make a big impact on Scott's life.

Summary

Every person receiving a cochlear implant has his or her own personality, family characteristics, academic potentials, and levels of functioning. What each individual perceives as success from the cochlear implant varies greatly.

But certain factors will facilitate the maximum use of and benefit from cochlear implants for all recipients. People who are congenitally deaf must begin with basic, easy-to-achieve auditory skills development. An individualized program must be devised that is suited to the individual's present level of functioning. A strong support system of parents, caregivers, spouses, or friends must be available to reinforce weekly auditory targets throughout the day. A strong motivation for learning to listen and to use spoken language is required.

The rewards will be many, including the ability to interact through listening to and speaking with the hearing world and the potential to develop as independent, capable communicators.

Changing the Lives of Children Who Are Deaf

Catherine McEnroe, B.A., M.A.T.

Catherine McEnroe received a B.A. in Deaf Education from Michigan State University and an M.A.T. in Audiology from Indiana University. Currently she has a private auditory-verbal communications and audiology practice in New York and Vermont.

Case Studies

Morgan

Morgan was born with a profound hearing loss and appeared to obtain no benefit from conventional amplification. She was in an educational program based on the use of sign language, in which she functioned happily for the first years of her life. When she was 6 years old, her parents learned that she had Usher's syndrome, which is characterized by deafness and the possibility of eventual blindness. Thus her sign language might ultimately be of little use. Within a few weeks of that diagnosis, Morgan was scheduled for cochlear implant surgery.

At first the implant was an intrusion into Morgan's comfortable, manual world. Gradually, however, Morgan began to make use of her new access to the sounds around her. Her mother had high expectations for Morgan's use of the implant and gave her numerous opportunities throughout the day to rely solely on listening to hear. Her mother and I were both pleasantly surprised the first time Morgan overheard our conversation—which wasn't directed to her—and repeated it at school the next day.

As Morgan's verbal language–processing ability grew, her dependence on sign language decreased. Morgan's parents maintained high expectations for Morgan's use of the implant. Morgan's mother gradually decreased her use of sign language to the point that Morgan no longer needed it. Morgan's sister was a bit more skeptical but finally stopped signing when Morgan hadn't been signing for quite a while.

Morgan's verbal-language level caught up with and then grew beyond her sign-language level. At age 10 years, 6 months, Morgan scored an age equivalency of 13 years, 5 months, on the Peabody Picture Vocabulary Test-Revised, which tests receptive vocabulary. At age 11 years, 7 months, Morgan scored age equivalencies between 11 years, 6 months, and 12 years, 6 months, across the six subtests of the Word Test-Revised, which tests expressive vocabulary and semantics; she obtained perfect scores on three of the subtests.

To investigate the role that her cochlear implant played in her understanding of verbal language, Morgan was tested with a subtest of the Minimal Auditory Capabilities (MAC) battery. That test requires the listener-viewer to repeat common sentences (CID Everyday Sentences). During lists 3 and 4, Morgan turned off her processor and relied solely on speechreading. She scored 44 key words correct out of 100. During lists 5 and 6, Morgan turned the processor on and scored 96 key words correct out of 100. This documented the fact that the implant was playing a major role in Morgan's speech perception.

Morgan transferred from the program for deaf students to her neighborhood school after wearing her implant for two years. Today, Morgan has been in the mainstream of education for four years and participates in all aspects of school life. Through a program for creative and talented youth, she was invited to take the Scholastic Aptitude Test (SAT) that high school students take before applying to colleges and universities. At the age of 12, Morgan scored 550 on the verbal language portion (the national average for college admission is about 500). Her math scores were not as high, since she has not yet encountered much of the math.

Morgan gradually came to enjoy our therapy activities and interactions and would come running to the session eager to begin. After she was dismissed from therapy because she no longer needed it, she said to her mother: "When I was little, you made me go when I didn't want to. Now I want to go and you won't let me."

Charlie

Charlie's hearing loss was detected following a bout of meningitis when he was 2 years, 8 months old. He obtained little benefit from hearing aids and was implanted when he was 3 years, 8 months old. He began auditory-verbal therapy when he was 4 years, 5 months old.

Charlie attends his neighborhood school and has been in the mainstream of education since nursery school. He is an avid reader and loves to play sports of all kinds. He has set his sights on becoming a "scholar-athlete" in high school.

Test results document Charlie's language growth using his implant. The tests used to evaluate Charlie were the Expressive One-Word Picture Vocabulary Test-Revised (EOWPVT-R), which examined vocabulary that Charlie spontaneously produced, and the Receptive One-Word Picture Vocabulary Test (ROWPVT), which examined vocabulary that Charlie understood. I first tested Charlie when he was 4 years, 6 months, when he had been implanted for about ten months. He scored an age equivalency of 2 years, 7 months on the EOWPVT-R but was unable to obtain any score for the ROWPVT because he didn't know the vocabulary. When Charlie was 8 years, 10 months, he scored an age equivalency of 9 years, 8 months on the EOWPVT-R and 10 years, 11 months, on the ROWPVT, thereby meeting the goal of age-appropriate vocabulary.

Marty

Marty had no verbal language when she was implanted. She had lost her hearing following meningitis at age 3 months. She wore hearing aids that did not provide enough amplification for her to hear speech, and she used signs in her self-contained class for preschool children who were deaf. She obtained an implant a few months before her fifth birthday and entered kindergarten at the mainstream school attended by her siblings. A sign-language interpreter accompanied Marty in kindergarten.

I first tested Marty at age 5 years, 3 months. At that time she was unable to obtain a score on either the EOWPVT-R or the ROWPVT. At age 7 years, 5 months, however, two years post-implantation, Marty scored an age equivalency of 6 years, 7 months, on the EOWPVT-R and 4 years, 8 months, on the ROWPVT. On the Test of Auditory Comprehension of Language-Revised (TACL-R), she scored age equivalencies from 5 years, 3 months, to 7 years, 5 months, with her total language score equaling an age equivalency of 6 years.

Marty has just completed third grade. She loves to talk and pretend she is the teacher. The interpreter still attends her class but functions as a teacher assistant and doesn't use any signs. Marty is closing the gap between her chronological age and her language age with the help of her implant and her very supportive family.

Cochlear implants can change lives. Just ask Morgan, Charlie, and Marty!

Defining Success with Cochlear Implants

Nancy M. Young, M.D.

Dr. Nancy Young is head of the section of Otology and Neurotology at Children's Memorial Medical Center in Chicago, Illinois, and is assistant professor at Northwestern University Medical School. She is the medical director of Children's Memorial Medical Center Cochlear Implant Program and medical director of the Department of Audiology.

Since our pediatric cochlear implant program began at Children's Memorial Medical Center in 1991, we have seen tremendous improvements in implant technology and in our understanding of what factors are important for a child to receive maximum benefit from his or her implant. Our increased knowledge has made it possible to provide families with better information about what type of improvements in their child's listening, speech, and language might occur over time.

Multiple research studies have demonstrated that a shorter period of deafness before implantation is beneficial.[1] In the child who is congenitally deaf, this translates into younger age at implantation. Several FDA-approved implant protocols for children receiving new devices permit implantation of children between 18 and 24 months of age.[2] Devices that already have received commercial approval by the FDA can be used off-label by physicians (i.e., outside the clinical candidacy guidelines approved by the agency) when such use is in the best interest of a child who is less than 24 months of age. At experienced implant centers, implantation of very young children is becoming increasingly common.

It is important to understand, however, that the benefits of implantation are not limited to the very youngest children. Research at Indiana University by Amy Robbins and her colleagues has demonstrated that cochlear implants have a positive impact on the rate at which children of all ages acquire language, both spoken and sign language.[3] Robbins and her colleagues studied children in both oral and total-communication (signed English with simultaneous spoken English) programs and compared children using hearing aids with children using implants in both types of educational programs. Before implantation, both groups were acquiring language at half the rate of normal-hearing children. The children who received implants doubled their rate of language acquisition (spoken or signed English) in comparison with their peers who did not receive implants. Improved language skills should contribute to an improved level of literacy and educational achievement and ultimately should translate into better skills for entry into the work force.

The experiences of two families at our medical center illustrate the potential that implants have to change a child's life and the need for professionals to individualize the care and counseling they provide. Our center has a program that permits early diagnosis of Usher's syndrome, a devastating condition in which children are born deaf and later exhibit progressive visual loss leading to blindness secondary to retinitis pigmentosa.[4] One of our families has two children diagnosed with Usher's syndrome when they were infants. The older girl was implanted at 24 months of age and her younger sister at 20 months of age. Knowing that their children were destined to be blind was important to the parents' and my decision-making. Although at that time, relatively few 2-year-olds were receiving cochlear implants, we felt that it would be advantageous for these children to hear as soon as possible. These two sisters have very dedicated parents and an equally dedicated auditory-verbal therapist. The older child has been using her implant for over three years. She has intelligible speech and is experiencing success in a mainstream public school. The younger sibling is well on her way to achieving the same level of communication ability. Neither child will ever be deaf-blind.

Recently I received an e-mail message from a physician who had read an article I had written on implantation of children with Usher's syndrome.[5] This man has an 18-year-old daughter who was diagnosed with Usher's syndrome at 11 years of age. When the diagnosis was first made, the father asked his local medical center whether an implant would be of benefit to his child. Because his daughter communicated in sign language only and was too old to realistically expect that she would ever develop intelligible spoken language, an implant was strongly discouraged. Unfortunately, this father was provided with well-intentioned but poor advice. It is true that at age 11, a child who uses sign exclusively is not likely to develop the ability to talk clearly. However, having hearing will still be of great benefit for someone facing a future of blindness. With training, the ability to understand speech can still develop. If not, just being more in touch with one's environment should prove useful to one who is deaf-blind. I suggested that this young woman and her father speak with deaf-blind adults who have received implants and that they consult with professionals at an experienced implant center.

We cannot uphold a single definition of "success" with a cochlear implant and use that single definition to deny children hearing. Having the ability to talk clearly and therefore fit seamlessly in the mainstream is wonderful and is now possible for increasing numbers of children as they receive implants followed by appropriate auditory training and educational support. There are children who may never achieve this goal, however, but who can still derive tremendous benefit from implants. Families need to educate themselves about their children's medical and educational options. Parents need to understand that professionals are not all-knowing, nor can professionals predict the future with certainty. Technology is changing rapidly, as is our understanding of the progress that children make after implantation. Appropriate advice at one point in time may be out-of-date a year later. For these reasons, it is important that parents read books, obtain information from the Internet, keep in contact with educational support groups that foster differing educational philosophies, and speak with other parents of deaf children who have made a variety of choices. Soon parents may find they know more about many aspects of the medical and educational management of deaf children than most professionals. Parents should not be surprised if their knowledge makes some professionals uncomfortable, and they must remember that the child they brought into this world is ultimately their responsibility, not the responsibility of the professional or the deaf community.

NOTES

1. H. Fryauf-Bertschy, R. S. Tyler, D. M. Kelsay, et al., "Cochlear Implant Use by Prelingually Deafened Children: The Influences of Age at Implantation and Length of Devise Use," *Journal of Speech Language and Hearing Research* 40, no. 1 (February 1997): 183–89; S. B. Waltzman, N. L. Cohen, et al., "Long-term Results of Cochlear Implantation in Congenitally and Prelingually Deafened Children," *American Journal of Otology* 15 (supp. 2) (November 1994): 9–13.

2. Personal communication with Advanced Bionics Corporation re CLARION Multi-Strategy Cochlear Implant Pediatric Study IDE G940176; personal communication with Cochlear Corporation re Nucleus CI24M Cochlear Implant System Pediatric Study IDE G940026.

3. Amy M. Robbins, Mario Svirsky, Karen Iler-Kirk, "Children with Implants Can Speak, but Can They Communicate?" *Otolaryngology-Head and Neck Surgery* 117, no. 3, pt. 1 (September 1997): 115–60.

4. Nancy M. Young, Marilyn B. Mets, Timothy C. Hain, "Early Diagnosis of Usher Syndrome in Infants and Children," *American Journal of Otology* 17, no. 1 (January 1996): 30–34.

5. Nancy M. Young, K. C. Johnson, M. B. Mets, T. Hain, "Cochlear Implants in Young Children with Usher Syndrome," *Annals of Otology, Rhinology & Laryngology*, supp. 166 (September 1995): 342–45.

Chapter 7

Education:
The Teaching Perspective

Some children with cochlear implants, particularly those children who have been implanted after the age of 4, are not immediately ready to be mainstreamed in classes with children who have normal hearing. They may temporarily require a more structured educational environment, which emphasizes the acquisition of listening skills and the development of receptive and spoken language. The following excerpts are presented by three of the foremost U.S. educators who direct specialized teaching programs for children with profound hearing losses, many of whom utilize cochlear implants.

One prefatory note is required, however. There are some differing viewpoints between those professionals who favor auditory-verbal approaches to training children who are deaf and those professionals who favor auditory-oral approaches to training such children. Auditory-verbal therapists embrace the concept of an equal "partnership" with parents, an emphasis on developing the child's *sense of hearing* (with hearing aids or cochlear implants) from the earliest possible time of fitting, and participation in nursery and preschools with hearing children (full inclusion into mainstream society from the beginning). By this means, hearing becomes an integrated part of the child's personality—listening becomes a way of life. Auditory-oral educators also believe that parents are partners in helping their children learn to talk but feel that for many children who are deaf, intensive (segregated) specialized training is necessary to provide children with profound hearing losses with proper foundations for eventual mainstreaming. Both groups of professionals agree, however, that every child who is deaf has unique needs and that no one plan or program is appropriate for all children who are deaf.

Auditory-Oral Education: Making a Difference for Children with Cochlear Implants

Jean Sachar Moog, M.S.

Jean Sachar Moog received a B.A. from Smith College and an M.S. in Speech and Hearing from Washington University. She is director of the Moog Oral School in St. Louis, Missouri, and director for Oral Deafness Programs for the Oberkotter Foundation. Formerly, Moog was principal at Central Institute for the Deaf for fifteen years.

Cochlear implants are changing the way deaf children learn to talk. The increased access to sound available through cochlear implants is making it possible for more deaf children to learn to talk better and more easily than ever before. Most children with implants are able to hear differences in vowel sounds and in some consonant sounds within the first two years after implantation; this acoustic information is invaluable in helping the children learn to produce those sounds. Nevertheless, the speech that is heard with an implant is deficient compared with speech heard with normal hearing. That is why some deaf children, even with cochlear implants, cannot learn to talk spontaneously the way children with normal hearing do—just by hearing others speak.

For a prelingually deaf child, who has been deaf since birth or since before learning to talk, specific instruction is equally as important as the implant itself in assisting the child to acquire competent spoken language. Teachers in auditory-oral programs are often best able to provide the requisite instruction.

I have worked for over thirty years in programs teaching children who are deaf to talk. During the past ten years I have worked with over one hundred children with implants in numerous auditory-oral school programs. It is remarkable how much more easily and quickly these children are learning to talk in comparison with the deaf children of years ago. Cochlear implants have made our jobs as teachers easier—teaching is less intense and less laborious. In addition, learning requires less effort from the children. Before cochlear implants, children who were profoundly deaf often required ten to twelve years of special education before obtaining sufficient spoken language skills to communicate effectively and to compete successfully in mainstream classrooms (with normal-hearing children). Today, many children who are profoundly deaf and who are implanted early (before age 4) are ready for mainstream classes by the early primary grades, if not sooner. Their speech is quite intelligible, their voices have appropriate inflection and rhythm, and their language and reading skills are within a year of those of their normal-hearing peers. Children who are deaf and who are implanted later—after age 4—take a little longer to close the gap, but they too are progressing faster than ever before, particularly when provided with quality auditory-oral education.

Educational Programs

For some children, education in an auditory-oral school provides the best opportunity to capitalize on the benefits provided by cochlear implants. In auditory-oral programs, children who are deaf learn to use a combination of listening, speechreading, and contextual cues to comprehend and use spoken language. The goal is for these children to acquire sufficient spoken communication skills to be mainstreamed educationally and to function independently in the world. Although programs may differ in the organization of their day-to-day activities, their specific curricula, and their teaching strategies, all auditory-oral programs incorporate, in one way or another, a number of features, which can be organized as follows: (1) teachers and the educational environment, (2) the instructional program, and (3) family support.

Teachers and the Educational Environment

Teachers believe children who are deaf can learn to talk and expect them to talk. Teachers in auditory-oral programs *believe* that their students who are deaf *can* learn to talk and *expect* them to talk. These strong beliefs foster an environment in which the teachers can effectively teach their deaf students to talk. Effective teaching can occur both through "lessons" and through the provision of a language-learning environment in which the teacher capitalizes on naturally occurring situations and contrives situations to make learning effective, interesting, and fun. The goal of auditory-oral teachers is to *help* their students who are deaf attain the *expected* goal of speaking.

Children are immersed in spoken language throughout the day and are dependent on spoken language for communicating. Throughout the day, children in auditory-oral programs are dependent on speaking to communicate. Children are provided with many opportunities to converse in a variety of communicative contexts as they participate in activities designed to improve their listening and talking skills. Speech is not a subject taught to the child or a therapy the child receives for fifteen or thirty minutes a day but is part of an ongoing, interactive educational process.

Emphasis is placed on the development of auditory skills. The easiest way for a child to learn to talk is through hearing. The more speech a child can hear, the better and more easily it will be for that child to learn spoken language. Teachers in auditory-oral programs recognize the need for children to wear their implant processors constantly and know how to identify whether their students' implants are working properly. The teachers know *what* sounds a child can be expected to detect and discriminate through listening and *how* that auditory information can best be utilized to assist the child in learning to talk. Much attention is given to the auditory environment, and systems are in place for daily monitoring of cochlear implants. Audiologists are available to identify when map adjustments are required and to make those adjustments immediately so that the child has minimal "down time" in terms of listening and hearing. Instruction is provided to improve listening skills as the teacher involves the child in listening activities. Throughout the day, the teacher calls the child's attention to sounds and speech that occur naturally in the environment.

All classroom teachers are knowledgeable about and experienced in teaching speech and spoken language to children who are deaf. Teachers in auditory-oral programs are skilled and talented in turning everyday happenings into language-learning opportunities. Teachers design activities to permit children to practice vocabulary and syntactic structures, as well as to practice using spoken language. Opportunities for the teacher to help individual children to improve speech clarity occur in all classroom activities; teachers are selective in identifying those situations that can be used effectively as teaching opportunities.

Small classes allow for individualized instruction. Auditory-oral programs offer small classes, typically three to six children per teacher. This class size permits individualization of instruction and maximizes the opportunities for each child to speak and to participate in activities.

Acoustics of the classroom are designed for maximum reduction of ambient noise. Children who are deaf require maximization of speech sounds and minimization of background noises. Auditory-oral programs pay close attention to classroom acoustics. The ambient noise in classrooms may be reduced through carpeted floors, acoustically treated walls and ceilings, double-glazed windows, noise baffles in air ducts, and doors engineered to bar hallway noise. Ambient noise may also be reduced if children wear FM units that block all sounds other than the amplified speech signal. Technology in this area is improving daily.

The Instructional Program

The auditory-oral approach to teaching children who are deaf to speak is based on the following assumptions.

Direct teaching accelerates the acquisition of spoken language. A major consequence of severely deficient hearing has been its interference in the development and use of spoken communication. The children who attend auditory-oral schools typically lag behind their hearing peers in the ability to talk and to understand the speech of others, which is why they are not yet mainstreamed. They need specific, direct instruction in listening, producing speech, and understanding and using spoken language, as well as in reading and other academic skills. Direct instruction does not always look direct, however. In fact, instruction is usually more effective if it looks natural and conversational, even though the teacher has specific teaching objectives in mind. In all activities, the auditory-oral teacher tries to capitalize on events that occur to make that specific activity into a language learning experience. This direct, focused instruction helps children who are deaf accelerate their learning and "catch up" to their normal-hearing peers.

Proper evaluation improves the effectiveness of teaching. Evaluation occurs at several different levels. First, evaluation is necessary to determine the child's existing skills. For example, the teacher must determine whether a child talks at the two-word level, the phrase level, the simple-sentence level, or the complex-sentence level, in order to devise the appropriate level for talking with the child. The auditory-oral teacher will gear the conversation a little above where the child demonstrates competence, but not so far above as to be out of reach. Second, evaluation helps teachers determine the effectiveness of their instruction. Teachers evaluate each child's skills after a period of instruction and compare the results with that child's skills before instruction to provide documentation of the child's progress. The improved skill level becomes the basis for new instructional objectives. A third level of evaluation is the assessment the teacher makes of a child's responses during each communicative interaction. The teacher utilizes the child's responses as a guide for further action.

The curriculum provides for instruction in English vocabulary and syntax as well as in speech production and auditory training. Since children who are deaf are usually deficient in the areas of English vocabulary, English syntax, speech production, and listening skills, these areas must be the focus of their educational program. Some teachers follow a developmental sequence of instructional objectives according to an anticipated order in which skills in each area are typically acquired. As each skill is acquired, the next skill in the sequence is targeted for instruction. Other teachers do not follow a formal organized sequence or checklist of skills but have internalized a sequence and automatically program their teaching to be at the next highest skill level.

Instruction focuses on both comprehension and production to accelerate language learning. Children in auditory-oral programs are expected to both understand and verbally respond to the speech of others. Emphasizing production provides the child with practice in talking, help in comprehension, and opportunity for meaningful use of speech skills and provides the teacher with feedback regarding the child's articulation, vocabulary, and syntax.

Competence with spoken English facilitates the development of literacy.

Proficiency with English syntax and English vocabulary is a necessary pre-requisite for competence in reading and writing. The instruction that children receive in auditory-oral schools prepares them to read and write competently—skills that are essential for independent and classroom learning in a main-stream setting.

Family Support

Parents are as important as and possibly more important than teachers, in terms of helping children successfully learn to use their cochlear implants. Parents must (a) ensure that their child's implant is working as it should, (b) begin their child's oral training immediately, (c) encourage and support their child in using spoken language, (d) serve as their child's advocate at school and elsewhere, and (e) work with their child at home to develop oral skills.

Conclusion

Numerous auditory-oral school programs throughout the United States focus their instruction on developing spoken language skills and incorporate many of the features discussed above. Among these are a group of private-independent schools, called Option Schools. (A list of these schools is found in List A.) These schools are called Option Schools because they offer an alter-native option to the type of education program that may be offered in the local public school. As more children have received, and continue to receive, cochlear implants, the demand for educational programs to help these chil-dren obtain maximum benefits from their implants has increased dramati-cally.

Thus, during the past three years, at least twelve new auditory-oral schools have opened. The intensive daily instruction provided in auditory-oral pro-grams is necessary for some children with cochlear implants and can greatly accelerate the progress of other such children. List B provides a list of twelve new auditory-oral programs that have opened in the past three years, some of which are not yet large enough or are too new to be included in the list of Option Schools.)

As stated by Dr. William House, who is sometimes called the father of cochlear implants: "Success with a cochlear implant depends only 10% on hardware and 90% on software. The software is the educational program that is provided to the child after the implant." Based on my experience, I agree 100 percent.

List A

Option Schools

Archbishop Ryan School for
Children with Hearing Impairment
233 Mohawk Avenue
Norwood, PA 19074
610-586-7044

The Atlanta Speech School
3160 Northside Parkway, NW
Atlanta, GA 30327-1598
404-233-5332

CChat Center—Rialto
485 N. Eucalyptus Avenue
Rialto, CA 92376
909-421-0205

CChat Center—Sacramento
9350 Kiefer Boulevard
Sacramento, CA 95826
916-361-7290

The Center for Hearing and Speech
3636 West Dallas
Houston, TX 77019
713-523-3633

Central Institute for the Deaf
818 S. Euclid Avenue
St. Louis, MO 63110
314-977-0000

Child's Voice
442 North West Avenue
Elmhurst, IL 60126
630-834-8255

Chinchuba Institute
1131 Barataria Boulevard
Marrero, LA 70072
504-340-9261

Clarke School for the Deaf
Round Hill Road

Northampton, MA 01060
413-584-3450

The DePaul Institute
Castlegate Avenue
Pittsburgh, PA 15226-2097
412-561-4848

Desert Voices
5811 N. 20th Street
Phoenix, AZ 85016
602-224-0598

ECHO Center
3430 McManus Avenue
Culver City, CA 90232
310-838-2442

Jean Weingarten Peninsula Oral
School for the Deaf
3518 Jefferson Avenue
Redwood City, CA 94062
415-365-7500

John Tracy Clinic
806 West Adams Boulevard
Los Angeles, CA 90007
213-748-5481

La Voz de Ninos Oral School
1114 Copper Avenue, NE
Albuquerque, NM 87106
505-242-5212

Lexington Hearing and Speech
Center
162 North Ashland Avenue
Lexington, KY 40502
606-268-4545

Little Rock Oral Program
1000 North Mississippi
Little Rock, AR 72207
501-224-5767

Louisville Deaf Oral School
414 West Ormsby Avenue
Louisville, KY 40203
502-636-2084

Magnolia Speech School
733 Flag Chapel Road
Jackson, MS 39209
601-922-5530

Memphis Oral School for the Deaf
711 Jefferson Avenue
Memphis, TN 38105
901-448-8490

Montreal Oral School for the Deaf,
Inc.
5851 Upper Lachine Road
Montreal, Quebec Canada H4A
2B7
514-488-4946

The Moog Oral School
11411 North Forty Drive
St. Louis, MO 63131
314-692-7172

The Omaha Hearing School for
Children, Inc.
1110 North 66th Street
Omaha, NE 68132
402-558-1546

Oralingua School for the Hearing
Impaired
7056 S. Washington Avenue
Whittier, CA 90602
310-945-8391

St. Joseph Institute for the Deaf
1809 Clarkson Road
Chesterfield, MO 63017
314-532-3211

Summit Speech School for the
Hearing Impaired Child
705 Central Avenue
New Providence, NJ 07974
908-508-0011

Sunshine Cottage School for Deaf
Children
103 Tuleta Drive
San Antonio, TX 78212-3196
210-824-0579

Tucker-Maxon Oral School
2860 SE Holgate Boulevard
Portland, OR 97202-3697
503-235-6551

The Vancouver Oral Centre
4824 Commercial Street
Vancouver, British Columbia
CANADA V5N 4H1
604-874-0255

List B

New Oral Programs Not Yet Members of Option

CChat Center—San Diego
6725 A Encinitas Boulevard
Encinitas, CA 92024
760-634-7953

Clarke Auditory Oral Center—
Jacksonville
9857 Old St. Augustine Road
Jacksonville, FL 32257
904-880-9001

Clarke East at Lasell College
1844 Commonwealth Avenue
Auburndale, MA 02166
617-332-2875

Listen and Talk Education for
Children with Hearing Loss
4501 46th Avenue, NE
Seattle, WA 98105
206-729-9894

St. Joseph Institute for the Deaf at
Carle Clinic
809 West Park
Urbana, IL 61801
217-356-6110

St. Joseph Institute for
the Deaf—Kansas City
7323 West 97th Street
Overland Park, KS 66212
913-383-3535

Children with Cochlear Implants at
St. Joseph Institute for the Deaf

Sister Joyce Buckler, Ed.D.
and Sister Roseanne Siebert, M.A.

*Sister Joyce Buckler received an M.A. in Audiology from Northwestern
University and an Ed.D. in Special Education and College Teaching from
Columbia University. Sr. Joyce was a teacher, supervisor, director, and
principal at St. Joseph Institute for the Deaf in St. Louis, Missouri, for
twenty years. Recently retired (1997), she is now Academic Outreach Con-
sultant for St. Joseph, providing services to the school's satellite programs.*

*Sister Roseanne Siebert received an M.A. in Speech Pathology and
Audiology from the University of Iowa and a B.A. in Deaf Education from
Fontbonne College in St. Louis. She is supervisor of the Speech Program
at St. Joseph Institute for the Deaf.*

In 1991 in Atlanta, at the annual meeting of Option—a consortium of private auditory-oral school programs—a prediction was made concerning the
impact of cochlear implants on future educational choices for children with
severe and profound hearing losses.[1] The prediction was that programs committed to the auditory-oral philosophy could best meet the academic and communication needs of these children. Other sections of this book speak to the
value of *auditory-verbal* therapy and its positive impact in assisting children
who are profoundly hearing-impaired to make maximum use of their cochlear
implants. That claim has been substantiated throughout the world and need
not be defended here. This section focuses on meeting the academic and communication needs of children with cochlear implants via *auditory-oral* programs.

What of the prediction made in Atlanta in 1991? Are auditory-oral programs assisting children to be successful users of cochlear implants? The
answer, based on research analyzed by members of the Consensus Development Panel of the National Institutes of Health, is an unequivocal "yes." The
National Institutes of Health Consensus Statement of May 1995 was developed at a conference convened to summarize the accrued knowledge about
the range of benefits and limitations of cochlear implantation.[2] The members

of the conference saw such knowledge as an important basis for informed choices for individuals and their families whose philosophy of communication was dedicated to the auditory-oral approach.

One study supported by the National Institutes of Health tested young adults who had been educated in two different educational settings: auditory-oral (utilizing hearing, speechreading, and speech only) and total communication (utilizing sign language and some speechreading and speech). The study on auditory-oral adolescents from across the United States and Canada was conducted at Central Institute for the Deaf in St. Louis, Missouri. The results of this portion of the study, "Factors Predictive of the Development of Literacy in Profoundly Hearing Impaired Adolescents," published in 1989, support the academic and language achievements of adolescents educated in an auditory-oral setting.[3] These results show that the hearing-impaired students who were educated in auditory-oral programs, and all of whom had spent a number of years in the academic mainstream, scored significantly higher in all areas than the adolescents in the unpublished comparison study. Spoken language and use of residual hearing by orally educated adolescents were most impressive. Although this study was not specific to children who use cochlear implants, it supports the benefits of an auditory-oral educational placement for children with severe and profound hearing losses.

Extensive research shows positive results for children using cochlear implants.[4] Researchers who not many years ago were hesitant in taking a strong stand about the educational needs of children with cochlear implants are now publicly supportive of auditory-oral educational settings for such children. It has been noted:

> A strong educational program that emphasizes the development of auditory and oral language skills and a family committed to helping their child maximize his/her hearing capabilities is extremely important to the [child's] overall success with the implant. The recommendation of a strong auditory-oral component to the child's educational program reflects the fact that auditory and oral speech skills in young hearing-impaired children do not develop without appropriate intervention. Maximum benefit from a cochlear implant will not be realized if listening is not stressed throughout the child's day. In some cases, it may be necessary to implement changes in the child's educational program before proceeding with cochlear implantation.[5]

Clearly, auditory-oral educational placements provide the best support for some children with cochlear implants. Further research, however, is needed to explore more specifically the extent to which the success with implants, specifically multichannel models, is generally dependent on the auditory-oral educational placement. Such a study, not yet published, is now under way in the research department of Central Institute for the Deaf in St. Louis, Missouri, with the support of the National Institutes of Health.

Before analyzing the success of children using cochlear implants, we should stress that for many years, children with severe and profound hearing losses have learned to listen and to use spoken language—without the support of cochlear implants. Those children became good oral communicators in auditory-verbal and auditory-oral programs, both public and private, having three basic goals: academic success, spoken communication, and eventual full-time mainstreaming. Those programs were, and remain, committed to an environment conducive to learning and listening—an educational environment dedicated to excellence in all aspects of a child's development. Today, children with cochlear implants in such an environment are achieving the same goals, albeit with less stress and at a faster rate of speed.

Miyamoto et al. have noted similarities between the listening process of children who wear hearing aids and the process of those who use cochlear implants.[6] For example, both groups of children (1) perceive vowel sounds before consonant sounds; (2) manifest a wide range of individual differences in the process of listening; (3) have much less consistent auditory responses in noisy than in quiet environments; and (4) must learn to make sound meaningful in order to comprehend their auditory environment.

The same study, however, notes the differences between children who wear hearing aids and those who use cochlear implants. First, children with cochlear implants learn to listen in a more holistic and natural way than most children who wear hearing aids. Second, although both sets of children must progress through a hierarchy of "listening" steps to achieve maximum listening skills, the steps for children learning to listen with cochlear implants generally need not be as minute as the steps required by children learning to listen with hearing aids. Third, cochlear implants provide children with access to a wide range of frequencies, permitting them to hear all sounds in the speech range. Important too is the more rapid development of the skill of reauditorization, wherein a child with a multichannel implant, although perhaps not perceiving the entire auditory message, can imitate some aspects of speech, retain these aspects, and recall them at a later time. These auditory skills enhance a child's overall spoken language development in conjunction with his or her improved listening.

Research from a number of centers has shown that the longer a child with a profound hearing impairment is deprived of the ability to hear through listening, whether due to deafness occurring prelingually, perilingually, or postlingually, the slower that child's rehabilitative process will be after receiving a cochlear implant.[7] Because the particular needs of children who have received cochlear implants vary depending on factors such as length of auditory deprivation, age of implantation, additional language-learning delays, and specific learning styles, various approaches to rehabilitation are required.

At St. Joseph Institute, we have found it necessary to implement changes in the educational-therapy programs of implanted children to maximize their success with cochlear implants. Such changes were particularly necessary in the early stages (1986) of our cochlear implant program because the first children at St. Joseph's were implanted with the single-channel House/3M instrument,[8] which, as research has shown,[9] provided a much more limited range of sound than the multichannel cochlear implants now provide.

Our experience at St. Joseph Institute has shown that children who receive their cochlear implants after age 5 and who have had prior limited auditory success require a structured and hierarchical educational-therapy approach. Auditory curricula such as *The Developmental Approach to Successful Listening* (DASL)[10] and *Auditory Skills Instructional Planning System* (ASIPS)[11] are used, with individualized modifications. *Teacher/Clinician's Planbook and Guide to the Development of Speech Skills* is the primary speech program used with all children at St. Joseph's.[12] A slow and methodical process is followed to assist children who, because of long-term auditory deprivation and or some complications in their learning style, require more time to learn to make sense of what they are hearing.

Two approaches to auditory (re)habilitation are used at St. Joseph's. One approach, analytic or bottom-up, is used for children whose listening development indicates the need for auditorily analyzing discrete parts of words, phrases, and or sentences. Once the child comprehends the various "parts" of a message, the whole message is easier for that child to interpret. Other children manifest the ability to learn in a more global or top-down approach, comprehending in a less discrete manner. Although no research has analyzed the relationship between learning styles and successful use of the cochlear implant, our experience has been that each child's style of learning is unique.

All children with cochlear implants require both isolated skill-practice therapy and "real-life" communication strategies. This combination is crucial. Siebert recommends that the steps used to assist children in utilizing their cochlear implants should be presented in increasing levels of difficulty, as follows:

1. Move from the sound-plus-vision to the sound-only condition
2. Move from a limited number of choices to a larger number of choices and then to the unlimited choices
3. Move from detection to discrimination, to identification, to recognition, and to comprehension
4. Move from words to phrases to sentences
5. Move from structured to spontaneous
6. Move from sounds or words that are very different to those that are minimally different.[13]

Whether a child learns analytically or synthetically, the objective of learning to listen with a cochlear implant (or hearing aid) is to become a successful communicator. Auditory comprehension lays the groundwork for the child's development of understandable speech and complex spoken language.

At St. Joseph Institute, individual speech and listening therapy are part of each school day. Essential goals of each child's therapy sessions are the basic auditory skills of detection, discrimination, identification, recognition, and comprehension. Targets are identified and practiced for each auditory skill. This practice, using content and materials that have meaning for the child, is continuously increasing in difficulty and is discussed in such a way that the child becomes aware of the relationship of practice to meaningful, rewarding conversation and communication. Constant practice provides each child with the confidence and motivation necessary not only for good communication skills but also for academic and social success. For a child to develop independent communication skills, the child must become skilled in self-monitoring clarification strategies for determining what is heard, "guessing" a particular message, and applying repair strategies for a variety of social and academic interchanges. (More specific strategies for assisting children in developing their listening skills are discussed by Moog et al.[14] and by Robbins[15] in the publication "Effectiveness of Cochlear Implants and Tactile Aids for Deaf Children." (That publication lists appendices outlining detailed approaches to therapy.)

Since the cochlear implant program was established at St. Joseph Institute in 1986 until the present time (1997), 104 children with cochlear implants have received listening and speech therapy at our school. The majority of these children have rapidly become competent communicators. A definite trend toward earlier mainstreaming is evident due to the use of cochlear implants. Although most students through the years have completed grade eight at St. Joseph's, each year the number of students who are between the ages of 7 and 12 and who are able to leave the self-contained classroom setting at St. Joseph and be mainstreamed continues to increase. Interestingly, a number of these mainstreamed children were once struggling to develop an ease with communication; after being implanted, they made progress at a sufficiently rapid pace to ensure success in the mainstream. Examples of these children follow.

Claudia, who received very limited auditory information with her hearing aids, was implanted at age 10. She rapidly learned to comprehend auditory information and to develop outstanding spoken-language and reading skills. She was mainstreamed at age 11; presently she is succeeding at one of the top girls' prep schools in the United States.

LeeAnne, who before receiving a cochlear implant was in a total-communication program, was implanted at age 5. Having extremely limited spoken language and vocabulary, she was immediately enrolled at St. Joseph. At age 10, she is mainstreamed successfully with her hearing peers.

Becky was implanted at age 7. Becky's cochlear implant provided her with auditory information that she quickly associated with spoken language; she developed high-level skills, allowing her to mainstream at age 9.

Sarah, who before receiving her implant was being considered for a total-communication program, was implanted at age 4 years, 6 months. As a result of her cochlear implant, her spoken language rose to a level of efficiency permitting her to fully mainstream at age 7.

Noelle, struggling with spoken language, received a cochlear implant at age 7. In five years she was mainstreamed; presently she is preparing to enter a university.

Many other children at St. Joseph have progressed as rapidly as these children. Still other children with cochlear implants have progressed more slowly, however. Factors affecting progress include an extremely limited number of active electrodes following surgery, a limited sense of the structure of language, undeveloped auditory memory, and more limited cognitive processing skills. For these students, more frequent assessments of progress are required, since, of necessity, the steps in their therapy are reached at a slower pace. Setting achievable targets for these children becomes critical for their sense of success.

Research by Quittner et al. suggests that the cochlear implant has a global multisensory effect on language learning.[16] This could account for the more rapid progress for a large majority of children, especially those in auditory-oral programs. Too, the rate of language learning with the cochlear implant relates to a child's ability to acquire language incidentally—a new experience—through overhearing ongoing conversations. Just as for children who have normal hearing, this natural exposure to spoken-language communication becomes, for the implanted child, an avenue for language learning.

Professionals and parents alike need to be aware that the surgical procedure is merely the first step toward the successful use of a cochlear implant; rehabilitation involves an even more crucial process.[17] Too often parents have unrealistic expectations, expectations that are too limited, and or the expectation that surgical implantation is the end rather than the beginning of a long road toward real listening—a road along which parents play a critical role. Rehabilitation therapy that will enable a child to learn to listen to his or her potential requires significant commitment on the part of the child, the parents, and the professionals. Bracket has identified behaviors and activities that can assist parents and others in contact with a child who has received an implant:

1. Assume the child can hear.
2. Make listening a part of all waking hours.
3. Call the child's name instead of attracting him or her visually by touch.
4. Focus the child's attention on sounds and voices in the environment.
5. Wait for the child to respond to environmental sounds in the home (phone, doorbell) before reacting.
6. Place the sound source or speaker in a less visible location.

7. As the child becomes more aware of sounds, gradually reduce nonauditory cues.

8. Use vocal attention-getters ("Look," "Hey," "Watch").

9. Give the child an opportunity to process information auditorily before adding visual cues.

10. Change your environment to maximize listening. (Turn off the TV in the background, for example.)[18]

The prediction made in Atlanta in 1991 has indeed become a reality. Auditory-oral educational environments *do* assist children in becoming successful users of cochlear implants. Research to date supports this prediction. Further research is needed, of course, as the National Institutes of Health has recognized.[19] But children who are severely and profoundly deaf need help *now*. The challenge for all of us today is to successfully advocate to obtain immediate assistance for children with severe or profound hearing losses.

NOTES

1. Option Meeting Minutes, April 13–14, 1991, Atlanta, Georgia.

2. "Cochlear Implants in Adults and Children," *National Institutes of Health Consensus Statement* 13, no. 2 (1995): 1–30.

3. A. E. Geers and J. S. Moog, "Factors Predictive of the Development of Literacy in Profoundly Hearing Impaired Adolescents," *Volta Review* 91, no. 2 (1989): 69–86.

4. A. E. Geers, and J. S. Moog, comment on "The Cochlear Implant: An Auditory Prosthesis for the Profoundly Deaf Child," *Ear and Hearing* 7, no. 2 (1986): 122–25; M. J. Osberger, A. M. Robbins, S. W. Berry, S. L. Todd, L. J. Hesketh and A. Sedey, "Analysis of Spontaneous Speech Samples of Children with Cochlear Implants or Tactile Aids," *American Journal of Otology* 12 (1991): 151–64; M. J. Osberger, M. Maso, and L. K. Sam, "Speech Intelligibility of Children with Cochlear Implants, Tactile Aids, or Hearing Aids," *Journal of Speech and Hearing Research* 36 (1993): 186–203; M. J. Osberger, A. M. Robbins, S. L. Todd and A. I. Riley "Speech Intelligibility of Children with Cochlear Implants," *Volta Review* 95 no. 5, (1993): 169–80; K. L. Kirk and C. Hill-Brown, "Speech and Language Results in Children with a Cochlear Implant," *Ear and Hearing* 6, no. 3 (suppl.) (1985): 36–37; M. A. Thielmeir, L. L. Tonokawa, B. Peterson, and L. S. Eisenberg, "Audiological Results in Children with a Cochlear Implant," *Ear and Hearing* 6, no. 3 (suppl.) (1985): 27–35; K. I. Berliner, L. S. Eisenberg, and W. F. House, "The Cochlear Implant: An Auditory Prosthesis for the Profoundly Deaf Child," *Ear and Hearing* 6, no. 3 (suppl.) (1985): 6–69; R. T. Miyamoto, E. Meyers, M. L. Pope, and C. C. Carotta, "Cochlear Implants for Deaf Children" (paper presented at the meeting of the Middle Section of the American Laryngological Rhinological, and Otological Society, Chicago, (January 26, 1986), pp. 10–11; R. T. Miyamoto, M. J. Osberger, S. L. Todd, and A. M. Robbins, "Speech Perception Skills of Children with Multichannel Cochlear Implants" (paper presented at the 3rd International Cochlear Implant Conference, Innsbruck, Austria, 1993); B. J. Gantz, R. S. Tyler, G. G. Woodworth, N. Tye-Murray, and H. Fryauf-Bertschy, "Results of Multichannel Cochlear Implants in Congential and Acquired Prelingual Deafness in Children: Five-year Follow-Up," *American Journal of Otology* 15, no. 2 (suppl.) (1994): 107.

5. S. J. Staller, A. L. Beiter, and J. A. Brimacombe, "Use of the Nucleus 22-Channel Cochlear Implant System with Children," in A. E. Geers, and J. S. Moog, eds, "Effectiveness of Cochlear Implants and Tactile Aids for Deaf Children: The Sensory Aids Study at Central Institute for the Deaf," *Volta Review* 96, no. 5 (1994): 15–39.

6. Miyamoto et al., "Speech Perception Skills of Children with Multichannel Cochlear Implants."

7. Osberger et al., "Analysis of Spontaneous Speech"; Osberger et al., "Speech Intelligibility," *Journal of Speech and Hearing Research*; Osberger et al., "Speech Intelligibility," *The Volta Review*; Gantz, et al., "Results of Multichannel Cochlear Implants"; R. T. Miyamoto, M. J. Osberger, A. M. Robbins, W. A. Myers, and K. Kessler, "Prelingually Deafened Children's Performance with the Nucleus Multichannel Cochlear Implant," *American Journal of Otology* 14 (1993): 437–45.

8. See Gantz et al., "Results of Multichannel Cochlear Implants"; Miyamoto et al., "Prelingually Deafened Children's Performance."

9. See Staller et al., "Use of the Nucleus 22-Channel Cochlear Implant System"; M. J. Osberger, S. Zimmerman-Phillips, L. Geier, and M. Barker "Clinical Results with the CLARION Multi-Strategy Cochlear Implant in Children" (paper presented to Option members, Salt Lake City, 1996).

10. J. V. Windel and G. G. Stout, *The Developmental Approach to Successful Listening (DASL)* (Houston: DASL, 1986).

11. *Auditory Skills Curriculum* (North Hollywood, Calif.: Foreworks, 1979).

12. D. Ling, *Teacher/Clinician's Planbook and Guide to the Development of Speech Skills* (Washington, D.C.: Alexander Graham Bell Association for the Deaf, 1978).

13. R. L. Siebert, "Increasing the Level of Difficulty During Training" (adapted from materials presented at the NECCI Thinktank, Manhattan Eye, Ear and Nose Hospital, New York, N.Y., 1993).

14. J. S. Moog, J. Biedenstein, L. Davidson, and C. Renner "Instruction for Developing Speech Perception Skills," Geers, and Moog, "Effectiveness of Cochlear Implants."

15. A. M. Robbins, "Guidelines for Developing Oral Communication Skills in Children with Cochlear Implants," in Geer and Moog, "Effectiveness of Cochlear Implants."

16. A. L. Quittner, L. B. Smith, M. J. Osberger, T. V. Mitchell, and D. B. Katz, "The Impact of Audition on the Development of Visual Attention," *Psychological Science* 5 (1994): 347–53.

17. See, e.g., Siebert, "Increasing the Level of Difficulty."

18. D. Bracket, "Rehabilitation/Education Strategies for Children with Cochlear Implants" (N.Y. League of the Hard of Hearing, Clinical Bulletin, Cochlear Corporation, November 1991).

19. NIH Consensus Statement (see note 2 above).

Tucker-Maxon Oral School Children's Cochlear Implant Center

Patrick Stone, Ed.D.

Patrick Stone is executive director of Tucker-Maxon Oral School in Portland, Oregon. He received an Ed.D. in Special Education from the Uni-

versity of Cincinnati, an M.S. in Elementary Education from Portland State University, and a B.S. in Education of Deaf Children from the University of Utah.

"Without his implant I know he would not be where he is today—a junior in our neighborhood high school with a B+ average and wonderful spoken language skills." This was spoken by the mother of the first Tucker-Maxon student to receive an implant. He was 3 years, 5 months of age and received the House/3M single-channel device in February 1984 at the House Ear Institute. Five years following implantation, he scored above 95 percent on the Ling Phonologic Evaluation.[1] At his completion of eighth grade, his reading (and language) comprehension was in the average range when compared with a national sample of normal-hearing eighth-graders.

This excerpt will describe the beginning of our Children's Cochlear Implant Center and will present data on the performance of some students who are currently wearing cochlear implants.

Background

Within nine months of working with the above-mentioned student, the staff at Tucker-Maxon recognized that the cochlear implant brought meaningful sound, unmatched by the most powerful hearing aids, to children who are profoundly deaf. We began to plan how to find out more about the implant and how to make it available to more of our children. We were fortunate in securing the support of the Jackson Foundation of Portland. In the spring of 1985, the foundation provided the funding for the startup of our Children's Cochlear Implant Center—the first such program to be housed at a school. That summer three staff members attended a two-week training course at the House Ear Institute in Los Angeles—one of seven centers providing implants to children at that time. At the conclusion of this training period, we were equipped and able to provide the pre- and postoperative audiological, speech, and language evaluations and to provide the services necessary for children receiving the House/3M device.

During the training course, Dr. William House impressed on the Tucker-Maxon staff his belief that the implant would be only as effective as the education provided the child after surgery. Our first student's early success led us to believe that an intensive auditory-oral environment was the type of education most suited to children with an implant. We felt then, and still feel now, that to implant a child with the intent that the child will utilize any form of communication other than spoken language as the primary goal is unconscionable.

In the late 1980s, Tucker-Maxon students began to receive the Nucleus

22-Channel cochlear implant. At that time we acquired the equipment necessary to map these devices. Following FDA approval of cochlear implants for
children, more and more of our families have elected to have their children
receive this wonderful technology.

As of July 1997, twenty-two children wearing the Nucleus 22-Channel
cochlear implant were enrolled at Tucker-Maxon. Nine of these children
received their implants while enrolled at Tucker-Maxon, have had their
implants for more than two years, and have no documented learning disabilities. Reports of these children follow.

Age and Placement Information

Table 1 lists the birthdate, hookup date, age at hookup, and current placement of each of these nine children.

Table 1

	Birthdate	Hookup Date	Age at Hookup	Current Placement
1. Male	7/79	9/91	12.1	Full inclusion; itinerant support
2. Female	7/84	4/90	5.9	Full inclusion; itinerant support
3. Female	1/87	4/91	4.3	Full inclusion; itinerant support
4. Female	2/87	2/91	3.11	Self-contained
5. Female	7/87	11/93	6.4	Full inclusion; itinerant support
6. Male	11/87	10/92	4.11	Full inclusion
7. Female	6/88	5/94	5.11	Self-contained
8. Female	10/90	10/94	3.11	½ self-contained; ½ inclusion
9. Female	5/91	6/94	3.1	½ self-contained; ½ inclusion

At the time their processors were activated, these children ranged in age
from 3 years, 1 month, to 12 years, 1 month. Two children currently attend
school in self-contained classrooms (attending classes with other children
who are deaf); two children divide their school days between self-contained
classrooms and inclusion classrooms (attending classes with hearing children); the remaining five children attend inclusion classes only, with most
receiving itinerant support. We anticipate that the two children splitting their
days between inclusion and self-contained classrooms will be fully included
with itinerant support in another year. Further, the two children currently in
self-contained classrooms will move into inclusion settings in the next two
or three years.

We are convinced that many of these children would not be succeeding
in regular classrooms were it not for their implants. Their growth in speech
and language has been accelerated because they now have easier access to a
much broader range of speech and language information, as explained below.

Speech Perception

At Tucker-Maxon, all instruction is provided to children with cochlear implants through auditory-oral teaching strategies. The teaching staff increasingly challenges their students to perceive speech information through audition. Listening is an integral component of all speech, language, and academic instruction.

Several tests are administered by the staff audiologist to determine growth in speech and language abilities over time. Table 2 shows growth in two widely used tests.

Table 2

	Hookup Age	*First WIPI* Date	Date	Score	*Recent WIPI* Date	Score	*First GASP* Date	Score	*Recent GASP* Date	Score
1. Male	12.01	9/91	6/91	36%	10/92	52%	10/92	8/10	12/93	8/10
2. Female	5.09	4/90	2/90	68%	3/95	92%	4/91	4/10	4/97	10/10
3. Female	4.03	4/91	10/94	72%	6/97	84%	5/92	4/10	6/97	10/10
4. Female	3.11	2/91	11/93	48%	5/97	78%	4/93	3/10	5/97	8/10
5. Female	6.04	11/93	2/93	16%	4/97	88%	5/94	5/10	4/97	9/10
6. Male	4.11	10/92	2/94	36%	3/97	84%	2/94	7/10	3/97	10/10
7. Female	5.11	5/94	11/93	28%	5/97	72%	5/95	3/10	5/97	10/10
8. Female	3.11	10/94	4/96	60%	5/97	80%	4/96	7/10	5/97	9/10
9. Female	3.01	6/94	5/96	20%	5/97	52%	5/96	2/10	5/97	5/10

The first scores reported on Table 2 are from the Word Intelligibility by Picture Identification (WIPI) test.[2] In this test, the child is shown six pictures and is asked to identify the picture representing the word spoken by the audiologist. The test is administered through listening alone. The words are selected to determine the child's ability to discriminate auditorily among consonants. For example, the pictures on one page are green, screen, queen, etc.—words that differ only in their initial consonant.

The "First WIPI" column indicates the date and score for the first administration of this test to each child. (In a few cases this was before implantation, but most of the children were unable to take this test before receiving their implants.) The "Recent WIPI" column shows the most recent score for each child. These scores show that these nine children significantly increased their ability to identify words through hearing alone, increases of 12 to 72 percent.

The second scores reported on Table 2 are from the Glendonald Auditory Screening Procedure (GASP) test.[3] In this test, the child is required to answer questions presented through audition alone. The scores are based on the responses to a total of ten questions. As with the WIPI, some students took this test before implantation, but most did not. As shown in Table 2, the "Recent GASP" scores of these nine children are significantly higher than the "First GASP" scores.

The results of these two tests provide evidence, beyond dispute, that these nine children are learning to use the information provided to them by their implants to understand spoken communication.

Speech Development

Each of these nine children (like all other children at Tucker-Maxon) receives intensive speech-development instruction. Daily speech instruction is provided by the child's teacher. The procedures and strategies described by Ling[4] are used by all staff members. This approach comprises two levels of instruction: the phonetic and the phonologic. New skills are taught within the context of syllables first—the phonetic level. When a sound is mastered in syllables, it is immediately practiced in words, phrases, and sentences—the phonologic level. Throughout the day, children are monitored and are reminded to use the most accurate production possible.

In addition to the child's teacher, the speech pathologist works with most children twice per week and carries out extensive evaluation activities of preschool children semi-annually and school age children annually.

Table 3 reports the growth over the past two years in speech intelligibility for the seven youngest children in this group. (The two older children are reported in Table 4.)

Table 3

	Birth Date	*Spring 1995* Vowel	Cons.	*Spring 1997* Vowel	Cons.
3. Female	1/87	86%	84%	91%	82%
4. Female	2/87	71%	65%	91%	86%
5. Female	7/87	60%	65%	80%	81%
6. Male	11/87	78%	62%	93%	62%
7. Female	6/88	44%	30%	68%	60%
8. Female	10/90	53%	52%	88%	86%
9. Female	5/91	Not Tested		74%	69%

The measure used is the Phonologic Level Speech Evaluation developed by Ling.[5] In this test, the examiner listens to a taped sample of 100 consecutive words spoken by each child during spontaneous conversational speech. The examiner then scores each spoken vowel and consonant as correct or incorrect. In the spring of 1995, these seven children had average vowel intelligibility of 65 percent and average consonant intelligibility of 60 percent. Two years later, their average vowel intelligibility rose to 84 percent, and their average consonant intelligibility rose to 75 percent. It is noteworthy that in the spring of 1997, four of the seven children received speech intelligibility scores of 80 percent or better, which means that most listeners are able to understand most of what those four children say.

With respect to the two older children, it is more informative to examine their increase in speech intelligibility during their first two years of implant use. Table 4 reports this information.

Table 4

	Birthdate	Pre-Implant	Two Years
1. Male	7/79	45%	64%
2. Female	7/84	60%	89%

Table 4 illustrates that during the first two years post-implantation, the first student's speech intelligibility increased nearly 20 percent and the second student's speech intelligibility increased nearly 30 percent.

Every one of the nine children reported here has achieved significant improvements in speech intelligibility since receiving his or her cochlear implant.

Language Development

To gain proficiency with the English language, children who are deaf require consistent and systematic instruction. The language instruction program at Tucker-Maxon is based on using conversation, both naturally occurring and teacher directed, to develop language skill. The specific procedures used have been described previously by this author.[6] Because conversational competence is the goal, conversation is the context used for instruction. The teacher designs role-playing situations in which the child must use a particular conversational objective not yet mastered. At the point in the dialogue when the child has difficulty, the teacher and child switch roles, and the child has the opportunity to hear and respond to the correct language. They then switch back and begin the conversation again. It is sometimes necessary for the child to engage in several of these scenarios to gain communication mastery.

Because of our focus on conversational language, one of the measures we use to monitor progress is the mean length of utterance (MLU), that is the average number of morphemes produced by a child in 50 (or more) consecutive spontaneous utterances. To determine a child's MLU, we transcribe a conversational sample and segment it into utterances: words, phrases, or sentences. The number of morphemes in each utterance is counted. For example, "The boy has a ball" has three morphemes (boy/has/ball). "The boy's ball is blue" has five morphemes (boy/'s/ball/is/blue). In this case the possessive "s" adds meaning, so it is counted as a morpheme. The total number of morphemes in the sample is divided by the number of utterances to establish the MLU. Miller has established age equivalencies for MLUs from 1 through 9.[7] The age-equivalency data allows us to determine the child's growth compared with that of normal-hearing children.

Table 5 reports the growth in language ability over time for the nine children being reported:

Table 5

	Date of Birth	First MLU	Language Age Eqvlnt.	Time in Months	Recent MLU	Language Age Eqvlnt.	Growth in Months
1. Male	7/79	5.60	55 mos.	42	7.50	132 mos.	77
2. Female	7/84	5.18	52 mos.	30	8.40	132 mos.	80
3. Female	1/87	1.17	20 mos.	72	6.60	98 mos.	78
4. Female	2/87	1.60	23 mos.	54	6.50	84 mos.	61
5. Female	7/87	3.70	40 mos.	30	7.60	132 mos.	92
6. Male	11/87	2.00	27 mos.	30	5.20	52 mos.	25
7. Female	6/88	1.93	26 mos.	36	5.34	52 mos.	26
8. Female	10/90	1.20	20 mos.	30	5.60	55 mos.	35
9. Female	5/91	1.48	23 mos.	20	3.74	40 mos.	17

The "First MLU" (column two) displays the child's MLU at the time of or shortly after receiving the cochlear implant. Column three shows the corresponding "Language Age Equivalent" for a normal-hearing child with the same MLU. The "Time in Months" column (column four) shows the time lapse between the "First MLU" and the "Recent MLU" (column five). Column six shows the corresponding "Language Age Equivalent" for a normal-hearing child with the same "Recent MLU." The "Growth in Months" column indicates the growth in language age between the child's "First MLU" and "Recent MLU." When averages are computed, the average length of "Time in Months" between "First MLU" and "Recent MLU" for these nine children is 38.2 months, whereas the average growth in "Language Age Equivalent" is 54.6 months. These children, therefore, developed language *faster* than normal-hearing children of similar language ages. Cochlear implants have helped these children vastly improve their language skills.

Conclusion

Since 1984, children with profound hearing loss have received cochlear implants and been educated at Tucker-Maxon. The data presented above show conclusively that such children make significant gains in all areas of spoken communication and language development when provided an intensive auditory-oral education.

NOTES

1. D. Ling, *Speech and the Hearing-Impaired Child* (Washington, D.C.: A. G. Bell Association for the Deaf, 1976).
2. M. Ross and J. Lerman, *Word Intelligibility by Picture Identification* (Pittsburgh: Stanwix House, 1971).
3. N. Erber, *Glendonald Auditory Screening Procedure* (1993).
4. Ling, *Speech.*
5. *Ibid.*
6. P. Stone, *Blueprint for Developing Conversational Competence* (Washington, D.C.: A. G. Bell Association for the Deaf, 1988).
7. J. Miller, "Implementing Language Sample Analysis" (paper presented at ASHA Convention, Seattle, 1996); J. Miller, *Assessing Language Production in Children* (Austin, Tex.: Pro-Ed, 1981).

Chapter 8

Cochlear Implants
and Deaf Culture

During the past decade, the growing concept of Deaf culture has taken root. Under this concept, members of the larger deaf community are viewed as either deaf (with a small "d") or Deaf (with a capital "D"). People who view themselves as deaf are those who, although impaired in their ability to hear (often *more* impaired in their ability to hear than those who declare themselves Deaf), have assimilated into hearing society and do not view themselves as members of a separate culture. People who view themselves as Deaf, however, consider themselves members of a separate Deaf culture rather than of the larger hearing society.[1] People who call themselves "Deaf" view and define deafness as a cultural identity rather than as a disability, for some purposes; they insist that their culture and separate identity must be nourished and maintained.

What is Deaf culture? Basically it is a concept developed by a minority of Deaf people and their hearing advocates. There are approximately 28 million people with hearing impairments in the United States, of whom approximately 2 million are profoundly deaf.[2] Only approximately three to four hundred thousand of those individuals use sign language, and a smaller number of that group claim to be members of the Deaf culture.[3] The majority of people with hearing impairments, even those who are profoundly deaf, live and work in the mainstream of society and go about their daily lives amid hearing people, just as I do.

Deaf culture does not fall within the usual realm of "culture." There are no Deaf songs, Deaf dances, Deaf foods, Deaf modes of dress, or the like. Rather, Deaf culture is primarily premised on a shared language—American Sign Language (ASL), or another country's equivalent—and shared experiences from growing up in state residential schools for deaf children. (The vast majority of deaf children in the United States no longer attend such schools; the Individuals with Disabilities Education Act [IDEA][4] has resulted in sharp declines in special school enrollments.[5])

Individuals who communicate via ASL clearly *do* speak a different language. ASL is a visual rather than spoken, concrete rather than abstract language bearing little resemblance to English. ASL has its own syntax and grammar. For example, an English-speaking person might ask, "What are your hobbies?" An ASL-signing person might phrase the same question by signing, "Time off—do, do, do?" An English-speaking person might ask, "Have you been to San Francisco?" An ASL-signing person might sign, "Touch San Francisco yet you?" ASL is quite different from signed English; the latter involves signing each English word as it is spoken, using English grammar and structure.

Further, some members of the Deaf cultural community claim to be part of a separate culture as a result of attending segregated (often residential) schools for deaf children or as a result of their participation in Deaf clubs or wholly Deaf environments in which they socialize or work. Indeed, many members of the Deaf cultural community will marry only other Deaf people and prefer to raise Deaf children, and many work at agencies serving deaf people or at schools for deaf children or college students.

Yet, there are many individuals who do not agree that these factors give rise to a true culture. As one speaker succinctly stated: "I do not believe that a disability forms the basis of a culture. The [Deaf culturists] may choose to define themselves that way, but I believe they are a group that *chooses* to isolate themselves from mainstream society."[6] The now deceased Larry G. Stewart, a leading member of the signing deaf community (a strong proponent and user of sign language), noted: "'Deaf culture' was not discovered; it was created for political purposes. The term has yet to be satisfactorily defined."[7] Dr. Stewart went on to say, "In the larger sense of world cultures, the meaning of culture is so powerful and complex that to apply it so narrowly to a group of highly diverse deaf American citizens, whose members are as heterogeneous as the general population, simply makes no sense."[8]

Members of the Deaf cultural community reject arguments disparaging or denying a true Deaf culture. They have coined—or have attempted to coin—the phrase "Deaf Is Dandy," which they seek to popularize in much the same manner that black people popularized the slogan "Black Is Beautiful." According to the leaders of the National Association of the Deaf (NAD),[9] Deaf people like being Deaf, want to be Deaf, and are proud of their Deafness. Deaf culturists claim the right to their own "ethnicity, with [their] own language and culture, the same way that Native Americans or Italians [or blacks] bond together."[10] They claim the right to "personal diversity," which is "something to be cherished rather than fixed and erased."[11] In short, they claim the right to their "birthright of silence."[12]

Although the Deaf culturists equate being deaf to being a member of a racial minority,[13] many deaf people find the analogy nonsensical. Deaf people lack one of the five senses, plain and simple. Black people (and members of other minority groups) do not. There is no similarity between the two. True deaf people such as myself are physically incapable of talking on the telephone alone. We have to use the phone with the aid of a third party—an interpreter or a relay service, both of which present extremely awkward situations. Most of us would *love* to be able to pick up the telephone and make a personal or business call when and how we feel like it without having to scramble to find an interpreter and without having to make the call with a third person listening to every word. We would like to be able to go to a movie or a play when we feel like it. (Deaf people cannot understand movies unless they are captioned; they can understand a play only if an interpreter is present, and even then it is awkward to watch the interpreter and the actors at the same time.) We would like to be able to talk to anyone we want to talk to at any time, to participate in group conversations, to hear the conversation at the dinner table, etc. We would like to be able to hear music, to hear our children and grandchildren laugh and cry, to listen to the radio when we are driving, to have a car phone, to be able to use the drive-up window at McDonald's, to hear the announcements at the airport, to be able to talk to the person in front of or behind us on a hiking trail, to be able to go to a Bar Association meeting on the spur of the moment, to take any job we are offered without having to consider how our deafness will interfere with the job duties. We would particularly like to hear our own voices and to be able to control the tone and pitch and loudness of our voices. The list is endless. Why would people *want* to deny such pleasures to themselves or their children?

Many members of the Deaf cultural community strongly desire to have Deaf children, who will be a part of their parents' Deaf culture. Several Deaf expectant parents have said to me, "We pray every night that our baby will be born deaf."[14] A *Washington Post* reporter stated, "Hearing people are always surprised to learn that deaf parents in neonatal wards cheer when they are told their babies cannot hear."[15] Some expectant Deaf parents visit geneticists to determine whether their children are likely to be born deaf. As explained by Jamie Israel, a genetic counselor at Gallaudet University's genetic services center, "Many of our [Deaf] families are not interested in fixing or curing deaf genes ... [m]any ... couples come in and want ... [D]eaf children."[16] If their children are *not* likely to be born deaf, Deaf parents may choose not to have children or to abort children in gestation, just as hearing or deaf people who determine through genetic research that their children *are* likely to be born deaf may choose not to have children or to abort children in gestation. As a senior scientist at the Shriver Center in Waltham, Massachusetts, noted, "If we can do prenatal diagnoses for a hearing couple that doesn't want a deaf child, it's only fair that we do it for a deaf couple that doesn't want a hearing child."[17] The chairman of the Department of Human Genetics at the Medical College of Virginia summarized: "Certainly there are people who would argue that genetic technology to select a normal fetus [for abortion] is a perversion of science. There are equally vocal people who say this is simply paying appropriate attention to the cultural values of a group who define themselves by [ASL]."[18]

The desire of parents to have children who will be like them and fit into their world is certainly understandable. But most parents want more for their children than they have. My parents, for example, never went to college, but they wanted all their children to have that opportunity. Similarly, although we cannot hear, most people who are deaf want our children and grandchildren to have that ability. In the view of many of us, it is nothing short of cruel for parents to hope and pray that their children will be unable to hear.

Other members of the Deaf cultural community advocate removing deaf babies from the homes of their hearing parents, who are not immersed in the Deaf subculture, and requiring such children to be raised by Deaf parents who will ensure that the children become a part of the Deaf cultural community. This clearly violates the constitutional rights of parents to raise their children as they see fit (absent abuse, of course). As Rick Apicella, a parent of a child with a cochlear implant, wrote to me, the Deaf culturists have couched the debate about cochlear implants in children as an "ethical dilemma," thus "adroitly ... sidestep[ping] ... the Supreme Court's recognition ... that parents possess a fundamental liberty interest in the care, custody, and management of their children ... [and] have a constitutional right to privacy regarding their child-rearing decisions."

Moreover, the theory that children who are deaf must be raised in a Deaf cultural community denies these children the right to choose for themselves whether to accept or reject the larger hearing world. Deaf culturists argue that parents should not make decisions about cochlear implants for their deaf children but that the children should be allowed to make such decisions for themselves when they are old enough to do so. As shown in previous chapters of this book, however, experience has proven that early implantation is necessary for maximum efficacy of a cochlear implant. Thus, waiting for ten or fifteen years to make the decision for a child to have a cochlear implant is the same as deciding that the child will *not* have an implant. If a child who is deaf is going to learn to talk, he or she must begin learning at a *very* early age. A person who is deaf does not learn to speak at the age of twelve or older, the age at which the child is arguably old enough to decide how to live his or her life. But a child who is deaf and who learns to speak and is part of the hearing world during childhood *can* learn to sign later in life and join the Deaf world.

(It should be noted that Deaf culturists argue against the last point, claiming that children who grow up speaking in the hearing world do not become a *real* part of the Deaf world because ASL is not "natural" to them and because they have begun to "think" more like a hearing person than a deaf person. This is contradicted by the fact that many of the leaders of the Deaf culture spoke before they signed. This point is discussed later in this chapter.)

One mother of a child who is deaf responded to comments made on America Online, in which commentators opined that deaf children should be raised by Deaf culturists, as follows: "If I adopted a child from another race, yes I would like he/she to learn about his/her culture. [B]ut who is to say I should go to a couple of the same race and ask them to help me raise my child? Being a parent is a full-time job ... [we] ask for advice, but do we have to take it?"[19] Another parent of a child who is deaf, after hearing a plea by Deaf educators to "give us your deaf children" to be taught in residential schools for the deaf, responded to the Deaf culturists: "Fine. Give us all your hearing children to train and educate." The offer was declined.[20]

Contrary to the mistaken belief of some Deaf culture advocates, we deaf people who choose to live in the mainstream (most of us, anyway) are not opposed to sign language. What we want is simply for all children who are deaf to have the right to choose for themselves where and how they want to live their lives. Only if children are provided with the oral skills that are required to live in the hearing world can they make that choice for themselves when reaching maturity. Children who cannot speak, do not know English, and have not been exposed to the hearing world have no options. They are stuck.

It is up to the parents of a deaf or hard-of-hearing child to determine whether the child should be given the option to become oral. It is not for the Deaf culturists to make that choice for other parents. It is always the right and the responsibility of parents to decide how best to raise their children. Nothing in the Deaf-versus-deaf dispute calls for a different arrangement.

Deaf culturists are very militant about preserving their Deaf culture. Choosing to communicate orally and to live fully in the hearing world, I have been accused many times by members of the Deaf cultural community of "having rejected my Deaf heritage," of being "a traitor to my race," and of being like "a black person pretending to be white." Kevin Nolan, dean of students at Clarke (oral) School for the Deaf in Northampton, Massachusetts, profoundly deaf himself and the father of three children who are hearing-impaired, notes: "Many parents of children who are deaf or hard-of-hearing, myself included, have had to endure pressure from ASL advocates to 'conform' to what they consider to be their exclusive [D]eaf culture and their world. They want our children who are deaf or hard-of-hearing to 'conform' to their narrow-minded expectations."[21]

Since sign language has now become a hot topic (it is even sometimes shown or used on TV and in movies, thereby becoming more visible), many hearing people are under the mistaken impression that the only way deaf people can communicate is via sign language. Nothing could be further from the truth. In actuality, more people who are deaf speak than sign.

In fact, many, if not most, of the leaders of the Deaf culture movement can speak, because they received early oral training (or in a few cases because they became deaf later in life), and the majority of those leaders know perfect

English—although they know ASL as well. Indeed, it is their oral skills that have enabled them to argue for Deaf isolationism so persuasively. These leaders of Deaf culture, however, do not want today's deaf children to learn spoken English. Rather, they believe that spoken English should be rejected by Deaf people and that Deaf people should use only ASL as their mode of "spoken" (actually, signed) language. This is known as the "bi-bi" approach, or the purported "bilingual-bicultural" approach.[22] Under this approach, Deaf children are to learn only ASL and not spoken *or* signed English. Bi-bi advocates believe that children who are deaf should be taught their "natural language" of ASL, which they consider to be the "birthright of all deaf children."[23] Their rationale is expressed as follows:

> Natural sign not only serves deaf children as a means of communication between other sign language users but can support intellectual development and the acquisition of ideas in the same way that spoken language serves hearing people. It is, therefore, a folly, say bilingualists, to create an artificial sign system, such as SE [signed English] ..., when a bona fide sign language already exists. It is not only a folly but, say most supporters of bilingualism, a moral crime to attempt to force young deaf children to do something they cannot do, that is, learn spoken language as a first language.[24]

The statement that children who are deaf are unable to "learn spoken language as a first language" is, of course, belied by the thousands of deaf children, including myself, who have learned spoken language as a first (and, in many cases, only) language. Nevertheless, advocates of biculturalism espouse the view that once a child who is deaf has acquired a strong "natural" language (ASL), the child can then be taught *written* (but not spoken) English as a second language. What biculturists do not explain, at least in any understandable manner, is why, even if we accept the proposition that sign language is more natural to deaf children than speech (a proposition that has proven to be untrue for most children who are deaf), learning ASL is more "natural" than learning signed English. Nor do biculturists explain why a child who is deaf should have to struggle with learning to read and write English as a second language when, even if the child is taught to sign only, it would be so much easier for the child to learn and sign English and then to apply those English signing skills when learning how to read and write. Why make it more difficult by trying to teach written English as a second language?

The leaders of Deaf culture who reject spoken skills in any form for children who are deaf (but would permit signed English), and particularly those who espouse the bi-bi movement and want to deny children who are deaf both spoken and signed English, would deny deaf children the very skills that allow many of the Deaf culture leaders to perform successfully in this hearing world. Kevin Nolan, for example, noted that "nearly all" the Deaf culture leaders he knows "have had the benefit of early oral education."[25] Nolan asks:

Why should they deny children who are deaf the opportunity to realize the same oral successes that they themselves have experienced? ... Having benefitted from oral education in their own childhoods, why do they ... deny their oral backgrounds—those very backgrounds that helped them to become the leaders that they are today. Why? Why? ... They are self-serving in that they would deny the birthright of so many children with hearing impairments who have so much potential![26]

Like the Deaf leaders known by Kevin Nolan, virtually all of the Deaf culture movement leaders whom I have known have good oral skills, gained from years of oral training. Why they reject this training, and reject the acquisition of similar skills for today's deaf children and young adults, is unfathomable.

Commenting on the statements that the rhetoric that "Deaf people are oppressed by hearing people" and that "hearing parents are not fit to raise deaf children" and that therefore Deaf adults "should take over and raise them," Larry Stewart called such rhetoric a

type of hurtful foolishness ... being used to brainwash young deaf and hard-of-hearing high school and college students to ... reject their English backgrounds.... This brainwashing has even generated feelings of guilt within many deaf adults who possess effective oral and signed English skills, leading them to avoid public use of [those] skills but instead to use ASL in an exaggerated manner and to become militant proponents of the ASL-only philosophy. Many of our so-called [D]eaf leaders are being taken in by this cult-like movement.[27]

When I and many of the leaders of the Deaf culture movement were growing up, technology was very limited. Most people of our generation (born during the years between 1940 and 1960) who are profoundly deaf were not able to obtain much, if any, benefit from hearing aids. (For example, I have never been able to wear a hearing aid.) Unfortunately, the Deaf culture advocates are still working from that outdated perspective. The times have changed, drastically! Technology has *vastly* improved. Today's deaf children are able to wear much-improved hearing aids or to have cochlear implants. I have personally met *hundreds* and *hundreds* of children and young adults who are profoundly deaf but who, as a result of new technology and very capable auditory training, can hear on the telephone and can hear their own and others' speech. And the technology continues to improve rapidly. In ten to twenty years (and very possibly less), cochlear implants will most likely have improved to the point where almost all people who are deaf can benefit substantially from an implant.

The Deaf culture advocates, however, are strongly opposed to research geared toward "curing" deafness or even geared toward finding better ways to mainstream children who are deaf. They view such activities as a form of genocide, which will lead to the obliteration of the "Deaf race."[28] Most of us who are deaf would view the end of forced deafness as a blessing rather than a tragedy. But the Deaf culture advocates disagree and strongly oppose cochlear implants. The former executive director of NAD, Charles Estes, claims that cochlear implants are a form of "assault ... by zapping the auditory nerve tissue electrically" and that this practice is analogous to the Iraqi invasion of Kuwait and the beating of a blind man to induce him to see stars.[29]

Deaf culture advocates particularly oppose cochlear implants for children. As stated by Roz Rosen, another former president of NAD, since "hearing is not a life or death matter ... [it is] consequently not worth the medical, moral and ethical risk of altering a child."[30] One Deaf activist noted, "It is brutal to open a child's skull ... just to rob that child of a birthright of silence."[31]

Deaf culturists frequently refer to the deaf child's "natural language" of ASL as a God-given right that should not be taken away by those people who seek to teach deaf children to speak, to use their residual hearing, and to speechread. Dr. John Niparko, an implant surgeon at Johns Hopkins University, responds:

> Deaf spokespeople are always talking about their "God-given talent for sign" and that we're robbing them of that ability by having them focus on speech.... But the fact is that there is a very complex neural pathway in each child from the auditory nerve to the brain. That part is normal in most deaf children—and it's a God-given pathway. If the hair cells in the cochlea are not doing their job, that incredible pathway just sits there unused. All a cochlear implant does is activate a God-given thing.[32]

There is a misconception that placing cochlear implants in children constitutes "experimentation." As one Deaf activist has stated, "like the Nazis," doctors who implant cochlear implants "seem to enjoy experimenting on little children."[33] Another Deaf activist has said, "Using deaf children as 'lab rats' and medical guinea pigs is profoundly disturbing."[34] Still another Deaf activist commented:

> I would be remiss not to equate cochlear implants with genocide.... The FDA's approval of implants reeks of manipulation and oppression. There is absolutely no question that our government has a hidden agenda for deaf children akin to Nazi experiments on Holocaust victims.... [A] marketing machine [has been] created by the implant industry and its coyotes to prey on hopeless parents.[35]

The director of the Missouri Bureau of Deaf Services has opined that cochlear implants "would be truly debilitating in the mental health sense."[36]

Professor Harlan Lane (who is hearing but considers himself the primary spokesperson for the Deaf community) erroneously describes the process of cochlear implantation as follows: "The exquisitely detailed microstructure of the inner ear is often ripped apart as the electrode weaves its way, crushing cells and perforating membranes."[37] He describes medical professionals ("surgeons, audiologists and speech pathologists") who work with cochlear implants as "the bigots of the world," since they "make money off of cochlear implants."[38]

Other proponents of Deaf culture have made interesting comments. One Deaf person wrote about supporting the idea that "cochlear implants are genocide" and stated: "I ain't want to become a cochlear implanted person cuz I ain't want to be a Robo-cop like in the movie. He was suffered by the ignorant scientists who wanted to altered him from the human culture race (i.e. lost his wife and can't feel himself). Geez!"[39]

An individual responding to a chat-room comment likening deaf children who receive cochlear implants to guinea pigs replied: "I'm sorry, you are incorrect. Guinea pigs have more rights!"[40] The same individual stated, "Implants give parents a reason to put off facing up to their child's deafness they delay the grieving process and set families up for more disappointment."[41]

Gallaudet students and their families or friends have informed me that cochlear implants are greatly frowned on at Gallaudet and that implanted students at Gallaudet are usually pressured (often by their peers rather than by staff or faculty members) to remove the implants or at least not to wear their processors. As one reporter succinctly stated:

> As anyone at Gallaudet knows, a student with a [cochlear implant] device ... runs the risk of being shunned. "I have some friends with implants," says Scott Mohan, a sixth generation deaf senior at Gallaudet. "They just don't use them anymore."
> "You can understand why," says Keith Muller, Executive Director of the League for the Hard of Hearing in New York City. "Kids who try to speak in deaf schools are ridiculed. And the greater their oral success, the more they are criticized."[42]

Indeed, the hatred with which the Deaf culturists view cochlear implants is expressed in the ASL sign for a cochlear implant: a two-fingered stab to the back of the neck, indicating a "vampire" in the cochlea. Further evidence is shown by the fact that some Deaf culturists "picket oralist deaf schools and stop parents of children with implants in malls, demanding to know why they butcher deaf babies."[43] The parents of one teenager who told a *Washington Post* reporter how much she liked her cochlear implant were "afraid enough of the radical elements of [D]eaf culture to not allow her name to be used" in the newspaper article.[44]

One person compared cochlear implants to breast implants:

> Parents, think about this, do you remember there was upon a time a woman could get breast implant so it became very popular. Then many many years later it was found that was causing problems in their autoimmune system so they had to remove the silicone implants from their breast....

I feel using [cochlear implants] is too soon and the kids will have to live with it for the rest of their lives. Suppose if they start having problems when they're 40 or 50 years old because they had CI operation when they were kids.[45]

Another individual, seeking information about cochlear implants, sent a list of questions to selected cochlear implant recipients and parents of children with cochlear implants.[46] Questions asked included the following:

(i) "Do you think that having a cochlear implant takes away your Deaf pride?"

(ii) "Do you think that cochlear implants remove you as a member of Deaf culture?"

(iii) "Do you think that cochlear implants are a way for hearing people to break down Deaf society?"

(iv) "Do you think that a person should be allowed to choose whether or not to have a cochlear implant or should it be left up to the parents to decide? (Take into consideration that the longer you wait, the less likely it is that [the implant] will work)."

At least several recipients of that questionnaire were angered by the above questions. The responses of three individuals are quite interesting. To the question about whether cochlear implants take away "your Deaf pride," one respondent, Mildred Oberkotter, stated, "I never possessed any Deaf pride, tho I have pride in myself as a woman who is deaf (small 'd')."[47] A second respondent, Melissa Chaikof, replied: "Having a cochlear implant has nothing to do with my [deaf] daughter's pride, be it deaf or otherwise. What she is very proud of is what she has accomplished."[48] The third respondent, Bill Boyle, first stated, "I do not believe in a 'deaf culture' or a 'deaf society' any more than a 'nearsightedness culture' or a 'one-armed society.'" He added: "The so called 'deaf culture' tried to prevent me (and others) from receiving [the cochlear implant] and continue to ridicule me for 'mutilating' myself. My experiences indicate that this artificial culture is a desperate attempt to stall progress for those who wish to go forward, similar to denying an artificial limb to an amputee or eyeglasses to those with vision problems." Subsequently, Boyle replied to the question by stating: "What the hell is deaf pride? Proud not to hear your child's voice, pianos, the birds in the trees? That's not pride, it's bull-headedness and selfishness.... I feel the implant enhances my pride. I am proud to be overcoming what was considered a severe handicap, proud to be part of the community as a whole, not to a 'club' of narrow minded people."[49]

To the question about whether cochlear implants "remove you as a member of Deaf culture," Mildred Oberkotter stated, "I have never been an active member of Deaf culture." Melissa Chaikof replied: "If the cochlear implant has removed my daughters from '[D]eaf culture,' and it probably has, then that is fine by me. The [D]eaf culturists' opportunities in life are so limited, and my daughters' are not. Furthermore, it has been the choice of those in the '[D]eaf culture' to exclude those with implants from their group." Bill Boyle answered in part: "I was never a member of this so called culture before my implant and refuse to join this club now."

To the question about whether cochlear implants are "a way for hearing people to break down Deaf society," Mildred Oberkotter replied: "Absolutely *no*! It's incredible you'd suggest this." Melissa Chaikof stated: "In obtaining implants for our daughter, we did not have the ulterior motive of 'breaking down Deaf society.' If that is an indirect result, then [I have already stated that I do not believe that disability forms the basis of a culture. Rather, it is a chosen isolation from the hearing society].... My concern for my daughters' futures is far greater than for the future of 'Deaf society.'" Bill Boyle replied, "This question is a disgrace and should be stricken."

To the question about whether a person should be allowed to choose to have a cochlear implant or whether parents should make that decision (keeping in mind that the longer the wait, the less likely it is that the implant will be successful), Mildred Oberkotter stated: "For young children, it is essential that parents choose what is best for their child's interest and [the child's ability to] function in his/her culture in which s/he is born. So much time and possible maximum value would be lost in language and auditory development if and when the child is cognitively ready to make such a decision for him/herself." Melissa Chaikof answered: "I absolutely think that the decision as to whether or not to implant should be in the hands of the parents ... and the implant team. Some children and some families make better candidates. For example, one implant team here will not implant children in total communication [sign and some speech] or manual [sign language only] programs ... [since the consensus is that children with implants who are placed in signing programs do not benefit as much from implantation]. On the other hand, the kids whose parents are committed to an auditory-verbal approach [learning to listen], as we are, stand a very high chance of success." Bill Boyle replied: "If this [question] is about children, it is an enormous responsibility for the parents to decide. *But*—it is a decision [for] the parents who truly believe that their decision will be in the best interest of their child, and not a decision [for] NAD [the National Association of the Deaf] or others to decide. Yes, the longer you wait, the less benefit, so leave the parents alone and let them decide."

Other proponents of cochlear implants have made interesting comments. A "Deafworldweb" Internet writer stated:

> I am absolutely dumbfounded after reading all of the comments regarding cochlear implants [on the Deafworldweb]. My blood is boiling after reading some of the comments, so I know I will not be able to clearly communicate my feelings! First, I have a comment. I was told several weeks ago by my 5 year old daughter's otologist that she will possibly be

a good candidate for a cochlear implant. Before this I had never even heard of a cochlear implant. I have been researching, talking to people, and visiting the deaf school to acquire as much information on this as I can before I am faced with making a decision. Upon visiting the deaf school, I observed a kindergarten boy who was born profoundly deaf and was implanted 2 years prior. I was amazed at what good speech and understanding he had. It was as good, possibly even better, than my hearing daughter's speech. I find it incomprehensible why so many of you are against these implants. I do not believe for one minute that given the opportunity, you "Deafies" would choose to live a life of silence!!! Why must you feel that a person who chooses to find a way to end their silence is turning against you and your [D]eaf world? I just don't understand. If you had cancer wouldn't you do everything you could to get rid of it? Just because you choose to get rid of the cancer does that mean you are turning against those in the community that have incurable cancer? Of course it doesn't! So many of you seem to feel that the world is prejudiced against you. To me it seems the other way around. Why can't we just view people as people? I find this attitude of the hearing world vs. the deaf world to be tiresome![50]

Another writer in the same chat room wrote:

I would like ... to respond to [your comments]. First, [you stated that] "Hearing is not all it's cracked up to be." Hearing is a sense that enables us to communicate better. If you feel this way, plug up your own ears for a couple days until you can't hear and see how difficult your life will become. "Give her knowledge and belonging in the deaf community," [you say]. A disability ... impair[s] one['s] ability. Deafness *does* impair the ability to hear. The world that we live in is a hearing world. If the whole world was deaf [deafness] would then not be a disability.

You sound angry in your letter. I do not mean to anger you or anyone. [I am] [j]ust stating the opinion that [a] cochlear implant can be a wonderful alternative. It may not work for you or your daughter, but I feel that it is closed minded to not think it might work for another person or [another] person's child.[51]

A third commentator wrote:

I am a hearing parent of a hearing-impaired child. I am not signing off on this because I do not want to receive hate mail. It is interesting to read your opinions regarding cochlear implants. While my son does not have enough hearing loss to be the recipient of a cochlear implant ... if I was faced with this decision I certainly would consider its benefits. Over the years my son has gone to school with three children who were implanted. They have all had their implants for about 5 to 7 years now. From my observations, all three of these children have benefited greatly from the device. Those of you who are so against it must not have children yet.

... Being from a hearing world it is only natural to want our children to exist in our world and travel the least difficult road. If you have a child with no disabilities you do not wish he had disabilities. By the same token, if you have a child with a disability, you wish him the best solution to help him ... survive and grow in this world that we live in. You do the same for any problems that arise during your child's growth and development into adulthood.

We as parents are all working towards the day when our children can be independent. We hurt when our children hurt, we suffer their pain of growing and want only to do what is best and most helpful to them. For an example, I will help my child study for a test as long as it takes him to understand that information. And I will rejoice in an "A" the same way I will mourn with him an "F."

... The [implanted] children that I know were implanted so young that to hear with a cochlear implant is normal to them. They know no other way. ... No one wants to take anything away from [D]eaf culture. But to be militant [about anything], whether it be a race, religion or culture, and say "You must accept me" is a sure fired way to make enemies. Open your minds and see the other side.[52]

The NAD's position paper "Cochlear Implants in Children" opines that cochlear implants for children who are deaf should be outlawed.[53] Written in response to the FDA's June 27, 1990, approval of the marketing of Cochlear Corporation's "Nucleus 22-channel prosthesis for surgical-implantation in children aged two through seventeen,"[54] the position paper states, "The NAD DEPLORES the decision of the Food and Drug Administration which was UNsound scientifically, procedurally, and ethically."[55] The NAD contends that research into cochlear implants in children was "conducted WITHOUT regard to the quality of life that the child will experience as a deaf adult user"; that it is unclear whether a child's cochlear implant "will DELAY the family's acceptance of the child's deafness and their acquisition of sign communication"; and that the "FAILURE ... to consider the impact on the child's future quality of life qualifies the implant program as highly EXPERIMENTAL."[56]

The position paper also cites the FDA's purported procedural error "in FAILING to obtain formal input from organizations of [D]eaf Americans and from [D]eaf leaders and scholars KNOWLEDGEABLE about the acquisition and use of sign communication and English in deaf children, and the social organization and culture of the American Deaf Community."[57] The position paper states that the "FDA's FAILURE to consult [D]eaf spokespersons represents, if an oversight, GROSS IGNORANCE concerning growing up in [D]eaf America, or, if willful, an offense against fundamental American values of individual liberties, cultural diversity and consumer rights."[58]

Finally, the NAD's position paper adds that the FDA committed an "ethical error":

> Experimentation on children is ethically offensive. New and high technology that entails invasive surgery and tissue destruction is used, NOT for life saving, but for putative life enhancement.... The parents who make the decision for the child are often POORLY informed about the [D]eaf

community, its rich heritage and promising futures, including communication modes available to deaf people and their families. Far more SERIOUS is the ethical issue raised through decisions to undertake invasive surgery upon defenseless children.[59]

Deaf culturists assert that members of their minority group "are in no more need of a cure for their condition than are Haitians or Hispanics."[60] To many members of the Deaf cultural community, cochlear implants represent "the ultimate denial of deafness, the ultimate refusal to let deaf children be Deaf."[61] "We are not disabled," claim the Deaf culturists. Rather, we are a cultural minority, and our culture should be respected and upheld. In accord with this reasoning, the Deaf culturists strongly criticize and oppose the National Institutes of Health's National Institute on Deafness and Other Communication Disorders, which gives federal grants for research geared at the prevention and treatment of deafness and other communication disorders.[62]

On the other hand, the Deaf culture advocates are strong activists for the promulgation of laws protecting people with disabilities, such as the Americans with Disabilities Act (ADA).[63] For purposes of those laws, Deaf culturists claim to be disabled and to require expensive accommodations to be provided by both the public and the private sectors. There is an inherent conflict between these contrasting positions.

While vehemently proclaiming the right to preserve Deaf cultural heritage and while denouncing those who choose to alleviate—to the maximum extent possible—their deafness or their children's deafness, members of the Deaf cultural community also vigorously advocate for the provision of special services to alleviate the effects of deafness. The Deaf cultural community, for example, is opposed to educating deaf children in mainstream classrooms but insists that such children should be placed in segregated schools for the Deaf so that they may become full-fledged members of the Deaf cultural society. The resulting cost to society is enormous.

The costs of special schools for children who are deaf are exorbitant. It has been estimated that the yearly cost of educating one child in a residential school for the deaf is $35,780 and the yearly cost of educating one child in a self-contained class for the deaf (in a public school) is $9,689, compared with only $3,383 to educate the same child in a regular classroom.[64] Another study estimated that the cost of kindergarten through a twelfth-grade education in Rhode Island is about $9,000 for a hearing child, $44,000 for a deaf child educated in a mainstreamed setting, and $429,000 for a deaf child educated in a residential school for the deaf.[65]

The fiscal year 1997 budget for the Phoenix Day School for the Deaf in Phoenix, Arizona (a nonresidential school), for example, was nearly $5.8 million to educate approximately 230 children. The 1995 federal budget for the Model Secondary School for the Deaf and the Kendall Elementary School on the Gallaudet University campus in Washington, D.C., was nearly $24.8

million. (Kendall Elementary School is a day school that has approximately 182 students. The Model Secondary School has both residential and day-school programs, attended by approximately 258 students, most of whom are residential students.)

Deaf cultural advocates also emphasize the need for very costly special colleges for deaf students. The 1995 federal budget for Gallaudet University's college programs for deaf students was $54.2 million; the 1995 federal budget for college programs for deaf students at the National Technical Institute for the Deaf in Rochester, New York, was $42.7 million.

Relay services mandated by ADA Title IV provide another illustration. In 1995 the Arizona Relay Service (ARS), for example, a relatively small service, employed approximately 140 to 160 relay operators—plus administrative and technical personnel—and processed approximately 60,000 calls per month. The cost for this service to Arizona telephone users was approximately $300,000 per month, or $3.6 million per year, not to mention the expenditure of hundreds of thousands of dollars to purchase the necessary equipment for the service to operate. The California Relay Service processed approximately 650,000 calls per month in 1995—over ten times as many calls as processed by ARS—and certainly had a much higher budget than ARS, possibly close to ten times as high as the budget of ARS.

Auxiliary aids and accommodations mandated by the ADA may also be expensive for individual entities to provide. Interpreter fees, for example, range from $20 to $40 per hour in most cities (more in some), and almost all interpreting agencies require the payment of at least a two-hour minimum fee. In some cases, interpreters will be paid for a half-day's work even when only one hour or less of the interpreter's time is required (rules regarding the provision of interpreters in court, for example, usually require interpreters to be paid for a half-day even if they interpret for only fifteen minutes, probably because it would be impossible for the interpreter to commit to any other job during that period due to the inability to predict how much time a court appearance will require). Further, most interpreting agencies insist that two interpreters be hired to interpret for any period longer than one hour or, in some cases two hours, due to the purported need for the interpreters to switch off every twenty minutes. Real-time captioning is even more expensive. The average cost of a real-time stenographer ranges between $40 and $100 per hour, assuming the reporter provides his or her own equipment.

It is estimated that deafness results in the following costs to society: "2.5 billion per year in lost workforce productivity; $121.8 billion in the cost of education; and more than $2 billion annually for the cost of equal access, Social Security Disability Income, Medicare, and other entitlements of the disabled."[66] As Tom Bertling, a deaf person raised in the Deaf culture, has noted, "Virtually every aspect of the [D]eaf community is dependent on government support for ... disabled [persons]."[67]

All of these expenditures are necessary today to allow people who are deaf to take their rightful place in society. Currently, therefore, the majority of Americans, including our representatives in Congress, rightfully endorse these expenditures. But the right of deaf people to receive costly assistance is not unlimited. Although society has moral and ethical obligations to those who are deaf, people who are deaf also have moral and ethical obligations to society. To fulfill those moral and ethical obligations, people who are deaf should support, rather than protest, research to ameliorate or eliminate deafness and should agree to accept full responsibility for the ramifications of *chosen* deafness or for the refusal to take reasonable steps to modify the ramifications of their deafness.

When most deafness becomes correctable, which for some people has already occurred and for others may well happen within the next ten to twenty years, an individual who chooses not to correct his or her deafness (or the deafness of his or her child) lacks the moral right to demand that others pay for the costly accommodations needed to compensate for the lack of hearing. In this age of budget crises and cries for tax reform, when there is talk of, and some action toward, cutting funding for welfare, Medicaid, Social Security, federally supported food banks, and other social-welfare programs, it is unrealistic, at best, for Deaf culturists to expect society to fund expenditures that could be eliminated. At worst, such an egocentric approach appears to give credence to Philip Howard's *Death of Common Sense*.[68]

A primary criticism of this approach is that it leads to a slippery slope. If we force people who are deaf to either correct their deafness to the extent possible or forgo public and private benefits, what else will we force people to do in the name of common sense? If prospective parents choose to bear a child who they know will be born deaf, will we label that as a form of willful deafness and deny the child accommodations? Though recognizing the slippery slope, I believe that lines can easily be drawn. Forcing a person to choose between *surgery* and accommodations, for example, is not analogous to forcing parents to choose between *abortion* and the right of their deaf children to receive appropriate accommodations. Abortion is the prevention of life; surgery is not, despite the contention that it will lead to the end of Deaf cultural life.

Another criticism of this argument is that no individual should be required to have surgery or any other invasive bodily procedure. In response to the irrefutable fact that every person always has the right to refuse any treatment, Deaf culturists assert that a person who is deaf will be given no real choice because accommodations for deafness will not be available as a result of that choice.

In our society, however, individuals are always obligated to assume responsibility for their choices. In the legal context, for example, one who suffers physical injury through the negligence of another may sue the negligent actor for damages, but recovery for permanent injury is not permissible if the injury could have been avoided by reasonable measures.[69] As one court stated, it is "well established that the plaintiff in a personal injury case cannot claim damages for what would otherwise be a permanent injury if the permanency of the injury could have been avoided by submitting to treatment by a physician, including possible surgery, when a reasonable person would do so under the same circumstances."[70]

Whether submitting to surgery is a "reasonable measure" depends on the circumstances. We must look to the risk of the surgery, the pain involved, the cost of the surgery, the amount of effort to be expended by the person having the surgery, and the probability that the surgery will have successful results.[71] Then we must weigh those considerations against the consequences of not having the surgery.[72]

This analysis, when applied to the refusal of a deaf person to have a cochlear implant, works as follows. First, the risk involved in cochlear implant surgery is minimal. There is less than a 1 percent risk of other injuries (such as facial nerve paralysis) and less than a fraction of a percent that death will occur (the remote possibility of death exists in every surgery).[73]

Second, the pain involved in the surgery is also minimal for the overwhelming number of implant recipients. Many doctors are now performing cochlear implant surgery on an outpatient basis; even those cochlear implant recipients who are hospitalized remain in the hospital only overnight.[74] Most patients experience slight pain and discomfort, as they would after having any other surgical procedure.[75]

Third, the cost of the implant is relatively high (approximately $40,000 for surgery, equipment, and follow-up services such as remapping the implant and receiving auditory training). When compared with the costs of special schools, interpreters, relay services, and governmental support for people who are deaf, however, that cost appears minimal.

Fourth, the amount of effort to be expended on learning to "hear" with the implant may be substantial for some and minimal for others. Even when that effort is substantial, however, when compared with the effort expended on attempting to obtain an education, find a job, communicate with the public, etc., etc., without being able to hear, the effort to be expended is relatively small.

Fifth, by contrast, the probability that the surgery will be a success is today unclear for some people, particularly for adults who are congenitally deaf. Because of this factor, we have not yet reached the day when deaf adults may be required to have cochlear implants before asking society for accommodations or assistance. When the probability of success is greatly improved, however, as is expected within the next one to two decades, the situation will be entirely different.

When cochlear implants have a high probability of significant success for all deaf people who are candidates for an implant a court would be likely to hold that an individual who became deaf due to the fault (tort) of another (a tortfeasor) could not recover from the tortfeasor for a permanent injury (permanent deafness) if that individual refuses cochlear implant surgery.

The deafened individual could not be *required* to have surgery, of course. Similarly, an injured person who refuses possible surgery because of religious or other personal reasons cannot be compelled to have surgery. Having made that choice for religious or personal reasons, however, an individual usually cannot recover damages for the now-permanent injury, despite the fact that, absent the tortfeasor's negligence, the injury would not have existed. A similar reasonable principle may apply to people who choose to remain deaf when a choice is possible or who choose not to alleviate many of the ramifications of their deafness.

Currently, the Americans with Disabilities Act (ADA) and other laws preventing discrimination on the basis of disability[76] do not provide that people with "voluntary" disabilities are not protected by those laws—nor, for the most part, have the laws been interpreted in such a manner.[77] We do not look to "how" an individual became disabled when deciding whether society will assist that individual to prevent discrimination. Asking *how* an individual became disabled, however, differs from asking whether an individual has taken—or will take—all reasonable efforts to eliminate or mitigate the effects of that disability.

In the not-so-distant future, courts may begin to decline to apply disability antidiscrimination laws to individuals who refuse to take reasonable efforts—including surgery—to eliminate, or at least minimize, the effects of their disabilities. This is particularly true when disabilities such as blindness or deafness are at issue, since it is difficult and expensive to provide accommodations for individuals with such disabilities. But the same concept should apply to all disabilities. By way of example, if a person with manic depression refuses to take medication that would alleviate the symptoms of that disability (medication that meets the test of reasonableness), should an employer be expected to provide that individual with flexible and shorter work hours, release from certain job duties, or other provisions to accommodate his or her "chosen" manic depression? In my opinion, the answer is "no."

Today, there is a tremendous backlash against laws such as the ADA. Some members of society, particularly those in the business sector, view the ADA as providing "special benefits" to people with disabilities[78]; those individuals and entities do not understand that the ADA is intended simply to equalize the playing field for people with disabilities, to allow them the opportunity to take part in mainstream society. The ADA does not provide "special benefits" for people with disabilities. For example, providing an interpreter or a special typewriter-telephone (and a relay service) for an employee who is deaf is not a "special benefit"; rather, it is an accommodation (which must be provided only when it is reasonable for the employer to do so), to allow the deaf person to take part in the work force to the same extent that a hearing person is already able to do so (without accommodation). If we require the provision of an interpreter or a special phone and relay service to people who do not *have* to remain deaf but who simply *choose* to remain deaf, we give validity to the criticism that "special benefits" are being provided to deaf people. This in turn could cause greater societal rejection of laws such as the ADA—laws that are urgently needed for the millions of people who are not able to eliminate or mitigate their disabilities.

Indeed, the United Kingdom's recently enacted Disability Discrimination Act of 1995 (DDA) already recognizes this concept to some degree.[79] Under the DDA, an individual is deemed to be disabled, even if the disability is controllable by medication or other medical treatment, if the disability would have a substantial effect on the individual's ability to carry out normal day-to-day activities without the medication or medical treatment.[80] Practical exceptions are noted, however. For example, this rule

> does not extend to those with impaired sight where the impairment is correctable by spectacles or contact lenses or by some other prescribed method, *whether or not those aids are in fact used.* This exception reflects the fact that the correction of impaired sight by spectacles and contact lenses is usually so effective that "people who wear spectacles or contact lenses would not generally think of themselves as disabled."[81]

The DDA provides that the secretary of state may issue regulations making other exceptions (in addition to the exception dealing with certain vision impairments). The DDA's annotations offer one illustration of such a regulation that might be enacted:

> For example, at the moment, people wearing hearing aids will be covered by the definition because hearing aids usually provide only a partial correction of a disability. Those people are still usually, and should be, seen as disabled. But if at some future date, as a result of improved technology, hearing aids became as completely effective as spectacles or contact lenses are today, it might be appropriate to exclude people in that situation from the general definition of disability.[82]

The U.S. Equal Employment Opportunity Commission (EEOC), which is responsible for enforcing the employment section (Title I) of the ADA, also takes the position that the determination of whether an individual's physical or mental impairment "substantially limits a major life activity" (as required to fall within the definition of a person with a disability under the ADA)[83] should be made *without* considering the effects of medical treatment on the individual.[84] The EEOC has not noted exceptions to that rule, as has the UK's

DDA. Nevertheless, even without such exceptions, several courts have disagreed with the EEOC and have refused, for practical reasons, to hold that a physical impairment that is correctable by medical treatment constitutes a disability under ADA Title I.

For example, the EEOC's regulations state that an insulin-dependent diabetic is disabled for ADA Title I purposes even if the only way the individual can perform major life activities is with the aid of insulin (without insulin, the individual would lapse into a coma).[85] In *Coghlan v. H. J. Deinz Co.*[86] the court disagreed with that reasoning, holding that the EEOC's interpretation contradicts the express language of the ADA, because "an insulin-dependent diabetic who takes insulin could perform major life activities, ... would therefore not be substantially limited" in the ability to perform such activities, and is therefore not disabled within the meaning of Title I of the ADA.[87]

Other courts have also disagreed with the EEOC's reasoning.[88] These courts seem troubled by the need to give special protection to individuals whose physical or mental impairments (otherwise considered disabilities) are completely correctable, even though in the cases cited, the plaintiffs *were* receiving appropriate medical treatment and were *not* seeking accommodations for problems alleviated by such medical treatment. Indeed, in at least one case, a court held that an individual who refused to submit to surgery that would have remedied a physical impairment could not claim protection under ADA Title I. In *Pangalos v. Prudential Insurance*[89] the court held that an individual's severe ulceritis colitis did not constitute a covered disability under the ADA because it could have been remedied by a colostomy, a surgical procedure that the individual refused to have. (The EEOC took the position that the court ruled incorrectly. The EEOC unsuccessfully argued in part, "It is established medical wisdom that colitis cannot be cured by surgery."[90] The EEOC also unsuccessfully argued that even if surgery mitigates, rather than cures, colitis, the existence of mitigating measures does not dislodge the protections of the ADA.)

In the future, it seems likely that more courts will hold that the law does not require that an individual with a physical impairment must be provided with accommodations that would not be necessary if the individual would obtain reasonable medical treatment that would obviate the need for such accommodations. If courts routinely accept an individual's refusal to accept reasonable medical treatment, and require the provision of accommodations to equalize the playing field for that individual, the social and political mood regarding laws such as the ADA is likely to deteriorate rapidly. Members of the public, including politicians, are likely to ask: Why should the public and private sectors be required to spend money to provide accommodations for a person whose disability is correctable, when correcting the disability would in itself help to equalize the playing field for that person?

This is not to say, however, that people who are deaf and who have cochlear implants, or other people who have disabilities and who accept mitigating medical intervention, should not be protected in any fashion by laws such as the ADA. I agree that such individuals may still be illegally discriminated against. Suppose, for example, that an employer refused to hire a deaf person simply because that person was deaf and had a cochlear implant. Such conduct should be held to violate the ADA. This type of situation is quite different from requiring the provision of costly accommodations that would not be necessary if reasonable medical intervention was accepted. It is crucial that we distinguish between the two types of situations.

Cochlear implants do not, and likely will not, eliminate deafness altogether. An individual who has an implant is still deaf. The difference is, however, that the ramifications of deafness are significantly reduced. At the present time, it is known that most children, and people who become deaf later in life and have memory of normal hearing, do very well with cochlear implants, thus reducing (if not eliminating) the need for special schools, interpreters, and other costly accommodations. Such people who refuse today to have cochlear implants yet demand costly accommodations may be viewed as acting unethically.

On one recent day, I met with two deaf adults at different functions. The first involved a meeting of a group of people, whose members included a person who was not deafened until her late teens and thus had had normal hearing for many years. She refuses to have a cochlear implant and instead must have two sign-language interpreters with her at all times when attending meetings and social functions relating to those meetings and when talking to people during breaks or before or after the meetings — all at very costly expense to the entity holding the meeting (frequently the taxpayer, since many of her meetings are government-sponsored). Later that evening, I had dinner with several people, including another deaf woman. That woman (who, like the previously mentioned woman, is in her fifties) had become deaf at the age of three and had received some, but not much, benefit from hearing aids during the years following. She had a cochlear implant a year ago. She has given away her TDD (she no longer needs it, since she now uses the regular voice-phone) and is able to understand speech without assistance in most situations (she no longer requires the services of her former interpreter). What a difference between those two women! One has fulfilled her responsibility to reduce the ramifications of her deafness (and realized much joy in the process), and the other has not.

In spite of all that was said above, it is impossible not to recognize the source and validity of the anger, hostility, and solidarity expressed by the Deaf culturists who choose to reject hearing society and who do not wish to be "hearing" to any degree. Any individual who has any compassion and who knows anything of the history of people who are deaf must understand how the concept of Deaf culture came into existence. The mountains of books and writings explaining the persecution, institutionalization, prejudice, and discrimination suffered by deaf individuals over the years are too voluminous even to mention in this chapter. As one who has been profoundly deaf since the age of two (and never able to wear hearing aids), I suffered from much of that prejudice and discrimination, which was detailed in my book *The Feel of Silence*.[91] Many people who are deaf continue to live as second-class citizens, as indicated not only by the rejection of deaf people by most hearing people but also by the following facts:

> The average deaf person today reads at a fourth grade level. One in three drops out of high school. Only one in five who starts college gets a degree. Deaf adults make 30 percent less than the general population. Their unemployment rate is high, and when they are employed, it is usually in manual jobs such as kitchen workers, janitors, machine operators, tailors and carpenters, for which a strong command of English is not required.[92]

Rejecting hearing society, technology that will alleviate the ramifications of deafness, and the potential eradication of most deafness, however, is not the solution to the problems of deaf people. This attitude, although rooted in and based on a long history of terrible prejudice and discrimination, serves only to continue and to maximize the problems. One is reminded of Keith Richburg's *Out of America: A Black Man Confronts Africa*.[93] Richburg speaks graphically about the African theory of a "'white conspiracy,' a Western conspiracy against blacks and a master plan to keep blacks down," which is premised on the tragic history of white-on-black oppression (and is a theory that, Richburg explains, is also expressed by some African-Americans).[94] According to this theory, all that goes wrong with black society, even today, is based on white oppression. Richburg, who is black and acknowledges and abhors the history of white oppression, finds "the antiwhite sentiment and the belief in a white, antiblack conspiracy" to be tragic for African nations; in Richburg's view, it is often used as an excuse for the failure of African nations to govern themselves adequately.

The Deaf culturists' rejection of hearing society—as well as their desire for a separate, isolated society and their consequential rejection of all speech and hearing, by whatever mode—is equally fallacious. As experience has shown, most people with cochlear implants, particularly most children who are implanted early and receive competent and thorough auditory-verbal training, need not fall within the deplorable statistics relating to deaf people. Rather, by using cochlear implants, deaf people, particularly children, have a wealth of opportunities and potential life experiences available to them. To deny such opportunities based on theories of segregation is indeed illogical.

In sum, therefore, the position taken against cochlear implants by members of the Deaf culturists appears irrational, unsound, immoral, and contradictory. That position is also dangerous, in that it could lead to the rejection of important laws and social policies that assist people with disabilities to become full-fledged members of society.

NOTES

1. For an article explaining the viewpoint of Deaf culture, *see* E. Dolnick, "Deafness as Culture," *Atlantic* 272, no. 3 (Sept. 1993): 37–53.

2. National Institute on Deafness and Other Communication Disorders, National Institutes of Health, "Statistics on Deafness and Hearing Disorders in the United States" (reported in the April 1989 "National Strategic Research Plan"; also mailed as an information sheet by the National Association of the Deaf in 1996).

3. There are no reported figures for the number of members of the Deaf subculture. Representatives of both Gallaudet University and the National Association of the Deaf have informed this author that three to four hundred thousand is the best and most commonly accepted estimate of deaf people who socialize and work primarily with other deaf people. Note, however, that not all (and perhaps not a majority) of these individuals take the extreme positions espoused by the leaders of the Deaf culture movement with respect to "ASL only," the rejection of cochlear implants (particularly for deaf children), the segregation of deaf children, or the desire to have only deaf children.

4. The IDEA [20 U.S. Code sect. 1400–1481], formerly called the "Education for All Handicapped Act" or "Public Law 94-142," was enacted to provide children with disabilities with a free appropriate public education. It is premised on the precept that, to the maximum extent possible, children with disabilities are to be educated alongside children without disabilities.

5. See, for example, F. Barringer, "Pride in a Soundless World: Deaf Oppose a Hearing Aid," *New York Times*, May 16, 1993, sec. 1, p. 1, (noting that Gallaudet University states, "Enrollment in the nation's 60 residential schools for the deaf, which are viewed as important incubators of deaf culture, has been declining").

6. E-mail to the author from Melissa K. Chaikof, November 11, 1996.

7. Larry G. Stewart, "Debunking the Bilingual/Bicultural Snow Job in the American Deaf Community," *A Deaf American Monograph* 42 (1992).

8. *Ibid.*

9. The National Association of the Deaf (NAD) is a nonprofit organization that states that it was "established in 1880, [and] is the nation's oldest and largest consumer-based organization safeguarding the accessibility and civil rights of 28 million deaf and hard of hearing Americans in education, employment, health care, and communications." The NAD's "primary areas of focus include grassroots advocacy and empowerment, captioned media, certification of American Sign Language and Deaf Studies professionals, deafness-related information and publications, legal assistance, policy development and research, public awareness, certification of sign language interpreters, and youth leadership development." NAD membership application publication, "About the NAD," faxed to the author by NAD on April 16, 1997 (in the author's files). The NAD does not assist in obtaining, publicizing, or participating in matters dealing with auditory-oral approaches to deafness (for example, it is involved in ensuring the qualifications of sign-language interpreters but not oral interpreters; it advocates for sign-language programs for deaf schoolchildren but not for auditory or oral programs).

10. R. Rosen, "President Rosen on Cochlear Implants," *NAD Broadcaster* (Dec. 1992), p. 6. See also, R. Rosen, "The President Signs On," *ibid.* (Jan. 1991), p. 3.

11. Rosen, "President Rosen on Cochlear Implants"; Rosen, "President Signs On."

12. Barringer, "Pride in a Soundless World."

13. Dolnick, "Deafness as Culture."

14. See, for example, "Deaf Parents Are Happy When Baby Is Born Deaf," *Toledo Blade*, October 11, 1994.

15. M. Arana Ward, "As Technology Advances, a Bitter Debate Divides the Deaf," *Washington Post*, May 11, 1997, p. A01.

16. Quoted in A. Trafford, "The Brave New World of Genetic Planning," *Washington Post*, November 15, 1994.

17. *Ibid.* (quoting Dorothy Wertz).

18. *Ibid.*

19. America Online, Friday, September 13, 1996, by K. Holtz.

20. Statement of Deborah Crosby, reported in Barringer, "Pride in a Soundless World."

21. Kevin Nolan, "Communication Choices: A Parent's Perspective," *Clarke Speaks*, p. T3 (winter/spring 1997), reprinted from *Volta Voices* (Alexander Graham Bell Association for the Deaf, Washington, D.C.), Nov.-Dec. 1996, p. 30.

22. See, for example, Wendy Lynas, *Communication Options in the Education of Deaf Children* (London: Whurr, Pub., 1994).

23. *Ibid.*, p. 60.

24. *Ibid.*, p. 63.

25. Nolan, "Communication Choices."

26. *Ibid.*

27. Stewart, "Debunking."

28. See, for example, J. Roots, "Deaf Canadian Fighting Back," *World Federation of the Deaf News* (1994), pp. 2–3 ("I would be remiss not to equate cochlear implants with genocide") (cited in T. Balkany, A. V. Hodges, and K. W. Goodman, "Ethics of Cochlear Implantation in Young Children," *Journal of Otolaryngology— Head and Neck Surgery* 114, no. 6 (1995): 748); A. Colon, "A Sense of Connection: The Deaf Nurture Their Distinctive Culture in a Hearing-Oriented Society," *Seattle Times*, Feb. 18, 1996, p. L1 (quoting the statement of M. J. Bienvenu, Deaf activist: "Mainstreaming deaf children into the school system amounts to 'genocide of the deaf culture'"); *DeafDigest* 1, no. 31 (March 2, 1997) ("Last week's *DeafDigest* mentioned gene therapy and computerized ears as possible ways to eradicate deafness. Now we are reading reports of sheep being cloned. Would advances in this field lead to human cloning as another way to eradicate deafness in the 21st century?").

29. *NAD Broadcaster* (January 1991), p. 3.

30. Rosen, "President Rosen on Cochlear Implants."

31. Barringer, "Pride in a Soundless World."

32. Quoted in Ward, "As Technology Advances."

33. A. Solomon, "Defiantly Deaf," *New York Times Magazine*, Aug. 28, 1994, pp. 36–68.

34. Roots, "Deaf Canadian."

35. A. Silver, "Cochlear Implants: Surefire Prescription for Long-term Disaster," *TBC NEWS* 53 (1993): 4–5, quoted in Balkany, Hodges, and Goodman, "Ethics of Cochlear Implantation in Young Children," p. 748.

36. Letters to the William House Cochlear Implant Study Group for dissemination, Sept. 1993 (cited in Balkany, Hodges, and Goodman, "Ethics of Cochlear Implantation in Young Children," (note 11, as "Letters to the William House Cochlear Implant Study Group for dissemination, Sept. 1993 [author's files]").

37. H. Lane, *The Mask of Benevolence* (New York: Vintage Books 1993).

38. Silver, "Cochlear Implants."

39. E-mail on the Internet, Sept. 13, 1996, by Harry Gibbons Jr., owner of The Deafworks Co. (in the author's files).

40. E-mail on the Internet, "Deafworldweb" chat room, March 25, 1997, by "Anonymous from Ontario, Canada" (in the author's files).

41. *Ibid.*

42. Ward, "As Technology Advances."

43. *Ibid.*

44. *Ibid.*

45. E-mail on the Internet, "Deafworldweb" chat room, March 2, 1997, by "Surf-skier from Somewhere in Southeast of Florida" (in the author's files).

46. E-mail by Kate T. Kubey, November 1996, submitted to the author by Mildred Oberkotter and Melissa K. Chaikof (in the author's files).

47. Response of Mildred Oberkotter (in the author's files).

48. Response of Melissa K. Chaikof (in the author's files).

49. Response of Bill Boyle (in the author's files).

50. E-mail on the Internet, "Deafworldweb" chat room, April 3, 1997, by "Anonymous from San Antonio, Texas" (in the author's files).

51. *Ibid.*, March 20, 1997, by "Anonymous from Anywhere U.S.A." (in the author's files).

52. *Ibid.*, March 18, 1997, by "Anonymous" (in the author's files).

53. NAD Position Paper: "Cochlear Implants in Children," April 1993, reprinted in *NAD Broadcaster*, March 1991, p. 1 (in the author's files).

54. *Ibid.*

55. *Ibid.* (emphasis in original).

56. *Ibid.*

57. *Ibid.*

58. *Ibid.*

59. *Ibid.*

60. Dolnick, "Deafness as Culture," p. 3.

61. *Ibid.*, p. 40.

62. The author is a member of the National Advisory Council to the National Institute on Deafness and Other Communication Disorders and has personal knowledge of such opposition.

63. 42 U.S. Code sec. 12101–12213.

64. Jean L. Johnson et al., "Implementing a Statewide System of Services for Infants and Toddlers with Hearing Disabilities," *Seminars in Hearing* 14 (Feb. 1993): 117 (cited in Balhany, Hodges, and Goodman, "Ethics of Cochlear Implantation in Young Children").

65. Ibid., pp. 105–18.

66. "Early Identification of Hearing Impairments in Infants and Young Children," *National Institutes of Health Consensus Statement 1992* 11, no. 1 (1992): 1–12 (cited in Balhany, Hodges, and Goodman, "Ethics of Cochlear Implantation in Young Children").

67. T. Bertling, *A Child Sacrificed to the Deaf Culture* (Wilsonville, Oreg.: Kodiak Media Group, 1994).

68. P. Howard, *The Death of Common Sense* (New York: Random House, 1994).

69. For a discussion of this issue, see Lisa E. Key, "Voluntary Disabilities and the ADA: A Reasonable Interpretation of 'Reasonable Accommodations,'" *Hastings Law Journal* 48 (November 1996): 75–104.

70. *Zimmerman v. Ausland*, 513 P.2d 1167, 1169 (Or. 1973).

71. *Ibid.*, p. 1170; *Lucas v. Deville*, 385 So. 2d 804, 815 (La. Ct. App. 1979); D. Dobbs, *Law of Remedies*, 3.9, pp. 272–73 (1993); Key, "Voluntary Disabilities," p. 99.

72. *Lucas v. Deville*, p. 815; Key, "Voluntary Disabilities," p. 99.

73. Personal communications between the author and Dr. William M. Luxford, M.D, a cochlear implant surgeon at the House Ear Institute in Los Angeles, California, who is renowned for his expertise on the subject.

74. William M. Luxford, M.D., "Surgery for Cochlear Implantation," chapter 35 in D. E. Brackmann and S. C. Arriaga, eds., *Otologic Surgery* (Philadelphia: WB Saunders, 1994).

75. Personal communications between the author and Dr. William M. Luxford.

76. The Americans with Disabilities Act is found at 42 U.S. Code secs. 12102–12213. Some other laws protecting individuals with disabilities from discrimination include the Rehabilitation Act of 1973 (29 U.S.C. secs. 591–595); the Fair Housing Act Amendments of 1988 (42 U.S.C. 3601–3631); the Individuals with Disabilities Education Act (20 U.S.C. secs. 1400–1485); and the Air Carriers Access Act (49 U.S.C. sec. 1374[c]).

77. See, for example, Key, "Voluntary Disabilities."

78. See, for example, George Will, "Disabilities Act May End Up Granting Special Rights to Jerks," *Idaho Statesman*, April 4, 1996, p. 15A (noting that under the ADA, our "compassionate government has recently rained new rights and entitlements … special privileges" on people with disabilities).

79. 1995 c.50 (United Kingdom), available in Sweet and Maxwell, *Current Law*, Statutes 1995, v.4, chapters 47–54.

80. 1995 c.50, pp. 50–58 (annotation by Gareth Thomas, L.L.B., B.C.L.).

81. *Ibid.* (citing Minister for Social Security and Disabled People, Hansard, H.C., Standing Committee E, col. 122) (emphasis added).

82. *Ibid.*

83. 42 U.S.C. Sec. 12102(2).

84. 29 C.F.R. app. sec. 1630.2(h). Several courts have followed the EEOC's reasoning. See, e.g., *Harris v. H & W Contracting Co.*, 102 F.3d 516, 521 (11th Cir. 1996); *Houlihan v. Lucky Stores, Inc.*, 87 F.3d 362, 366 (9th Cir. 1996); *Roth v. Lutheran General Hospital*, 57 F.3d 1446, 1454 (7th Cir. 1995); *Wilson v. Pennsylvania State Police Department*, 6 A.D. Cas. (BNA) 1125 (E.D. Pa. 1997); *Sackett v. WPNT, Inc.*, 4 A.D. Cas (BNA) 1597, 1600 (W.D. Pa. 1995); *Canon v. Clark*, 883 F. Supp. 718, 721 (S.D. Fla. 1995); *Sarsycki v. United Parcel Service*, 862 F. Supp. 336, 340 (W.D. Okla. 1994).

85. 29 C.F.R. app. sec. 1630.2(h).

86. 851 F. Supp. 808 (N.D. Tex. 1994).

87. Ibid., p. 813.

88. See, for example, *Deckert v. City of Ulysses, Kansas*, 4 A.D. Cas. (BNA) 1569 (D. Kan. 1995) (applying the same reasoning as *Coghlan*); *Chandler v. City of Dallas*, 2.F.3d 1385, 1391 (5th Cir. 1993), *cert. denied*, 114 S.Ct. 1386 (1994) (also dealing with diabetes); *Eckles v. Consolidated Rail Corp.*, 890 F. Supp. 1391, 1398 (S.D. Ind. 1995) (dealing with epilepsy).

89. 5 A.D. Cases (BNA) 1825 (E.D. PA. October 15, 1996), *affirmed*, 118 F.3d 1577 (3d. Cir. 1997).

90. Brief of the EEOC as Amicus Curiae in *Pangalos v. Prudential Insurance Company of America*, Case No. 96-2022, filed with the Third Circuit U.S. Court of Appeals February 13, 1997, note 6.

91. Bonnie Poitras Tucker, *The Feel of Silence* (Philadelphia: Temple University Press, 1995).

92. Ward, "As Technology Advances."

93. Keith B. Richburg, *Out of America: A Black Man Confronts Africa* (New York: Basic Books, 1997).

94. *Ibid.*, p.148.

Chapter 9

Conclusion

Cochlear implants can, and do, provide both deaf children and deaf adults with a wealth of experience and opportunities. Some people who are deaf view their cochlear implants as true miracles. Others, though relishing significant benefits from their implants, wish for still-improved assistance in hearing. A much smaller number of implantees realize only minimal benefit from their implants and await greater technological progress.

Cochlear implants represent a new beginning for many people who are deaf. But current implants do not yet constitute a panacea. We deaf people have a technological wish list for the future:

1. Vastly improved ability of implants to screen background noises
2. Improved speech discrimination for *all* implant users
3. Improved telephone accessibility
4. More efficient processing and mapping strategies
5. Effective behind-the-ear processors
6. Waterproof equipment
7. Improved battery life
8. Greatly enhanced access to programming centers
9. Training programs and equipment to allow adult implantees to map their own processors (or parents to map their children's processors)
10. Less-expensive equipment, services, and insurance
11. Speedier repair and replacement of equipment

Researchers and manufacturers, are you listening? We've made wonderful progress in the last decade. The day will come when cochlear implants or similar technologies are capable of *completely* eradicating the ramifications of deafness. We still have a way to go, however—and we are counting on you.

But technological advances alone are not sufficient. An equally important component of our wish list is the desire that doctors, clinicians, educators, and the general public be made aware of the actual and potential benefits of cochlear implants. Efforts to educate the public on the vast difference that implants can make for both deaf people in particular and society in general are sorely needed. Even perfect technology will be of little avail if people are not aware of, or are misinformed about, the capabilities of that technology. I hope this book will constitute a first step in this sorely needed educational process.

Index